Cambridge Human Geography

THE CITY AS TEXT: THE POLITICS OF LANDSCAPE INTERPRETATION IN THE KANDYAN KINGDOM

Edited by
BRIAN ROBSON
Professor of Geography, University of Manchester
DAVID LEY
Professor of Geography, University of British Columbia
DEREK GREGORY
Professor of Geography, University of British Columbia

Cambridge Human Geography will provide an important new framework for the publication both of the fresh ideas and initiatives often embodied in postgraduate work and of the more substantive research and wider reflective output of established scholars. Given the flux of debate within the social sciences as a whole, the series will seek to attract authors concerned to address general issues of the conflicting philosophies within and between the "political science" and "liberal" approaches. Much of this interdisciplinary debate will be developed through specific studies: of production and economic restructuring; of the provision and management of public goods and services; of state investment and collective consumption; of human agency and of the human-environment interface. The central aim of this series will be to publish quite simply the best of new scholarship within the field of human geography.

Cambridge Human Geography

Phenomenology, science and geography
Spatiality and the human sciences
JOHN PICKLES

Property companies and the construction industry in Britain
HEDLEY SMITH

Crime, space and society
SUSAN J. SMITH

Land use planning and the mediation of urban change
PATSY HEALEY, PAUL MCNAMARA, MARTIN ELSON AND ANDREW DOAK

Islands, islanders and the world
The colonial and post-colonial experience of Eastern Fiji
T.P. BAYLIS-SMITH, R.D. BEDFORD, H.C. BROOKFIELD AND M. LATHAM

Landlords and property
Social relations in the private rented sector
JOHN ALLEN AND LINDA MCDOWELL

Unions and communities under siege
American communities and the crisis of organised labour
GORDON L. CLARK

The Mediterranean city in transition
Social change and urban development
LILA LEONTIDOU

Lost words and lost worlds: modernity and the language of everyday life in late nineteenth-century Stockholm
ALLAN PRED

The city as text: the politics of landscape interpretation in the Kandyan Kingdom
JAMES S. DUNCAN

THE CITY AS TEXT:
THE POLITICS OF LANDSCAPE INTERPRETATION IN THE KANDYAN KINGDOM

JAMES S. DUNCAN
Department of Geography
Syracuse University

CAMBRIDGE UNIVERSITY PRESS
Cambridge
New York   Port Chester   Melbourne   Sydney

Published by the Press Syndicate of the University of Cambridge
The Pitt Building, Trumpington Street, Cambridge CB2 1RP
40 West 20th Street, New York, NY 10011 USA
10 Stamford Road, Oakleigh, Melbourne 3166 Australia

© Cambridge University Press 1990

First published 1990

Printed in Great Britain at the University Press, Cambridge

British Library cataloguing in publication data
Duncan, James S.
The city as text: the politics of landscape
interpretation in the Kandyan Kingdom – (Cambridge
human geography)
1. Sri Lanka. Kandy. Landscape. Effects on man
I. Title
304.2'09549'3

Library of Congress cataloguing in publication data
Duncan, James S. (James Stuart), 1945–
The city as text: the politics of landscape interpretation in the
Kandyan kingdom / James S. Duncan.
p.   cm. – (Cambridge human geography)
Bibliography.
ISBN 0 521 35305 X
1. Landscape assessment – Sri Lanka – Kandy. 2. Kandy (Sri Lanka) –
Kings and rulers. 3. Kandy (Sir Lanka) – Geography. I. Title.
II. Series
GF91.S72D85   1990
304.2'3–dc20   88-7398 CIP

ISBN 0 521 35305 X

ROBERT MANNING
STROZIER LIBRARY

JAN 29 1991

Tallahassee, Florida

VN

For Nancy

Contents

List of figures	page viii
Preface	ix
Glossary of terms	xi
A note on transliteration	xiv

PART I INTRODUCTION — 1

1 Introduction — 3

PART II TOWARDS AN INTERPRETIVE FRAME — 9

2 Landscape as a signifying system — 11
3 The discursive field of Kandyan kingship — 25
4 Concretizing the Sakran discourse: from landscape of the gods to landscape of the hero-kings — 42
5 The Kandyan landscape, 1312–1815 — 59

PART III THE POLITICS OF LANDSCAPE INTERPRETATION IN EARLY-NINETEENTH-CENTURY KANDY — 85

6 From discourse to landscape: a kingly reading — 87
7 From landscape to civic ritual: a kingly reading — 119
8 From landscape to discourse: contestatory readings and material interests — 154
9 Conclusion — 181

Appendix	185
Notes	194
List of references	206
Index	226

Figures

1	Lanka in 1815	page 26
2	Kandy in 1602	62
3	Kandy in 1736	73
4	Kandy in 1765	75
5	The palace/temple complex in 1765	77
6	The palace/temple complex in 1815	79
7	Sketch of the palace/temple complex in 1815	81
8	Kandy in 1815	83
9	Kandy Lake and the sacred rectangle	103
10	The wave swell and cloud drift walls	104
11	The cremation of the prince	121
12	The Asala Perahara	131
13	Sri Vikrama and his courtiers	135
14	The Kandyan Mountains	141
15	An ambassador's procession to the court	143

Preface

It was nearly six years ago that my family and I arrived in Sri Lanka, where I was to spend a year collecting material for a book. Our plane arrived at the Colombo airport at 12.30 in the morning and I was exhausted after the thirty-hour flight. I knew that we had another three-hour drive ahead of us until we reached the guest house in Kandy where we were to live. None the less, I was immensely pleased to have arrived. Now, six years later, I have finally come to the end of my book and once again I am immensely pleased to have arrived.

My journey was made easier and more pleasant because of the help and encouragement provided by a number of people both in North America and in Sri Lanka. I would like to take this opportunity to record my appreciation to them. My first debt is to the late David Sopher, who introduced me to cultural geography, landscape interpretation, South Asia, and the geography of religion. Although I did not undertake this study until long after I had left the stimulating atmosphere of his seminars, it is safe to say that I could not have conceived of such a study were it not for his enduring influence on me. I hope he would not be too displeased with the results.

My first and closest friend while I was in Kandy was M. Majid. The guest house which he and his wife run in Ampitiya in the suburbs of Kandy was an ideal environment in which to live while conducting my research. He helped me and my family in countless ways, and I shall always look back fondly upon my time there.

I am indebted to Gerald Pieris, head of the Department of Geography, University of Peradeniya, for inviting me to be a visiting research fellow in his department during 1983. The kindness shown to me and my family by Dr Pieris and his colleagues made our stay there a great pleasure. I am grateful to Shantha and Nalani Hennayake, for their help with the translation of Sinhalese documents and for their friendship during my stay in Kandy in 1983 and 1985. I benefited greatly from conversations with Anuradha Seneviratne of Peradeniya University and with Mr S. Panawatta, Director of the Kandy Museum, who graciously allowed me to use the Museum's facilities and gave me access to document, maps, and illustrations. Messrs. Karunaratna and Ratnayaka, librarians in the Ceylon Room of the University of Peradeniya library, were also extremely helpful.

I am indebted to three former colleagues at the University of British Columbia: David Ley, who shared my interest in landscape and culture theory, Shelagh Lindsey, who introduced me to semiotics and to whom I must still seem like a doubting Thomas, and Trevor Barnes, who encouraged my interest in textual analysis. I sorely miss the stimulating conversation of our weekly reading group at the Faculty Club.

Since my arrival at Syracuse University in the autumn of 1985, Jonathan Smith has exerted a great influence over my thinking. It was primarily through him that I became interested in literary theory and began to see the promise that it held for landscape analysis. He has read and reread several drafts of this manuscript and has greatly improved it. I am also grateful to Brian Stock for generously giving advice on the application of textual analysis to historical materials, and to Maruja Jackman for reading an earlier draft of this book in its entirety.

Two old friends at Syracuse, John Agnew and David Robinson, undoubtedly delayed the completion of this book by at least six months. Were it not for their good company I would have taken shorter lunches and many fewer coffee breaks. Nevertheless, I would like to thank John Agnew for reading the manuscript and David Robinson for procuring Sir A.C. Lawrie's *Kandyan Law and History* from the Foreign and Commonwealth Office Library in London. I am also grateful to Michael Kirchoff of the Syracuse University Cartographics Laboratory for drafting the maps and diagrams for this volume.

My final and greatest debt of gratitude is to Nancy Duncan. Few geographers are fortunate enough to be married to someone who is also their closest colleague. Nancy's influence upon this work has been strong, as it has been upon everything that I have written. She has been involved in every stage of the research and her input was especially great in chapter 2. Her editorial skills have also proved invaluable.

The Social Sciences and Humanities Research Council provided me with a Faculty Leave Fellowship in 1983 and the University of British Columbia offered me a Summer Travel Grant in 1985. Without their assistance my research in Sir Lanka would not have been possible.

Glossary of terms

abhiṣēka: Consecration (see *rajasuya*)
adikar: Chief officer of the state
Āhās Gaṅgā: The heavenly Ganges
Amaravātī: The city of Sakra on Mount Mandara
amṛita: The potion of immortality
Airāvata: Sakra's white elephant
Anōtatta: Mythical lake in the Himalayas sacred to the Buddhists
appuhāmi: Gentleman in waiting
asparasas: Heavenly nymphs
Āsala Perahāra: Festival of the full moon of the month of Asala (July–August)
Aśoka: The Mauryan emperor of the third century B.C. who came to be seen as the archetypal Buddhist monarch
Aśokan kingship: A model of kingship in which the king is mild-mannered, righteous, unfailingly protective of Buddhism and responsible for the welfare of his people
asura: Demon (see *yakkha*)
aṭamagala: Magical eight-sided diagram
basnayāke nilamē: Lay head of a *devale*
bodhisattva: A future Buddha
Brahmā: The creator in late Vedic works
cakravarti: A great king. A universal monarch
Cakravāla: The rock wall marking the edge of the universe
chank: A sea shell used in the consecration ceremony

Cūlavaṃsa: The second two volumes of the great chronicle of Lanka composed by monks
dāgoba: A solid hemispherical dome enshrining religious relics or the remains of kings
Daḷadā Māligāva: Temple of the Tooth Relic
deṇiya: Low, marshy land
dēva: God
dēvāle: A temple to the gods
Dēva Sanhiṇde: Abode of the gods. Northern part of the sacred rectangle in Kandy
Dhamma: The doctrine proclaimed by the Buddha
disāva: Governor of a province
Disāvanē: Province of the Kandyan Kingdom
Diyavadhana Nilamē: Lay chief of the Temple of the Tooth
dooley: An uncovered chair used to carry a person
gandharva Gods who attend Sakra. Guardians of the East
garuḍa: Mythical bird who serves as the vehicle of Visnu
goyigama: The cultivator caste, the highest caste in Lanka
haṃsa: Mythical water bird
howdah: A litter, usually with a canopy, for an elephant's back
Indra: The king of the gods in Hinduism
Jātakas: Tales of the prior lives of the Buddha
kalpas: The great ages of the world. At the end of a *kalpa* the world is destroyed, only to be created anew

Kande Uda Rata: Kandy. The kingdom in the mountains
kapa: Ritual pole
kapruka: A gift-giving tree
kapurāla: Priests of the *devala*
karanḍuva: Golden casket
Kataragama: Son of Siva. One of the four guardian gods in Kandy
Kauṭlīya Arthaśāstra: A book of government written during Mauryan times
Kiri Muhuda: The Ocean of Milk. Name of the lake in Kandy constructed by Sri Vikrama
kṣatriya: The warrior caste from which kings were drawn
lascarins: Native militia
Mahābhārata: Epic religious poem in Hinduism
Mahāvaṃsa: The first volume of the great chronicle of Lanka composed by monks
Mahaveli Gaṅgā: The river which flows around Kandy
Mahāyāna: The so-called northern school of Buddhism, practiced primarily in Japan, and China. It places less emphasis upon monasticism and more upon the cult of images and *bodhisattvas* than does Theravāda Buddhism
Maitreya: The future Buddha
makara toraṇa: Dragon gateway
maṇḍala: Circular cosmic diagram
maṇḍapa: Hall
Mandara: The eastern peak of Mount Meru. Sakra's city is located here
Manu: Mythical king of the Solar dynasty. The law giver
Meru: The cosmic mountain at the center of the three worlds which serves as a cosmic axis and is the abode of Sakra and his thirty-two gods
nāga: Serpent
Nandana: Sakra's park
Nātha: One of the four guardian gods of Kandy

Nāyakkars: A Tamil line of kings who ruled Kandy from 1739 until 1815
nirvāṇa: Extinction. Escape from rebirth
nītiya: Laws
ola: Manuscript
pandole: Ceremonial arch
pan sil: Five precepts of lay Buddhist life
pārijāta: The tree from the Ocean of Milk that grants wishes
pasada: Building with cells for monks
pataha: The pond ritual
Pattini: One of the four guardian gods of Kandy
Pāṭṭirippuwa: Octagonal structure attached to the Temple of the Tooth
perahāra: Procession
Purāṇas: A collection of tales of ancient times
radaḷa: A subcaste among the *goyigama* which constituted the aristocracy in Kandyan society
rāja dharma: The duty of kings
rājakāriya: Corvée labour due the king
rājasūya: Consecration (see *abhiseka*)
raṭa: District
raṭē mahatmayā: Governor of a district
Ṛg Veda: Early Hindu hymns
Śakra: The king of the gods. A Buddhist transformation of the Hindu god Indra
Śakran kingship: In this model of kingship the king views himself as a *cakravarti* who rules over his people just as Sakra ruled over the thirty-two gods in his heaven. Greater emphasis is placed upon the glorious and divine quality of the king than in the Asokan model
saṅgha: Buddhist clergy. Order of monks
sannasa: Royal grant, usually inscribed on copper

Glossary of terms

Sāsana: The religion (Buddhism)
semara: Yak
Seṅkaḍagala Sirivardhanapura: The city of Kandy
sepoys: Native troops in British employ
sima: A furrow demarcating a sacred area
siriṭ: Custom
Śiva: One of the major gods of Hinduism
soma: Heavenly elixir (see *amrita*)
sudharma: Sakra's audience hall
Tāvatimsa: Sakra's heaven on top of Mount Meru
Theravāda: The school of Buddhism which is practiced in Lanka and throughout much of Southeast Asia. It places more emphasis upon monasticism than does the Mahayana school
Tuṣita: Heaven above the Tavatimsa heaven
Uḍawattakellē: Sacred forest to the east of the palace/temple complex in Kandy
Vaḍuga: A Tamil. In Kandy it was used as a derogatory term to stress the foreignness of the Nayakkar kings
Veddas: A tribal group in Lanka
Vejayanta: Sakra's palace
vihāre: Buddhist temple
Viśvakarma; The architect of the gods
Visṇu: One of the major gods of Hinduism. One of the four guardian gods of Kandy
yakkha: Demon (see *asura*)

A *note on transliteration*

Following Dirks (1987), I use diacritics for Lankan terms only on their first occurrence.

Part I

INTRODUCTION

I

Introduction

This book has three general goals. The first is to provide a methodology for interpreting landscapes. The second is to illuminate the way in which a landscape, understood as a cultural production, may be integral to both the reproduction *and* contestation of political power. The third is to analyze the relationship between landscape and the pursuit of power in a particular place and time: the royal capital of Kandy in the central highlands of Śrī Lankā during the early years of the nineteenth century.

The approach I take here represents a sharp break from the way that American cultural geographers traditionally have studied landscapes. Landscape study, a mainstay of American cultural geography since 1925 when Carl Sauer (1969), the dean of cultural geographers, wrote his immensely influential "The Morphology of Landscape," is typically presented as an atheoretical undertaking. Sauer and his students have exerted such influence over how cultural geographers have thought about landscapes that they have shaped a corpus of scholarship that has shown remarkably little variation over the years. It was material culture and not man himself that should be the object of geographic investigation, Sauer admonished in 1925, and cultural geographers since that time have shied away from studying the relationship between social organization and landscape.[1] Questions of how landscapes are used to advance or retard the attainment of social and political goals are virtually never asked. In this study I offer a broader approach, more social, more political, more theoretical than has been customary. I hope by this to convince not only fellow cultural geographers but also scholars in other fields that, as a pervasive and surprisingly disingenuous cultural production, landscape is a signifying system of great but unappreciated social and political importance, and that it offers enormous promise as an object of study.

In chapter 2 I provide a general outline of this alternative approach; in chapters 3 through 8 I apply it to a particular landscape. In developing my hermeneutic perspective on landscape interpretation,[2] I have been influenced by many scholars outside of the field of geography. A few are themselves interpreters of landscape, such as Roland Barthes (1979a; 1982; 1986b; 1987), Michel De Certeau (1984; 1985), and Clifford Geertz (1973a; 1980 1983b).[3]

Within my own discipline, I have read with interest the work of the "new cultural geographers" such as Denis Cosgrove (1978; 1982; 1983; 1985), Stephen Daniels (1985; 1987; 1988), and David Ley (1987; 1989). It is interesting to note that Cosgrove and Daniels come from Britain, where the traditional cultural geography inspired by Carl Sauer and his students has had little impact. They now export a new brand of cultural geography, influenced by such thinkers as Raymond Williams and John Berger, which is enlivening American cultural geography.[4] While each of these scholars differs in his perspective on the nature of theory and interpretation, they share a common goal – elucidation of cultural process through the study of landscapes.

Whereas my perspective represents a departure from traditional cultural geography in many important respects, it also represents continuity in that its central concern is with a time-honored tradition in cultural geography "reading the landscape." What is meant by this phrase? Usually cultural geographers have taken it to imply that one can discern the impact on the landscape of cultural groups. Such readings have been skillfully practiced by cultural geographers such as Pierce Lewis (1979), J.B. Jackson (1984), Donald Meinig (1979a; 1979b), and Wilbur Zelinsky (1973). Underpinning this work is the assumption that landscapes are communicative devices that encode and transmit information. Cultural geographers have long accepted this proposition and Philip Wagner (1972) has written an important book on the subject which, unfortunately, has not had the influence that it deserves.

Accepting landscapes as texts, broadly defined, we are led to examine a number of issues which have been hitherto ignored. The first is the question of how landscapes encode information. At the heart of this question lies the concept of intertextuality, which implies that the context of any text is other texts. In the case of landscapes the contexts in which they are produced and read may be texts written in other media.[5] Raymond Williams' (1982) notion of culture as a signifying system provides a useful overarching framework with which to examine this transformation of ideas from one type of medium to another. I also make use of the concepts of discursive field, discourse, and narrative, for a culture's signifying system can be thought of as composed of what Foucault (1970) terms "discursive fields" containing discourses which are in turn composed of narratives (Geertz 1973b; 1983b; V. Turner 1974). I will then draw upon a version of critical socio-semiotic theory as elaborated by Barthes (1979a, b; 1986a) and De Certeau (1984; 1985) as well as the work on rhetoric of Hayden White (1978), Kenneth Burke (1945; 1969) and others in order to demonstrate the tropes by which narratives are encoded in the landscape.[6]

This examination of the mechanics of how a landscape works, however, represents only the first part of a properly constituted study of landscape. The second part of such a study must breathe some life into this skeleton, as it probes the role of landscapes in the constitution of social and political practice. To address this issue one must first ask how social life in general, and power relations in particular, are constituted, reproduced and contested. Then as cultural geographers we can explore the manner in which one signification system, the landscape, is a constitutive part of this process. In order to achieve answers we must go beyond a consideration of the formal semiotic or tropological properties of the landscape as a system of communication, to see the landscape in relation to both structured political practices and individual intentions.

The relationship between a discursive field and landscape as a signification system is, I believe, best examined in a particular place and time rather than in the abstract. The particular place and time that I have chosen to study is the royal capital of Kandy in the highlands of Sri Lanka during the early years of the nineteenth century. There are a number of reasons why early-nineteenth-century Kandy is a rich locale in which to explore the relationship between a discursive field and a landscape. First, there exists a large literature both on kingship and on the architecture of royal capitals in South and Southeast Asia which can serve as a context for a consideration of the discourse of kingship and its relation to landscape in Kandy. Second, whereas there have been a few studies which have included discussions of the relationship between kingship and landscape in early Lankan capitals (Paranavitana 1950; B.L. Smith 1987; Wickremaratne 1987), there have been none of Kandy, the last Sinhalese capital on the island.[7] A third reason why Kandy makes a good case study is that Kandyan society was highly textualized. By this I mean that authority was assumed, by the literate and illiterate alike, to lie in texts. The political and religious beliefs that formed the discursive fields within the society were written down and these texts served as the basis of customary law.[8]

The discursive field of kingship, which is the one that particularly concerns us here, was composed of two distinct discourses on kingship. One, the Aśokan, was based upon the story of Aśoka, the great Indian monarch of the third century B.C. This discourse included a set of beliefs that defined a proper king as pious, righteous, and devoted to the fostering of the Buddhist religion and to the welfare of the people. The other model, the Śakran, was, potentially, a competing discourse composed of a set of beliefs, the central idea of which is that a king should model himself upon Śakra, the king of the gods and in doing so become a divine ruler, a god-king.

Each of these discourses has a series of political and religious texts associated with it which provide precedent for, and thereby legitimation of, that discourse. Each discourse also has an attendant landscape model. The

Asokan discourse favors the production of a landscape dominated by religious structures and public works for the benefit of the people, while the Sakran results in a landscape of palaces and cities modeled upon that of the king of the gods in heaven. These different discourses, therefore, not only constitute different ways to think and talk about kingship, but produce different material results as well.

During much of the history of Kandy these two distinct perspectives on kingship were intertwined, as kings adopted elements of each. One could see this syncretism materialized in the landscape of Kandy in the balance that was achieved between religious buildings and palaces. During the early nineteenth century, however, the last king of Kandy, Śrī Vikrama, largely abandoned Asokanism in favor of Sakran ideals. He concretized this shift through a massive rebuilding program in the capital. In this study I will examine the relationship between this Sakran discourse and the Kandyan landscape, showing how the landscape became the site of a political struggle between interest groups who argued in terms of competing discourses within a broader, unchallenged discursive field of kingship.

Chapters 3, 4, and 5 provide the context for the interpretation of the landscape of Kandy in the early nineteenth century. Chapter 3 offers an historical sketch of kingship in Lanka from the founding of the first great kingdom in Anurādhapura in the third century B.C. to the fall of the Kandyan Kingdom in 1815. This chapter serves not only to put the discourses of kingship in Kandy within an historical framework, but also to outline the socio-economic context within which their contradictions came to the fore. Chapter 4 examines some of the written texts that underlie the Asokan and Sakran discourses on kingship and their attendant landscape models both in Lanka and elsewhere. Chapter 5 traces the development of the landscape of Kandy from its founding in 1312 until 1815 when it fell to the British. This chapter provides the context for chapter 6 which interprets the landscape of the capital as it existed in 1815.

In chapter 6 I show how the physical form of the city constituted a text which was in turn a transformation of the texts that informed the discursive field of Kandyan kingship. I demonstrate how architectural elements and spatial location within the landscape were tropes that allegorically represented the narratives of Sakran kingship. As such they lent conceptual support to the process of legitimizing the political structure of the society. In chapter 7 a similar analysis is applied to the civic rituals that took place in the capital. These rituals, like the landscape itself, were concretizations of the narratives within the political discourses. I argue that these civic rituals were largely dependent upon the landscape for their effect, since much of their communicative power depended upon the location of the rituals within a symbolically charged landscape. Thus the civic rituals as well as the landscape can be considered texts, the production and reading of which were interpretively dependent practices in the service of power.

In chapter 8 I examine the conditions under which the Sakran discourse on kingship adopted by the last king was challenged. A major factor leading to this challenge was the hardship caused by the last king's massive building program in Kandy between 1810 and 1812. This program can be satisfactorily explained only with reference to the king's commitment to a Sakran model of kingship. The program entailed such exorbitant demands for labor that it was challenged both by certain factions among the nobles and by the peasants. In this struggle over the meaning of the landscape I quote from the texts, both written and ritual, of three different groups in Kandyan society. I examine first the king's own interpretation of his city-building program; second, the interpretations of a faction of the nobles opposed to the king, and third the interpretations of a group of peasants. I argue that changing material conditions among the nobles and peasants brought into play a latent oppositional discourse. However, this oppositional discourse was articulated differently by these two groups, for each had different material interests at stake. The landscape of the capital, therefore, is revealed not only as the concretization of particular political discourses, but also as the site of political struggle.

As has been shown in a number of recent studies, many different types of landscapes, including those that cultural geographers are wont to refer to as "ordinary" are susceptible to political readings (Anderson 1988; Cosgrove and Daniels 1988; Duncan and Duncan 1984; Ley 1987; Mills 1988; Wiener 1981; R. Williams 1973). In other words although the cosmic symbolism of Kandy may seem radically "other" to us, fundamentally it is not different from any other landscape in that it constitutes a text concerning which there is a politics of reading. Thus the complexity of the relationship between landscape, discourse, and social structure can be profitably explored in many different times and places.

Part II

TOWARDS AN INTERPRETIVE FRAME

2

Landscape as a signifying system

Hostility to theory usually means an opposition to other people's theories and an oblivion to one's own (*Eagleton 1983, viii*)

The contextual conception of the world

The study of landscapes, the traditional purlieu of American cultural geography, has also been pursued in Britain, the United States, and elsewhere, by a number of historians, landscape architects, and journalists. With a few notable exceptions, however, researchers have lacked both the interest and the theoretical sophistication to confront what strike me as potentially the most provocative and challenging questions concerning landscape and its role in social process.[1] While traditionally landscapes have been recognized as reflections of the culture within which they were built or as a kind of artifactual "spoor" yielding clues to events of the past, particularly diffusion, only rarely were they recognized as constituent elements in socio-political processes of cultural reproduction and change.[2] Elsewhere I (Duncan, 1980) have analyzed the failure of cultural geographers to address the question of what has been described as "the inner workings of culture" (Wagner and Mikesell, 1962, 5). Cultural geographers who ironically had little interest in culture, turned their attention almost exclusively to artifacts. Dozens of journal articles over the years have been devoted to the topic of the regional distribution – and occasionally the diffusion – of such artifacts as house types, barn types, fences, or landscape "ensembles" which are claimed to reveal culture regions or culture hearths.

Perhaps because of their object fetishism, their fascination with historical reconstruction, and their belief in the possibility of unmediated observation as a guarantee of objectivity, geographers have largely limited their research methods to observation and archival study. Interviewing where possible or other means of collecting data on consciousness have rarely been attempted.[3] Although there are exceptions,[4] the question of the meaning of landscape is usually addressed only from the researcher's own point of view. Interpretive authority is assumed to result from an unmediated relation between what is simply "out there in the landscape" and the informed scholar's stamina for field or archival exercises. This perspective fails to take critically into account the researcher's own "contextual conception of the world" (Butler 1984, 7).

Sometimes a more creative effort is attempted. In such cases it is either claimed that a private and therefore unique interpretation is being offered, that the researcher is engaged in a form of artistic creation for which no clearly articulated methodology is applicable,[5] or that an illusive phenomenological essence is sought.[6]

Until relatively recently, landscape interpretation in British and American geography has been isolated from what Dominic LaCapra (1983, 5) has referred to as "the heavy sectors" of academic inquiry, the self-reflexive disciplines of philosophy and literary theory. Practitioners have been unconcerned with developments within the social sciences or the humanities – with what a Levi-Strauss, a Derrida, or a Foucault might have to say about the nature of cultural process or representation, on the grounds that landscape interpreters need not be concerned with such esoteric debates. Rather cultural geographers have presented themselves as keen and knowledgeable observers who can describe landscapes in ordinary language to anyone wishing to better appreciate the chronology of events and cultural value systems that are reflected in the human use of the earth's surface. Their vision of the scholar is one who, armed with a sound historical training, goes out into the world and records what is there. This is based on an empiricism which sees outward forms and surface appearances as largely unproblematic. Artifacts are observed and recorded as data, given things. Observational data, whether recorded by the researcher directly or retrieved from archives, is distinguished from theoretical statements which are seen as abstract and hypothetical, and therefore not descriptions of the world. There is a strong anti-theoretical bias in this separation of facts and theories, and, unfortunately, this commonsense view of facts as theory neutral is also naive.[7]

Descriptions are not mirror reflections; they are of necessity constructed within the limits of the language and the intellectual frameworks of those who describe.[8] Such a language is not a set of words which have a one-to-one correspondence with reality "out there." It is based on discourses which are shared meanings which are socially constituted, ideologies, sets of "commonsense" assumptions. The same words may have different meanings in different discourses. Descriptions can have meaning only in such a context-bound sense. Thus all description, whether explicitly theoretical or not, relies on language, on some form of categorization which is inherent in the very act of naming. And categorization is necessarily theoretical. Therefore, whether or not theoretical assumptions are consciously held or made explicit, they are inescapable. As Catherine Belsey (1980, 4) puts it, not worrying about the 'niceties" of theory "evades confrontation with [one's] own presuppositions, protects whatever procedures and methods are currently dominant, and so guarantees the very opposite of objectivity, the perpetuation of unquestioned assumptions."

Furthermore, not everything that is real and which has causal power can be observed or experienced. Thus resistance to the idea of explicit theorizing in the sense of positing theoretical – that is non-observable – entities usually indicates a highly self-limiting kind of empiricism which unnecessarily rules out of consideration many of the most interesting and powerful causal factors effecting social phenomena.

Nevertheless, landscape interpretation can lead us to the center of an interdisciplinary intellectual arena where scholars are struggling with such important issues as the nature of objectification, representation, consciousness, ideology, and the relationship between these aspects of a cultural system. At first sight these questions may seem foreign to some cultural geographers, and indeed they are not home-grown questions, products of our own discipline. They are hybrids produced by the cross-fertilization of such diverse intellectual strains as anthropology, literary and art criticism, psychology, and political science. Nevertheless, I would argue, these questions are central to a geographical understanding of the production and use of landscape and its role as a constitutive component of social processes. They also serve to open up a dialogue between cultural geographers interested in landscape and other academics, for the language of literary theory or cultural anthropology is no longer foreign to the ears of landscape interpreters, and landscape interpretation is no longer seen as irrelevant by literary theorists or cultural anthropologists who have adopted a greatly expanded concept of text.[9]

Such an approach to landscape interpretation represents a departure from traditional American cultural geography in three important ways. First, it stresses the role that landscape plays in social and cultural processes. Second, because of this concern with process, a dialogue is established with researchers in those other fields within the social sciences and the humanities in which the role of objects in social and cultural process is studied. Third, the more general issues of theory-ladenness and the hermeneutic circle, of the role of commonsense social knowledge in social scientific explanation, and the status of data become important issues in landscape interpretation.

Landscape's own projection

Cultural geographers have long, privileged vision. Since its inception under Carl Sauer, the subdiscipline has celebrated fieldwork and cherished the belief that through observation we can understand the world. In this respect, cultural geography has paralleled what Clifford and Marcus (1986) in their volume entitled *Writing Culture* termed the "realist ethnography" of American cultural anthropology. Cultural geography also shares a privileging of vision with positive philosophy of science, as both base their claims to truth on a bedrock of allegedly theory-neutral, non-cultural, non-ideological observation statements.

Cultural geographers might profitably consider the following statement by Michel Foucault (1970, 251): "The visible order, with its permanent grid of distinction is now only a superficial glitter above an abyss." At issue here is not whether "the visible order" is of intellectual interest, for Foucault would agree with traditional cultural geographers that it is. The question is, what do we make of that visible order? Need the privileging of vision be central to the practice of cultural geography? How can it respond to the challenge presented by the anti-ocularism that has characterized some of the more interesting literature in the social sciences and humanities in the twentieth century, especially in Europe? The intellectual historian Martin Jay (1986, 182) sums up the anti-ocular position of such thinkers as Foucault when he writes, "What is 'seen' is not a given, objective reality open to an innocent eye, but an epistemologic field constructed as much linguistically as visually." In a similar vein, the art critic W.J.T. Mitchell (1986, 38) argues that the "innocent eye is blind" for the world is clothed in our systems of representation. One need not regret that we can have no unmediated access to reality or that we can not observe innocently. To understand the relational nature of the world we need to "fill in" much that is invisible – to read the subtexts that lie beyond the visible text. The meaning of these texts and subtexts changes both over time and with the changing perspective of the interpreter. In order to know the meaning of a text we must preconceive the whole of which the text is a part. Thus we may bring to bear on our analysis of events in the early nineteenth century late-twentieth-century theoretical categories which, although they should be grounded in a "thick description" of the place and time and refined in the light of this ideographic detail, must also preserve the critical distance of the outside observer through their comparative qualities.

While cultural geographers have tended to privilege vision and thereby adopted an unproblematic stance toward data, structural and post-structural social science and literary criticism have privileged the linguistic and thereby also refused to question the relation between data and theory; while focusing attention on the unstable relation between signifier and signifieds (where signifieds are concepts not the actual referents), issues of epistemology, the theory-ladenness of data or the validity of concepts, theories or explanations has been largely ignored. Herein lies an enormous challenge for the present generation of cultural geographers. For just as one might argue that a landscape underdetermines its own context of interpretation, so one might equally argue that there is also danger in radical relativism. Although I have attempted to place some distance between myself and the cultural geographical tradition, I do draw from that tradition an impatience with groundless idealism. Ideas take place on earth, and invariably they are muddied by the mundane exigencies of biological, social, and political survival. I am arguing here for a middle road between empiricism and theoreticism, whereby our "contextual conception of the world" and the landscape's "own projection" confront one another.

Culture as a signifying system

According to Raymond Williams (1982, 13) culture is "the signifying system through which necessarily (though among other means) a social order is communicated, reproduced, experienced, and explored." He insists that cultural practice and cultural production are not "simply derived from an otherwise constituted social order but are themselves major elements in its constitution" (R. Williams 1982, 12, 13). He further emphasizes its material and practical nature by calling it "a realized signifying system" (R. Williams 1982, 207). He distinguishes it from other kinds of social organization such as the political or economic systems and from more specific systems of signs while emphasizing that, as a signifying system, culture is embedded in other systems as a constitutive component. For an example that relates to the geographer's interest in landscape, Williams cites dwellings. Dwellings, he says, primarily satisfy the basic need for shelter. Beyond this, however, within the context of a particular society dwellings signify a particular kinship or family system and further signify internal social differentiations (R. Williams, 1982, 211). He says that whereas in the vast majority of cases shelter is the primary function, in some cases such as palaces and certain country houses the signifying factor overrides the normally primary factor.

This view of culture as a signifying system which is present within all other social systems and which manifests all other systems within itself preserves useful distinctions while avoiding what Williams (1982, 209) calls "habits of separated analysis historically developed within the capitalist order which assume in theory and practice, an 'economic side of life', a 'political side', a 'private side', a 'spiritual side', a 'leisure side' and so on." Another advantage of such a definition is that it emphasizes both the systematic quality of culture (as a structured system of signs) and its processual quality as something which is temporal dynamic, contested and reaffirmed.

Very much compatible with Williams' perspective is an exciting new interdisciplinary approach to culture and cultural production which views these not only as a signifying system, but as texts which lend themselves to multiple readings. Some of this literature also acknowledges that certain readings are more hegemonic than others and that there will always be a politics of interpretation. Proponents of this perspective include Marcus and Cushman (1982), Clifford and Marcus (1986), and Geertz (1980) in anthropology; Darnton (1984), Stock (1983; 1984; 1986), and LaCapra (1983) in history; Brown (1987) in sociology; Hodder (1986) in archaeology; Said (1983) and Fish (1980) in literary theory; Eco (1986) and Barthes (1979a, b) in semiology; Mitchell (1980; 1986) in art criticism, and Ricoeur (1974) in philosophy.

Within the larger, widely shared, cultural sphere are discursive fields which are focused on institutions. The term discursive field here refers to a range of competing discourses constituted by a set of narratives, concepts, and ideologies relevant to a particular realm of social practices. For example, one could say that there are discursive fields within law, medicine, or religion. Discursive fields may also be centered around central organizing concepts within a society such as kingship, which figures prominently in the present study. Some of these discourses are hegemonic while others are contestatory. There may be a stable discursive order in which competing discourses coexist in some degree of mutual incognizance or in an uneasy syncretism. All the politically significant classes or other interest groups in a society may be supportive, albeit not entirely uncritical of the hegemonic perspective. Alternatively, there may be open and acknowledged conflict between groups whose assumptions are based in different discourses.

Discourses then can be defined as the social framework of intelligibility within which all practices are communicated, negotiated, or challenged. These discourses are both enabling resources as well as constraints or limits within which certain ways of thinking and acting seem natural and beyond which most who have learned to think within the discourse can not easily stray.

Although the terms "discourse" and "discursive field" have been most closely associated with the work of Michel Foucault (1967; 1970) and Louis Althusser (1971), I have attempted to escape the more deterministic, more structural implications of these terms whereby subjects are "produced" by an autonomous discourse which produces the "illusion" within them that they are agents.[10]

According to the literature on discourses, ideologies are inscribed in them;[11] ideologies inhere in the very language and in the narrative structure of discourses. Power relations are also thereby inscribed in discourses. While hegemonic discourses can restrict the terms of a debate, these terms may be subject to external attack. Here again I do not subscribe to a "strong" definition of discourses, in seeing them as separated by ruptures or discontinuities in history, as incommensurable, or as unassailable from the outside. Whereas words may have different meanings within different discourses as Foucault (1967; 1970) has argued, I do not assume the impossibility of translation between discourses, nor do I reject the possibility of real, resolvable conflict between those subscribing to the terms of different discourses. Of course, I would acknowledge that the difference between the discourses may be based in real and irreconcilable material interests, and thus resolutions may often be the product of an unequal power struggle within which one group loses its "voice."

Landscape as a signifying system

The landscape, I would argue is one of the central elements in a cultural system, for as an ordered assemblage of objects, a text, it acts as a signifying system through which a social system is communicated, reproduced, experienced, and explored. In order to understand this structured and structuring quality of landscape, we must first inquire into what is signified by the landscape. I will call this the signification of landscape. Second, we must examine the manner in which this signification takes place; I will call this the rhetoric of the landscape. First, let us briefly turn to the signification of landscape.

I can think of three lines of inquiry here. The first is an examination of local people's accounts of the nature of the landscape, what it looks like to them (by no means a simple question as Roland Barthes' (1987) "La lumière du sudouest" would suggest), what importance they attach to the landscape, and how their readings of the landscape contribute to a politics of interpretation that either naturalizes the social relations in a society or transforms them.

Here arises the question of hermeneutics. It involves the researcher's interpretation of what a landscape signifies to those who produce, reproduce, or transform it. The hermeneutic problematic acknowledges the historical, cultural, and intellectual frames of reference which the academic brings to bear on his or her interpretations and the role these must necessarily play in historical investigation. It also takes seriously "commonsense" beliefs, values, and explanations. As Anthony Giddens (1976, 316) has said, these are not "adjuncts to human action, they are integral to it." He goes on, "lay beliefs are not descriptions of the social world, but are the very basis of the constitution of that world, as the organized product of human acts."

Local accounts of the nature and importance of a given landscape, while situated within and structured by a general cultural discursive field, can at times differ sharply either within or between groups. There is always space within the limits of that discursive field for contestation to take place. Such discursive spaces, or "openings" to use De Certeau's (1985) term, could prove to be one of the most fruitful areas of research into the signification of landscapes.

As my use of the terms "discourse" and "structured accounts" suggests, I am not simply arguing for an acceptance of the locals' accounts at face value, for causes of actions and causes of collectively achieved structural conditions are by no means exhausted by actors' reasons. There will always be unintended and unacknowledged conditions of action.

I would also argue that the distance which the academic can bring to bear, either through training or the difference of cultural and historical background, can be of use in determining these unacknowledged causal conditions. This is, of course, the ironic stance, the outsider's view, the sociological perspective. Thus the perspective of the local provides important raw material out of which a hermeneutic interpretation is fashioned. The job of the cultural geographer is to show how the locals' accounts are constituted within a system of signification, connected to other elements within the cultural system produced within a social order.

The second line of inquiry into the signification of landscape, is non-locals' accounts. The interest here lies in the difference between the discourses within which the outsider interprets the landscape and those of the insider. Again, an outsider may achieve a certain critical distance which may place in a different perspective the local's taken-for-granted or naturalized view. Normally landscapes tend to appear natural or inevitable to those who live and work within them. Except under exceptional circumstances such as will be elaborated below, the tangibility and apparent transparency of landscape features will tend to convince the local viewer of the landscape that the social, political, and economic relations that are enabled by its organization are naturally or even divinely ordained. The juxtaposition of the outsider's and the insider's readings can help to defamiliarize the relationship between landscapes, dominant ideologies, and political or social practices. It can illuminate the way dominant ideologies which are communicated through the medium of landscape reproduce social and political practices.

The third line of inquiry concerns the cultural geographer's interpretation of the system of signification underlying the landscape itself. Again the distance which the researcher as an outsider can bring to bear on an interpretation affords a view of the relationship between different elements in a cultural system. An important focus of attention here is on the way in which the landscape reproduces codes of signification that are present in other areas of the cultural system; in the present study the religious and political texts of

Lankan society are of central importance. One of the questions which can be asked is, how are codes transformed when they are transferred from literary to iconic form?¹²

In this study the central focus of attention is on the way landscapes signify relationships of power. As Geertz (1973c, 448) would phrase it, landscapes are "a story . . . [people] tell themselves about themselves." In the case of the Kandyan Kingdom the landscape is an allegorical narrative of the power of the king and how his power is spatially and temporally contiguous with the power of the gods and the hero-kings of old.

The rhetoric of landscape

Let us now turn to a consideration of the mechanisms by which signification takes place within a landscape. The issue of the rhetoric of landscape is interesting because it raises questions about the processes whereby the landscape as a text is read and thus acts as a communicative device reproducing the social order. Again, one can point to several lines of inquiry that might prove fruitful. The first explores the impact of objectification, the effectiveness of the landscape as a concrete, visual vehicle of subtle and gradual inculcation. The second examines the tropes that one finds in a landscape, which encode and communicate information by which readers may, or may not be, entirely persuaded of the rightness, naturalness, or legitimacy of the hegemonic discourses.

Hayden White (1982, 300) in his article entitled "Method and ideology in intellectual history" has argued that "the form of the text is where it does its ideologically significant work." If we can accept that one of the primary goals of ideology is what Mary Louise Pratt (1986, 140) has termed "reductive normalizing," the attempt to make both subjects and objects appear as fixed, codified, reified, to make what is patently cultural appear as if it were natural, then landscape as an objectifier *par excellence* plays an important role in ideology.

I find myself in agreement with Pierce Lewis (1979, 12) when he says that landscape is "our unwitting autobiography." However, while he bemoans our lack of knowledge of our cultural past, our inability to read artifactual remains, I would draw an additional insight from his statement. It is this forgetting, this "cultural amnesia," which allows the landscape to act as such a powerful ideological tool. By becoming part of the everyday, the taken-for-granted, the objective, and the natural, the landscape masks the artifice and ideological nature of its form and content. Its history as a social construction is unexamined. It is, therefore, as unwittingly read as it is unwittingly written.

Let us now consider the second element in the rhetoric of landscapes: the nature of the tropes which allow a landscape to act as a sign system. The first of these tropes is allegory.[13] According to this view, landscapes do not simply fulfill obvious, mundane functional requirements (suburban housing developments provide an environment in which labor can reproduce itself), nor do they simply represent localized cultural creations (house styles or barn types that arose in New England and diffused to New York). Rather, through the vocabulary of various conventional forms – signs, symbols, icons, and specialized tropes in the landscapes – people, particularly powerful people, tell morally charged stories about themselves, the social relations within their community, and their relations to a divine order.

Most of the allusions in the landscape under consideration in this study are to narratives of the world of the gods which was thought to be a real world with real relations to the world of humans. One could argue that such a landscape is allegorical in the sense that it is a concrete representation of landscapes of a higher order. A structural similarity between the city of Kandy and the city of the gods was created in order that Kandy could partake of the power of its allegorical representation. Although this normally may have been an effective way of inculcating within the citizenry a sense of the normalcy and legitimacy of the prevailing order, it was not always so.

It can be safely assumed that in Kandyan society, as in many other societies, people were taught to think allegorically and that the allegorical method of interpretation was often applied to landscapes. However, I will show below that, while the common people of the kingdom interpreted the landscape allegorically, it was not necessarily in terms of the same allegory which the king had "written into" the landscape in the form of motifs alluding to Sakra, the king of the gods. Jameson's definition of allegory illustrates this point nicely. He says, "allegory is here the opening up of the text to multiple meanings, to successive rewritings and overwritings which are generated as so many levels and as so many supplementary levels" (Jameson 1981, 29).

Another important trope is synecdoche – the employment of a part to stand for the whole or the whole to stand for the part. Synecdoches are powerful signifiers because they parsimoniously conjure up in the mind of the observer a whole narrative. Such allusions are fundamental in the operation of landscape as rhetorical practice. Thus one of our primary tasks in understanding how a landscape works as a system of communication is to ferret out its synecdoches. Hayden White (1978, 73) argues that synecdoche sanctions the integration of apparently unrelated particulars into a whole, "the quality of which was to justify belief in the possibility of understanding the particular as a microcosm of a macrocosmic totality." This synecdochic tension is clear in Kandy, where the synecdoches are parts of a model on earth of the whole city of the gods which is in heaven. For example, a wall in the shape of an undulating wave around the lake in Kandy becomes a signifier which stands for a whole complex narrative of the churning of the mythical Ocean of Milk by the gods at the time of the world's creation. This narrative is an allegory for the creative energy that was thought to magically flow out of the person of the king and his capital. The complexity of the narrative can not be reproduced *in toto* in the architectural fabric of the city, but through synecdoche it can be effectively alluded to.

Metonymy is another figurative relation in which a word or an icon stands for something else, to which it is related by contiguity.[14] The most common examples of metonymy involve naming, as when the name of a part of a whole syntagmatic chain of objects is employed to refer to the concept for which this chain stands. Thus the crown is one element of a whole set of symbolic objects which refer to the monarch or to the power of a monarch. In the United States a reference to "the White House" is readily recognized as a reference to the power of the presidency, the executive branch, or the United States government. Examples of metonymy given by Eco (1986, 90) are when the place of origin is used to refer to the original object, cause is used to stand for effect, container for content, instrument for operation, and emblem for object emblematized.

An example of metonymy in Kandy was the title given to the king. He was often referred to in official correspondence as "The Great Gate". Here the great gate of his palace was used to stand for the king. However, the great palace gates were thought to be liminal, a point of passage between the world of humans and the world of the gods. Thus through spatial juxtaposition, a metonymic relation of contiguity through which power could flow from the heavens down to earth was reconfirmed. The great gates were also thought to stand for the cosmic mountain at the center of the world, upon which rested the cities of the gods. As such, through the metonymy of calling the king "The Great Gate", his own claim to be a liminal figure, not quite human and yet not quite a god, in a palace not quite of this world and yet not of the world of the gods, was communicated.

This particular example of metonymy also, of course, served as an example of synecdoche and simile, for the great gates were an element which stood for the whole narrative of "The world of the gods" on the central cosmic mountain, but they were not of the same order as the divine world, they merely paralleled that world and created an "as if" model on earth. One interesting aspect of simile is that it makes a claim and can be the object of debate and contestation. In other words, interpreters could hold conflicting views on the validity and meaning of the relationship between the form of the city as a model or allegory of divine power and the textual referents of that model.

A third trope that comes to mind is that of recurrent narrative structure. This trope consists of a system of repetitions strategically designed by the city builders employed by the king to ensure optimum reception of a message.[15] Such a trope was common, as Baxandall (1972) points out, in the religiously inspired art and architecture of fifteenth-century Italy where the preacher, the painter, and the architect were *repetiteurs* to each other.

The translation of cultural beliefs into the visible motifs of landscape exteriorizes that which was hitherto internal vision and thus helps to shape, control, and reinforce the internalization of vision. It is through tropes such as these, and there are no doubt many others, that landscapes do much of their ideological work.

Textuality and intertextuality

The concepts of textuality and intertextuality are useful in the study of the landscape of any society that has an important textual tradition. In such societies authority lies with those who control interpretations of the great texts and have the responsibility for defining the society's cultural identity through the writing of its past. Foucault (1975) and others (see Baker 1985; Hobsbawm and Ranger 1983; Stock 1989) have argued that memory, the representation of the past, is an important political resource. Foucault (1975, 25–26) writes, "Memory is actually a very important factor in struggle . . . if one controls people's memories, one controls their dynamism . . . It is vital to have possession of this memory, to control it, administer it, tell it what it must contain." Baker (1985, 135) shifts the emphasis to political contestation saying that it "takes the form of competing efforts to mobilize and control the possibilities of political and social discourse, efforts through which that discourse is extended, recast, and – on occasion – even radically transformed." Traditions are either selectively maintained or invented for a variety of purposes, social, political, and religious. Stock (1989) says that the important thing is that they are "perceived as belonging to the past. They are a part of a narrative of social development which begins in the past and leads to the present." The past, he argues is seen to influence or even determine the present. He also points to the fact that representations of the past tend to minimize diversity and complexity, "bestow[ing] on past experience an overriding sense of unity."

Kandyan society was highly textualized. It was what Stock has referred to as a "scriptural society." Such societies he says all have in common the fact that they "acknowledge the primacy of the written even when the act of writing is absent, suppressed, or unacknowledged. Truth arises from a sacred book" (Stock 1988, 200). For example, the historical claims of the members of Kandyan society to be divinely sanctioned guardians of a religious tradition and the assumption that the king had the primary responsibility in this regard were based on a series of religious, historical, and political texts. These texts, which told of the teachings of the Buddha, of the world of the gods, and of the proper behavior of kings were an important source of reference within the kingdom.

The transmission of traditions employed oral, visual and written media which were controlled to various degrees by the rulers, the king, the bureaucracy composed of nobles, and the *sangha* (the Buddhist clergy). Stock points to the importance of the geographical dimension of the transmission of traditions, and, in the case of Kandy, this took the form of a landscape text produced largely under the direction of the king. A localized version of syncretic Buddhism was established by selecting particular Hindu gods from within the total pantheon and exalting them through the building of temples to them and also through the juxtaposition of architectural allusions to particular Buddhist and Hindu narratives.

The narratives of a glorious past, when righteous hero-kings ruled over Lanka during its most prosperous and powerful period of history, were recorded in the great historical chronicles written by the *sangha* and were incorporated into the ritual practices and landscape designs of kings. The references to a golden past deepened and enriched Kandyan identity and legitimated the rule of these kings who modeled their behavior on these narratives of the hero kings. Thus it is useful here to use the term intertexuality to conceptualize the relation between the historical texts and the landscapes and rituals, produced by later generations of Kandyans, for which these texts became both context and pretext.

If not cautiously defined, the term intertextuality like discourse also may carry with it some unwanted theoretical baggage. In some structural, deterministic formulations of literary theory, it has been used to denote the interaction of autonomous texts. Here I will use it as Stock defines it, and as it has been used in Duncan and Duncan (1988), to mean not only the interaction between different texts and between different types of texts such as written and landscape texts, but also between these texts and social practices which have become textualised.

Stock (1983; 1986) has studied textual communities which grew up around a common interpretation of a set of texts. He points out that these communities were often composed largely of illiterate followers of certain authorities whose readings of a text or set of texts they championed. In the case of Kandy, where the literate population was small, there developed textual communities, each comprised of members whose shared readings of the landscape were based on that community's oral transmission of a particular discourse on kingshiip, each of these discourses being found in the common Hindu/Buddhist textual tradition. In other words, the transmission of these traditional values was intertextual in that it involved landscape texts as well as written and spoken texts.

Stock (1989) has identified an important distinction between what he terms "traditional" and "traditionalistic" behavior. The former is an unselfconscious adherence to customary ways, while the latter is a self-conscious adherence to historical or allegedly historical models of behavior, often with an eye to the political advantages that were to be gained.[16] During the latter years of the Kandyan Kingdom there was a strong sense of the importance of history and extensive use of traditionalistic behavior. For example, the king self-consciously modeled himself and his city upon textual accounts of Sakra and the city of the gods. He also modeled himself upon the hero-kings who ruled Lanka during its golden age. Thus, the written texts became the contexts within which the king's behavior and his city are interpretable. As we shall see, other competing texts were drawn upon as models of opposition by those who wished to overthrow him.

In conclusion, I would argue that if we wish to understand the active role that landscapes play within cultural systems, we should focus our attention upon both the signification and rhetoric of landscape. We should also investigate the role of textuality and intertextuality in the contest of discourses and in the struggle over the meaning of landscapes. These contests and struggles, which may have a basis in real material interests, often play a significant role in the political process.

3
The discursive field of Kandyan kingship

It is precisely through the process of making a power situation appear a fact in the nature of the world that traditional authority works   (*Bloch 1974, 79*)

The historical background

The written history of Lankan society is among the world's most ancient. This unbroken record has been and is the venerated text, the ethnic scripture, of this passionately political people. To follow and fulfill this textual tradition was to have political legitimacy, thus it is written history and written mythology that provided the reference for the struggle for political power. The text endured, conferring a charge and bestowing a gift, its mission borne forward by a chosen people.

As K.M. De Silva (1981, 4) observes, the historical mythology of the Sinhalese is "the basis of their conception of themselves as the chosen guardians of Buddhism," and of Sri Lanka itself as "a place of special sanctity for the Buddhist religion." This link between Lanka and Buddhism was established in the *Mahāvaṃsa* (1950), a chronicle composed by Buddhist monks in the sixth century A.D. and added to after each reign in the *Cūlavaṃsa* (1953a, 1953b) until the fall of the last king of Kandy in 1815. According to the *Mahavamsa* (1950, 55) the Buddha on his deathbed commanded Sakra, the king of the gods, to protect Lanka, for it was in Lanka that Buddhism would flourish.

It is probable that Lanka was settled by Indo-Aryans from Northwestern India. These early occupants were followed by a later wave of immigration from Northeastern India. The exact date of these migrations and settlements is unknown; however, the *Mahavamsa* places them in the fifth century B.C. Although the accuracy of this chronology is debatable, the significance of describing the death of the Buddha and the birth of Lanka as contemporaneous events is not. The place and its people were signified as sanctified, and the religious foundation of the satire was laid (K.M. De Silva 1981, 3–4).

Although there were other settlements in Lanka, Anuradhapura, capital of the northern kingdom of Rajāraṭa, was the first of lasting importance (see figure 1). As the site of monumental sculpture, splendid architecture and a

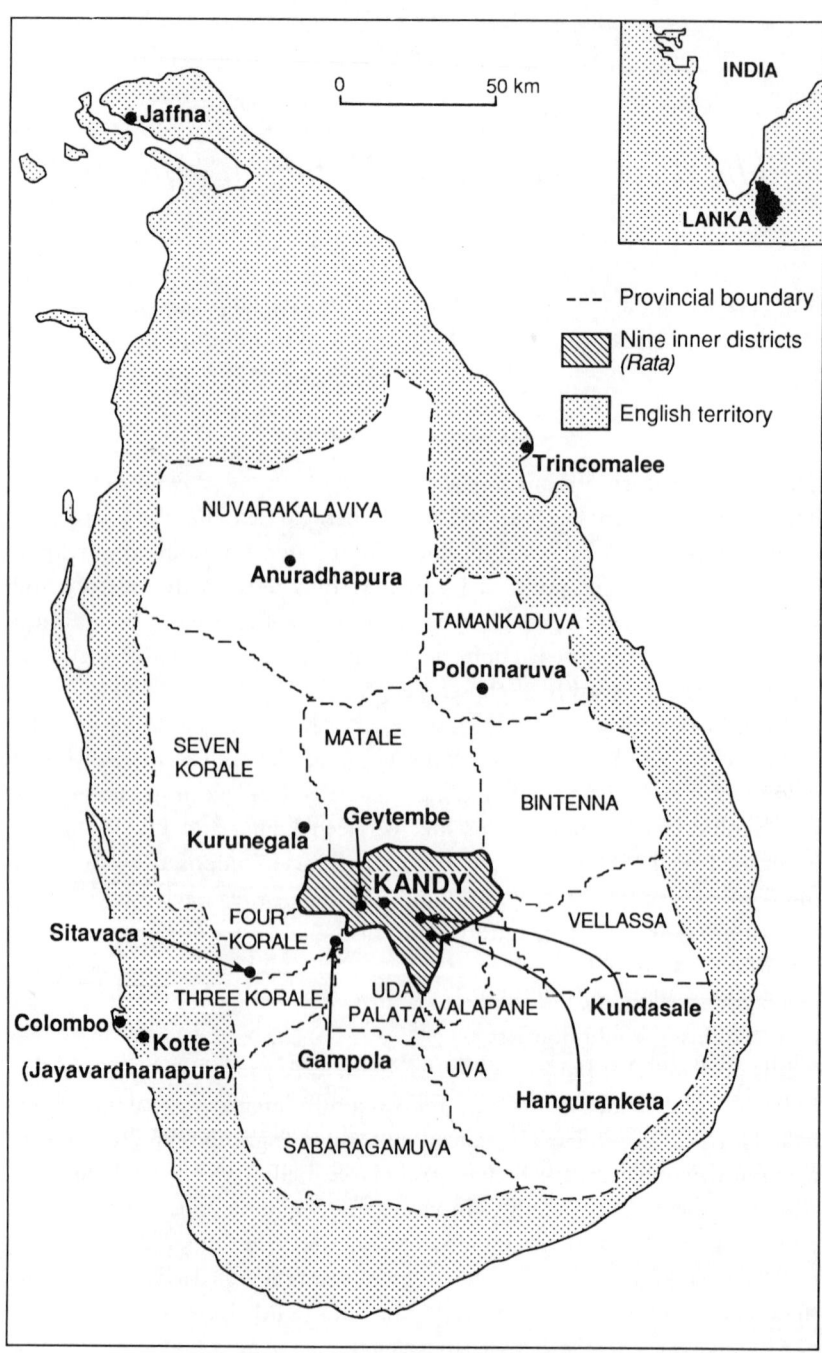

1 Lanka in 1815

technologically advanced irrigation system, Anuradhapura inspired reverence and awe throughout Lankan history. Even the city plan manifests religious significance. It was from Anuradhapura that some of the legendary hero-kings ruled during the height of Sinhalese power, and for later kings, eager to emulate these glorious predecessors, it has furnished a powerful model.

While traces of human settlement found under the citadel in Anuradhapura date from 500 B.C., it was not a capital until the reign of king Paṇḍukābhaya in the fourth century B.C. By this time it was a wealthy city in contact with other parts of the world. Luxury goods such as gems, pearls, spices, and ivory were traded with the Mauryan Empire in India and the Hellenistic monarchies to the west, while gold, glass, horses, wine, and Red Sea coral were imported.

In 270 B.C. the great Indian Emperor Asoka assumed the lands his Mauryan forebears had held and enlarged this domain until it extended from South Central India to the Himalayas and from Bengal to Bangladesh. After his war with the Kaliṅgas of Eastern India, he converted to Buddhism and subsequently dispatched missionaries to the states which fell within his sphere of influence, including Lanka.

Sometime after his coronation, which occurred in Anuradhapura in 250 B.C., King Devānampiyatissa became a proselyte of Asoka's missionaries and was reconsecrated as the first Buddhist monarch of Lanka. To fulfill his obligations as a legitimate Buddhist ruler, Devanampiyatissa inaugurated a monumental program to construct religious buildings. As most of these buildings were wooden and have since disappeared, we only know them through texts. However, there is evidence of a nine-storey monastery. There were also colossal *dāgobas*, which were solid hemispherical domes that enshrined religious relics.

Lying less than forty miles off the Indian subcontinent, Lanka could not ignore mainland politics, or escape the depredations of its rulers. In the century that followed Devanampiyatissa's reign, Lanka was frequently invaded by Tamil armies. The most famous of these invaders was Elāra, who ruled in Aunuradhapura until he was slain in a duel by the first of the great Sinhalese hero-king, Duṭṭhagāmini, in 161 B.C. Elara's defeat culminated a long war, which the *Mahavamsa* records as a glorious victory for Buddhism. K.M. De Silva (1981, 15) notes the significance of Dutthagamini's triumph to official Sinhalese history as

> nothing less than the consummation of the island's manifest destiny, its historic role as the bulwark of Buddhism: the Southern Kingdom ruled by the Sinhalese Buddhist had prevailed over the northern kingdom ruled by a Dravidian usurper.

Although De Silva is careful to point out the historical inaccuracies in the legend, he acknowledges its central importance to the reconstruction of Sinhalese political tradition.

Dutthagamini engaged in an even grander program of building than Devanampiyatissa. During his rule the great Mahāstūpa, a huge *dagoba*, was constructed as was the Lovāmahāpaya, a large building containing cells for monks, and the Maricavatti-vihāra, a Buddhist temple (*Mahavamsa* 1950, 180–219).

In Anuradhapura in the first century B.C. the sacred texts of Buddhism were written down for the first time. This established Lanka as one of the most important centers of Buddhism in the world and began the textual tradition which came to play a dominant role in the religious and political life of the island. A large body of exegetical works grew up around these canonical texts in the succeeding centuries. A politically important aspect of this growing Sinhalese textual tradition was the extensive body of historical literature supporting the Buddhist mandate.

During the early period the system of irrigation agriculture was highly developed both technologically and in terms of social organization. In many respects it was comparable to the more widely known hydraulic civilizations such as those found in the ancient Middle East and China (K.M. De Silva 1981, 32). The Sinhalese engineers constructed a multitude of cisterns, and were the first to invent the valve pit and other sophisticated irrigation techniques (Gunwardana 1971). This agricultural system produced a sufficient surplus to sustain priests and artisans, and allowed construction of symbolic religious architecture. This included colossal *dagobas*, one of which was over 400 feet tall, making it taller than the third pyramid at Giza (K.M. De Silva 1981, 53), and also monumental sculptures such as Buddhas forty feet high.

By the fifth century A.D. Anuradhapura was trading regularly with China and by the sixth century the Byzantine navigator Cosmas Indicopleustes (*A Guide to Anuradhapura* 1981, 9) referred to Lanka as a major link in the trade between east and west. The island, he said, was frequented by ships from as far away as Persia and Ethiopia, sending its own ships out to China, Southeast Asia, and Africa.

The strain of civil wars and repeated invasions by South Indian Tamil armies sorely taxed Anuradhapura, and by the middle of the seventh century there were signs of decline. To the southeast of Rajarata, Rohaṇa began to assert itself as an alternative base for Sinhalese power. This southward shift in Sinhalese power was temporarily stayed in the eighth century, as a result of peace with the Palava dynasty in South India, but pressure was reapplied in the ninth century by the Pāṇḍyans from the mainland, who ultimately defeated the Sinhalese and sacked Anuradhapura. Reconstruction was attempted when the Pandyans withdrew, but the city's position remained perilously exposed now to the waxing Cōḷa Kingdom. As Anuradhapura declined in importance, Polonnaruva to the south, guarding the strategic road to Rohana, assumed importance as an administrative center. Finally, the deathblow to Anuradhapura came in 993 A.D. when the Cola King Rājarāja I looted and burned the city.

The Colas under Rajaraja annexed all of the kingdom of Rajarata. Polonnaruva was designated as their provincial capital due to its strategic position on the route to Rohana, which the Colas were never able to completely control. The Colas remained for seventy-four years, promoting their own Hindu faith and eroding the Buddhist hegemony. However, in 1073 they were expelled by the Sinhalese King Vijayabāhu I who made Polonnaruva his primary capital and spent much of his long reign repairing the damage caused by years of political instability and foreign domination. He rebuilt the irrigation systems, thereby restoring agricultural production, and elevated the Buddhist monkhood to its former position of preeminence.

During this renascence religious, cultural, and economic links were forged with other Buddhist countries in Southeast Asia such as Burma, Cambodia, Malaysia and Thailand. Long-distance trade revived as Muslim merchants living on the coast of Lanka once again carried luxury goods to the Middle East and Europe. However, this flowering was brief, for upon Vijayabahu's death a half century of civil war ensued and much of the good which he had accomplished was undone. But the full glory of Polonnaruva was yet to come.

In 1161 Prince Parākramabāhu captured Polonnaruva and made himself king of the whole island. Not only did he restore the ravages of the preceding half century's conflict, but through an immense building program raised it to new heights. He also restored many of the religious monuments in Anuradhapura. He vastly expanded the irrigation systems in Rohana and Rajarata, and began the development of Dakkhina-dēsa in the southwest where later Sinhalese Kingdoms were to thrive. During the latter years of his reign he conducted a vigorous foreign policy, sending armies to attack Burma and the Cola Kingdom in South India. Shortly after his death in 1186, however, his army was defeated in South India, and Lanka once again was thrown into turmoil. The next century spelled the end for Polonnaruva, as it was racked by civil war and Cola invasions. Like Anuradhapura it was abandoned to decay.

In the following centuries there were Sinhalese capitals at Gaṁpola, Rayigama, Koṭṭe, and Kandy. The move of Sinhalese power to the southwest to avoid the political turmoil in the north represented a major change in the nature of the Sinhalese polity and economy. The Sinhalese in effect conceded that Rajarata was under the sphere of influence of South India. During the second half of the thirteenth century there arose in the north a kingdom ruled by a South Indian Tamil dynasty. This Tamil Kingdom was in constant conflict with the Sinhalese Kingdoms to the south as each attempted to extend their borders at the other's expense. Even in the south political power was far from secure, as rival chiefs challenged one another and the nominal authority of the Sinhalese king from their local strongholds.

From the thirteenth through the fifteenth centuries invasions out of South India were frequent; there were two sorties from the Malay peninsula and one from China as well. Records from Vijayanagara in South India in the first half of the fifteenth century refer to Lanka as part of its imperial domain. It is likely, however, that Vijayanagara's power extended only over the Tamil Kingdom in the north and had little impact upon the Sinhalese Kingdoms in the south (Arasaratnam 1964, 91).

The Sinhalese concession of the north had important economic, ecological, and cultural, as well as political, implications. The highly productive irrigation agriculture in the dry zone, which had sustained large populations at Anuradhapura for over 1,000 years and at Polonnaruva for several centuries more, began to collapse. The wealth of these states, which had supported the monumental religious art and architecture of the cities, disappeared with the agricultural surplus. A large percentage of the population was forced to migrate to the southwest as the land in the dry zone could not support it without irrigation and furthermore the people had become convinced of their vulnerability to foreign invasions.

By the early sixteenth century the irrigation system around Polonnaruva was in ruins and the area was largely depopulated. The centers of Sinhalese population were now located in the south, southwest, and the central highlands, where there was rainfall sufficient to support agriculture without costly irrigation schemes. The move to a different ecosystem was not without cost, however, for in the often hilly country into which the Sinhalese retreated the large-scale cultivation of rice was infeasible. Although rice continued to be grown in the wet zone, the large surpluses produced in the irrigated dry zone were no longer possible.

The state sank to a subsistence level of production and the reduced rice crop had to be supplemented by other grains with lower yields and by gardens of fruit and nuts. Fewer cattle were bred in the wet zone and with the reduction in consumption of milk products the quality of people's diets declined. Spices, however, did flourish in the wet zone and these became a major source of export out of the southwestern ports. As the land in the wet zone could produce little taxable income for the state, the king's exchequer increasingly relied on the export of valuable spices such as cinnamon. The nature of land tenure also changed with the removal from the dry zone. By the early seventeenth century the grain tax was replaced by a system of service tenure. During this period there was also a weakening of Buddhist institutions, and frequent revivals were attempted through missions to other Theravada Buddhist countries such as Thailand and Burma. The decline in Buddhism allowed continued syncretism with Hindu ideas.[1]

At the beginning of the sixteenth century the kingdoms of Jaffna, Kandy, and Kotte were the three centers of political power on the island. Kotte was the most powerful of the three and claimed Kandy as a vassal state. The Portuguese, who were moving to control trade in the Indian Ocean, arrived in Colombo in 1505 and began to trade with Kotte. Portuguese territorial ambitions on the island were aided in 1521 by the partition of Kotte into the states of Kotte, Sītāvaca, and Rayigama. In the territorial struggles that ensued, Kotte sought Portuguese aid and devolved to a Portuguese client state. In fact Portuguese influence became so strong in Kotte that the king converted to Christianity in 1557. His conversion infuriated many of the Sinhalese because until this outrage the legitimate ruler of Lanka had always been a practicing Buddhist. Deprived of popular support and threatened by a menacing neighbor, the kingdom of Sitavaca, the king and his Portuguese backers were forced to forsake Kotte and withdraw into the Portuguese fort at Colombo.

By the end of the sixteenth century, however, the tables turned and the Portuguese were strong enough to pressure the kingdom of Sitavaca into submission. Having reduced Sitavaca they then persuaded the king of Kotte to will his kingdom to them upon his death. They completed their conquest of the coastal kingdoms by annexing the kingdom of Jaffna at the beginning of the seventeenth century. Thus they came to possess the entire island with the exception of the central highlands and the east coast, which were left in the hands of the king of Kandy.

The Kandyans, who came to see themselves as the last representatives of independent Sinhalese power on the island, vigorously repulsed Portuguese attempts to subjugate their kingdom throughout the first half of the seventeenth century. Although the Kandyans were able to block determined Portuguese assaults, the cost of this resistance reduced the kingdom to penury. This poverty was exacerbated by the Kandyans' loss of control over the ports along the east coast. Once landlocked, the Portuguese were able to force upon the Kandyans increasingly unfavorable terms of trade. The Kandyan king retaliated against this economic extortion and military pressure by attacking Portuguese settlements along the coasts and constantly fomenting rebellion among the Sinhalese in Portuguese-held territory. The second strategy was quite successful as the Kandyan king, being both Sinhalese and a Buddhist, was seen as the sole rightful ruler of the island.

At the beginning of the seventeenth century the Dutch entered the Indian Ocean in order to challenge Portuguese domination over trade in the area. The common hostility which both the Dutch and the Kandyans felt towards the Portuguese led them to sign a treaty in 1638. This treaty gave the Dutch a monopoly over the immensely lucrative trade in cinnamon, which they coveted, in return for assistance rendered to the Kandyans in expelling the Portuguese. Although it took nearly two decades to accomplish, in 1658 the combined forces of the Dutch and the Kandyans expelled the Portuguese from their last stronghold on the island.

To their chagrin the Kandyans soon found that they had exchanged one European adversary for another, for within a few years they were completely cut off from the coasts by the Dutch. The Kandyans were too weak to drive the Dutch out, however, and for the next century there existed between them an uneasy truce marked by a mutual antagonism that often erupted in minor skirmishes.

During this period an event of signal importance took place in Kandy. In 1739 Narēndra Siṇha, the last of the Sinhalese dynasty, died without legitimate heir and the throne passed to the brother of his South Indian wife. Thus was founded the Nāyakkar dynasty which ruled until the fall of the Kingdom in 1815.[2] From 1739 on, much of the king's entourage was Tamil rather than Sinhalese and a gulf opened between the kings and the nobility.

By the time that the Kandyan Kingdom arose in the late fifteenth century, the Tamil Kingdom of South India had ceased to pose a political threat to the Sinhalese. The new enemies were the European powers. Nevertheless, in spite of the changed geopolitics of the area, for the Kandyan peasantry and nobility who were ethnically Sinhalese the idea of a Tamil monarch was received with acute ambivalence. The histories of Lanka, with which they were familiar, taught of two millenia of Tamil depredations and heroic Sinhalese opposition.[3]

There are two major reasons why these Tamil kings were installed by the Sinhalese nobility. The first is that in Lanka, as in India, kings were required to be members of the *kṣatriya* (warrior) caste. However, in Lanka, unlike India, *kṣatriyas* were always scarce, which is why *kṣatriya* queens were traditionally drawn from South India.[4]

The second major reason why a Tamil king was installed was that for a non-*kṣatriya* Sinhalese noble to become king would require the consent of the major factions among the nobles. The Sinhalese nobility was so factionalized that they preferred to see a foreigner – even a Tamil – as king than risk losing the kingship to a rival faction within the aristocracy. Having said this, there is little question that the ascendance of a Tamil dynasty politically destabilized the Kandyan Kingdom, for it exacerbated the traditional rivalries between the king and the nobles by superimposing upon it a rivalry between a Tamil royal court and a Sinhalese nobility.

Nevertheless, the eighteenth century was a time when the power of the nobles relative to that of the king was on the rise. The Nayakkars progressively delegated control of the provincial bureaucracy and foreign affairs to the nobles and retired to politically legitimating activities such as increasing elaborated court ritual and the patronage of Buddhist institutions (Dewaraja 1982, 211). In fact Kirti Śrī (1747–1782) probably did more to foster Buddhism than any other king of Kandy.

However, Kirti Sri could not devote his full attention to religion, for during the early 1760s the century of uneasy peace was broken by two Dutch military expeditions to Kandy. These campaigns ended in 1765 with the Kandyans formally ceding all of the coasts of the island to the European interlopers. Although of symbolic importance, this treaty changed the economic prospects of the kingdom very little. It merely formalized what had been a *de facto* situation for over a century. In 250 years, the Portuguese and the Dutch had reduced the Kandyan Kingdom, which had never been wealthy, to abject poverty.

Then at the end of the eighteenth century, the Kandyans made what turned out to be a fatal miscalculation. They signed a treaty with the British, who sought supremacy in the Indian Ocean and were keen to remove both French and Dutch influence from South Asia. No sooner had the Dutch been removed from the coasts than the Kandyans found themselves surrounded by an even stronger and more aggressive foe. Once the English were established on the coasts in 1796 they set out to "pacify" the Kandyan state and bring it under British influence. To this end they invaded Kandy in 1803 and held it for several months, but were later utterly defeated. For the next twelve years it was their policy to undermine the Kandyan Kingdom by more devious means.

The primary instrument of this British policy was John D'Oyly, an Englishman fluent in the Sinhalese language, who used spies skillfully and placed bribes well in order to aggravate political tensions. These tensions were mounting, even without his meddling assistance, as an increasingly unpopular Nayakkar king, intent upon curtailing the power of the aristocracy, was locked in internecine struggle with a rapacious group of Sinhalese nobles. In the end, D'Oyly's policy of subterfuge prevailed and the nobles were persuaded to betray their king to the British. As a result, in 1815 the British marched into Kandy unopposed and the nobles surrendered their king to them. Kandy was annexed by the British and the last of the Sinhalese Kingdoms was extinguished.

The Kandyan social structure

The Kandyan Kingdom in the eighteenth and early nineteenth centuries was economically weak due to the combination of a poor agricultural base, an unfavorable balance of trade resulting from European control of the coasts, and the high costs of the periodic wars against the Europeans. As stated above, the transition from irrigation agriculture in the dry north to rain-fed cultivation in the central highlands was a move from what had been, prior to political disruptions, a surplus-generating agricultural system to a system which produced at a mere subsistence level. In the central highlands, the flat land required by wet rice cultivation was largely unavailable. Such land was to be produced at great cost through the construction of artificial terraces or the use of lower-yielding varieties of grain that did not require ponded water. Population densities were lower in the Kandyan highlands than in the wet, flat coastal lowlands controlled by the Europeans where rice could support greater population densities.

Money was scarce in the kingdom, so payment normally took the form of exchanges of goods or labor. In theory the king owned all of the land in the kingdom; he was Bhupati: lord of the soil. In practice, however, members of the society had the right to cultivate land in return for service. For this reason the Kandyan social organization has been termed a type of feudalism organized along caste lines (Bandarage 1983, 38).

Unlike India, where the thousands of castes are divided into four *varnas* (*brāhmin, ksatriya, vaisya,* and *śhūdra*), in Lanka the first two divisions are almost entirely missing. There were only a very few *ksatriyas* and they belonged to the royal families. By 1739 the last of the Sinhalese *ksatriya* kings had died without legitimate *ksatriya* offspring. The absence of *brahmins* and *ksatriyas* caused problems for the Sinhalese. The need for *brahmins* to perform court rituals was easily overcome by employing *brahmins* of Indian origin; however, as I mentioned above, the absence of *ksatriyas* posed a much greater problem, for only a person of *ksatriya* blood was ritually fit to be king. It was for this reason that the Sinhalese nobles turned to a South Indian *ksatriya* king when the last of the Sinhalese *ksatriyas* died.[5]

In the Kandyan Kingdom there was a bipartite scheme in which the *goyigama* (cultivators) and *nilamakkārayō* (shepherds) were the equivalent to the Indian *vaisyas*, while the low castes corresponded to the *sudras*. The *goyigama* caste, which included the majority of the population, was subdivided into a number of ranks. The top rank was called the *radala* and they formed the aristocracy. The *radala* dominated the most important positions in the government as well as the monkhood (R. Pieris 1956, 169–179). As such they sat at the top of the feudal hierarchy, administering the production and

The discursive field of Kandyan kingship

distribution of many goods and services that were produced both by the lower order of the *goyigama* and the other castes.

This feudal agricultural system was subdivided into three types of tenure lands which were either directly or indirectly controlled by the aristocracy.[6] The first type of tenure was *gabaḍāgam* lands belonging to the crown. These were used for the king's personal maintenance and tenants were required to submit a portion of the rice produced on the land plus *rājakāriya* (*corvée* labor consisting of between thirty and ninety days' service for the king).

The second type of tenure was called *nindagam*. Because of the shortage of money in the kingdom, the king rewarded officials with land grants. In exchange for service, nobles were granted the right to exact tribute from these villages. The allocation of tributary villages to the nobles played an important role in the power struggle between the king and the nobles. The king tried to regulate their power by constantly reallocating grants, revoking grants to nobles whose loyalty was suspect and awarding them to those whose loyalty was assured. Thus, noble families found it difficult to secure their own local power base.

The third type of tenure was *vihāragam* and *dēvālagam*. These were outright grants of land made by the king to specific Buddhist monasteries and temples to the gods. The villagers who cultivated these lands did so at the pleasure of the clergy and owed them a portion of the crop and a certain number of days of service. Because the higher orders of the monkhood were filled by members of the upper ranks of the aristocracy and because temples to the gods were administered by laymen who were also drawn from the aristocracy, the nobles were able to control much of the resources and labor of the country.

During the mid-eighteenth century, King Kirti Sri attempted to strengthen his position by closer conformation to the canons of the ideal Buddhist monarch. To do so he offered large grants of land to the monkhood, but in so doing he inadvertently increased the power of the nobles by allowing them even greater control over rice and men (Dewaraja 1972, 101–109).

The administration of the kingdom was divided into many jurisdictions. There were thirty-one separate departments of the king's retinue, those who were attached to the palace and whose responsibility was to serve the king (R. Pieris 1956, 14–18). These departments were responsible for everything from the king's bath to the treasury department, to the protection of his person. The elaboration of some of these duties was nothing short of astonishing. For example the *diyavadana nilamē* who was in charge of the king's bath and whose duty it was to wash, comb, and dress the king's hair, accomplished this task with the aid of twenty assistants. These men were drawn from about 500 families whose sole service responsibility was to the king's bath.

The second type of administration was territorial. There were twenty-one territorial units in the kingdom, of which the twelve larger units were called *disāvanē* (provinces). These were under the jurisdiction of a *disāva* (governor), who was drawn from the upper ranks of the Sinhalese nobility. The *disavas* had a great deal of autonomy within their provinces and were charged with collecting revenues and sending men to perform *rajakariya* both within the province and in the capital. A *disava* was appointed for a year but could be reappointed at the king's pleasure. The *disavas*, whose families were forced to live in the capital to ensure their loyalty, formed the backbone of the territorial administration.

There were also nine smaller territorial units, called *rata* (districts), clustered around the capital. These were administered by *ratē mahatmayās*, who were chiefs drawn from the aristocracy but who were of lesser rank than the *disavas*.

At the apex of the hierarchy of the territorial administration were the *adikars*. During the eighteenth century there were two *adikars*,[7] drawn from the highest levels of the aristocracy, who divided between themselves general territorial authority over the kingdom. Each was responsible for the administration of a certain number of provinces and districts as well as for a half of the capital. It was the *adikars*' job to supervise the construction of public works projects throughout the kingdom and to conduct public festivals (R. Pieris 1956, 19–26). While in theory they were spokesmen for the king, charged with carrying out his orders, in reality – at least during the eighteenth and early nineteenth centuries – they wielded great power.

The kingdom when viewed spatially and abstractly consisted of two concentric rings. In the outer ring were arrayed the twelve provinces surrounding the inner ring of nine districts. At the center of this ring lay the capital of Kandy. Whereas I will postpone a discussion of the symbolic significance of this spatial pattern until chapter 6, a few words about the relationship between the capital and its hinterland are in order here. The city of Kandy was the central place for the kingdom both politically and ritually. Power flowed out of the capital and goods and services flowed in. Kandy was the political center of the kingdom, for the king and his *adikars* were based in the capital and the families of all provincial governors were commanded to reside there. Kandy was also the religious center of the island because the island's holiest relic, the Tooth of the Buddha, and the two major monasteries that controlled all the other monasteries on the island were located there. Not only did the power of the relic radiate out of Kandy into the periphery of the kingdom but quite literally so did the monks themselves, for all ordinations took place at these two monasteries in the capital. Certain festivals spoke of the centrality of the capital by diffusing sacrality centrifugally out of it, such as the Kārti festival where holy oil was annually sent from the Nātha Dēvāle in Kandy to all of the *dēvāla* and *vihara* in the kingdom.[8] Other festivals, such as the Asala Perahara, symbolized the capital's centrality centripetally because all important officials and thousands of peasants who were tenants of the king, the nobles, the temples and the monasteries, were obliged to come to Kandy and participate in that great annual festival in honor of the Buddha, the gods, and the king. As this festival will be analyzed in detail in chapter 7, suffice it to say here that it served an important political and religious purpose in reinforcing the centrality of the capital. Festivals such as this also help us to understand why kings felt compelled to build magnificent capitals, for a royal and sacred landscape was admired not only by the permanent residents of the city, but also by the thousands of peasants who were drawn annually to the center to be dazzled by the power of the Buddha, the gods, and the king that was manifested in that place.

Until the rise of the Nayakkar dynasty in 1739 the nobles had to worry merely about sharing power with the king. When the Nayakkars came to power, however, they surrounded themselves with Tamil advisors drawn from among their relatives and their retinues. Throughout the eighteenth and early nineteenth centuries these Tamil advisors came to occupy increasingly high level economic and political positions in the palace bureaucracy. Although they never held positions within the territorial administration, they became the king's most trusted personal advisors and through grants of land and trading privileges rose to positions of great wealth. By the early nineteenth century many of the Sinhalese nobles found themselves in debt to relatives of the king. This indebtedness thus decreased the nobles' power relative to the Nayakkar bureaucracy, which increasingly constituted a third power block within the kingdom. The threat posed by this growing political and economic power of the king's relatives was an important reason why the Sinhalese nobles betrayed him to the English in 1815.

The discourse of kingship

Political discourse in the Kandyan Kingdom was shaped by a number of texts, such as the *Nīti-Nighaṇḍuva* (LeMesurier and Panabokke 1880) and the *Culavamsa* (1953a; 1953b) and by an oral tradition specifying the proper behavior of kings (A. Gunasekara 1978). These and other texts outlined the reciprocal duties of a king and his subjects. As such, these texts specified the nature of kingship and set the bounds for political action. Political actors looked to these texts, both written and oral, not only for political guidance, but also to legitimate their political goals. These Kandyan texts had been drawn from an older set of Hindu and Buddhist political and religious texts such as the *Laws of Manu* (*Manu Dharmas or the Laws of Manu* 1887), the *Purāṇas*, the *Kauṭilīya Arthaśāstra* (1972), the *Jātakas* (1962). The diversity of these "foundational" texts produced a complex discursive field within Kandyan society.

In a society such as the Kandyan in which texts are used to support political power, there is an historical, institutionalized basis of opposition and struggles over meaning can be long and bitter.

It is important to note that while the religious foundations of political discourse served an important ideological function legitimating the social order and the exercise of political power, such power was not absolute, for the behavior of kings was constrained by *siriṭ*, the traditional way in which kings of Lanka governed as exemplified by the example of "good princes" (K.M. De Silva 1981, 144) and by the *dasa rāja dharma*, "ten kingly virtues" (A. Gunasekara 1978, 122). One can identify two major discourses within the larger discursive field pertaining to kingship, the Sakran and the Asokan.[9] Both formed an integral part of the definition of Kandyan kingship. The complexity lay in the fact that there was a tension between these discourses; in fact in some respects they are quite contradictory in their definition of the behavior of a good king. This tension led to a luxuriant politics of interpretation.

The Asokan model was based on the Mauryan emperor Asoka (third century B.C.) who was looked upon as an ideal Buddhist king. According to this view a king should be mild-mannered, righteous, and unfailingly protective of Buddhism and responsible for the welfare of his people.

By the tenth century, this model of the ideal Buddhist king was elaborated to the point that the kings came to be thought of as *bodhisattvas* (future Buddhas) because of good deeds done in past lives (Paranavitana 1928, 59; see *Epigraphia Zeylanica* 1912). There was, however, no guarantee that a monarch would become a Buddha. In order to assure that he would, he was required to pursue the Asokan ideals and continue to do good deeds during his present lifetime. The environmental evidence of these good deeds was a distinctively Asokan landscape which embodied and exemplified these values. In order to become a Buddha, kings devoted themselves to building religious structures, such as monasteries, *dagobas* and *vihara*, which would enrich the religion, as well as to public works such as irrigation tanks which would benefit the people. The landscape model of Asokan kingship was therefore simultaneously religious and utilitarian.

At the end of the Anuradhapura period during the tenth century A.D., under the influence of Mahāyāna Buddhist and Hindu ideas, it apparently became more acceptable for kings of Lanka to be considered the incarnation of a god – usually Sakra, the king of the gods (Paranavitana 1956, 71; Mendis

1945, 79).[10] After the Cola conquest of A.D. 1017 Hindu ideas of divine kingship were further reinforced in Lanka. In the eleventh century, Lankan kings first began to refer to themselves as *cakravartis*, universal rulers modeled upon the king of the gods. During this time the kings systematically took queens from South India and claimed such South Indian titles as "Lords of the Solar and Lunar Dynasties" (Obeyesekere 1984, 340).

From this Hindu influence arose the alternative, Sakran model of kingship based on the Hinduized god-king in which the king is seen a a kind of god on earth modeled upon Sakra, also called Indra.[11] Indra was the most popular of the Vedic gods in ancient India and is also the god most often mentioned in the great chronicles (Geiger 1960, 178). He was not only the king of the gods who vanquished the *asuras* (demons), he was also the god of rain who came out of the east, the direction of the monsoon in northern India. As such, he represented energy and fertility (Ali 1973, 129; Eliade 1973, 84).

When Buddhism incorporated Indra into its pantheon of gods as Sakra,[12] he was transformed from a violent warrior king into a benevolent Buddhist monarch who achieved his military victories and right to rule through righteousness. From the Buddhist point of view, Sakra, as well as all of the other gods, was subservient to the Buddha. According to the *Samyutta Nikaya* (1917, 279, 281–82), Sakra in his previous life was a human being, a *brahmin* named Māgha of Māghadha village in the region of India from which the Buddha came. Because of his good deeds he was reborn in the lowest *dēva* world on the top of Mount Meru and became its king. However, Sakra like all gods and humans who have not yet become enlightened, was thought to have faults. Any human has the potential to become Sakra in a future life by acquiring sufficient merit in their present life (Godage 1945, 55). Becoming a god was a stage on the way to attaining Buddhahood. In fact, it is thought that the Buddha as a *bodhisattva* became Sakra thirty-six times before finally becoming enlightened (Godage 1945, 55).

When incorporated into Buddhism, the great Hindu gods, Varuṇa and Śiva were seen as subservient to Sakra and were counted among his thirty-two gods who lived on Mount Meru. However, Sakra, in line with the Buddhist theory of elective kingship, did not command them, but rather consulted with them (Marasinghe 1974, 40). The Buddha converted Sakra and his thirty-two gods to Buddhism by preaching to them for three months in the Tāvatimsa heaven on top of Mount Meru (*Devorohane* 1954, 190), and subsequently Sakra along with Brahmā visited the Buddha (Godage 1945, 62). On his death bed, the Buddha entrusted the care of the island of Lanka to Sakra (*Mahavamsa* 1950, 55).

At times Sakra was known to appear on earth as an old man in great need (Ariyapala 1956, 215). Those who opposed a Sakran model of kingship seized upon this image and presented Sakra as an old, besotted fool. These opposing images of Sakra were later to become important tools in the actual politics of kingship.

In the Sakran, as in the Asokan discourse on kingship, the king was also expected to be just, pious, caring, and attentive to the needs of the citizens. However, the former view stressed the glorious and divine quality of kingship. The king was seen a a *cakravarti*, a universal monarch who rules over his people and other kings just as the king of the gods, Sakra, rules over the thirty-two gods in the Tavatimsa heaven. The Sakran model of kingship stressed the building of palaces, cities and lakes that glorify the god-king. These landscapes were modeled upon textual descriptions of the cities of the gods in heaven on the top of Mount Meru.

Under normal circumstances, the discursive field of kingship in Kandy tended to syncretize these two discourses. The *Culavamsa*, which was recorded by monks, and served as the official record of the kingdom, implies that the two models can be integrated although the kingly behavior conforming to the Asokan model received more praise. The kings of Kandy were described as both *bodhisattvas* and ideal Buddhist monarchs as well as being *cakravartis* and god-kings like Sakra. Similarly, within the *Culavamsa* the kings of Kandy were praised for building *dagobas* and *vihara* as well as making Kandy resemble the city of Sakra in the Tavatimsa heaven through palace building.

Such a blending of the Asokan and Sakran discourses on kingship had also taken place within the greater Buddhist tradition throughout Asia, for the *cakravarti* was seen as a *bodhisattva* and Sakra was a god who revered the Buddha and watched over his interests. The blending of these two discourses, however, was not a blend of equal entities, for the Hindu, Sakran strand was certainly seen by the *sangha* (monks), and probably by the nobles and people as subordinate to the Asokan. The *cakravarti* was believed to be a *bodhisattva* whereas the king of the gods, Sakra, was simply seen as a worshipper of the Buddha. So while there was an attempt to harmonize these two points of view, their oppositional nature became visible when the approved relationship was altered. For example, if a king appeared to overstress the Sakran model he was criticized. At that point the Sakran model became oppositional rather than complementary to the Asokan one.

The Nayakkar kings and the problem of political legitimacy

The Nayakkar kings of Kandy in the eighteenth and early nineteenth centuries were well aware of their precarious position on the throne due to their status as members of a Tamil dynasty. Because of their inherently unstable position as non-Sinhalese kings, the Nayakkars realized that their survival depended upon

The discursive field of Kandyan kingship

the ability to achieve political legitimacy in the eyes of the Kandyan people and to successfully play the different factions of the Kandyan nobility against one another. The Nayakkar kings attempted to achieve legitimacy by simultaneously increasing their attachment to both discourses. They converted to Buddhism and adhered to Asokanism by becoming patrons of the religion.[13] In fact, it is indisputable that the Nayakkar King Kirti Sri brought about a revival of Buddhism which had languished under some of the earlier Sinhalese kings of Kandy. To further strengthen their credibility they emulated the hero-kings of Anuradhapura and Polonnaruva. However, this strategy was somewhat problematic for Tamil kings in that much of the heroic quality of the early Sinhalese kings derived both from their being Sinhalese and from their defeat of Tamil usurpers. The Nayakkar kings, therefore, never had access to this strong Sinhalese claim to legitimacy and were always open to the charge that they represented the traditional enemies of the Sinhalese.

Thus the Nayakkars also employed the second discourse by emphasizing the charismatic model of the Sakran god-king. The latter took the form of a heightened court ritual where greater and greater social distance between the king and his subjects was established. The increased prominence of this discourse involved political risks, for, as we discussed earlier, the two discourses could under certain circumstances be construed as oppositional. As Obeyesekere (1984, 63) points out, it galled the Kandyans that they were required to prostrate themselves before their king while they were not required to pay comparable signs of respect to the monks or even to the image of the Buddha himself.

The Nayakkars, for the most part, however, were able to integrate the two models and play the noble factions against one another. Some kings achieved this delicate balance more successfully than others, however; King Kirti Sri (1747–1782), for example, while increasing the charismatic Sakran trappings of office, also counterbalanced this by closely adhering to the Asokan model by supporting Buddhism and building public works. As a result, he is remembered in the *Culavamsa* as a prototypical Asokan monarch.[14] The last king, Sri Vikrama, however, created an imbalance through self-aggrandizement—a misjudgment which ultimately cost him his crown and the Kandyans their political independence.

4

Concretizing the Sakran discourse: from landscape of the gods to landscapes of the hero-kings

Rhetoric is the art of persuasion, and religious cosmogonies are designed, in the last analysis, as exceptionally thoroughgoing modes of persuasion
(K. Burke 1970, v)

With the details of this system [of mythical geography] a learned Singalese is perfectly conversant; as well and as minutely acquainted as with what relates to his village or family, and infinitely better than with the geography and history of his country and nation   (Davy 1821, 142)

Introduction

Let us now turn to a more detailed consideration of how this Sakran discourse was manifested in the landscape. I would argue that central to this discourse were two narratives about landscape. The first was a narrative about the landscape of the gods, which was comprised of subnarratives such as those about the Ocean of Milk, the cosmic mountain, and the city of Sakra in the Tavatimsa heaven. We will see how these subnarratives were also encoded in the landscapes of royal capitals in South and Southeast Asia and in the early capitals of Lanka. The second major narrative was based on historical textual accounts and the archaeological remains of the earlier Lankan cities. It told of the glories of these cities of the *cakravartis* during Lanka's "golden age." The second narrative was related to the first in that the landscapes of these earlier cities had also been modeled on the cities of the gods. In order to interpret the landscape of early-nineteenth-century Kandy, we must understand that it encoded these two major narratives within the Sakran discourse.

Although, as we shall see in chapter 6, the former was the dominant narrative in city building, the latter narrative was particularly important in certain parts of the city. At times, because the narrative of the landscape of the *cakravarti* was derivative of the narrative of the landscape of the gods, both narratives are encoded simultaneously within a given element in the urban landscape. This "doubling," I would argue, served to further enhance the charismatic quality of the capital.

The narrative of the landscape of the gods

The narrative of the landscape of the gods forms a part of a cosmology, a larger narrative of the nature of the universe. Let us now briefly sketch a picture of this cosmology.

Sinhalese Buddhism, unlike Hinduism, has no creation myth as such (Obeyesekere 1963, 142; Tambiah 1976, 36). Hindu gods such as Viṣṇu and Brahma are incorporated into Buddhism, but are not believed to be world creators. Rather, they are thought to suffer a kind of amnesia, believing that because they have lived for such a long time they must have created the world (Marasinghe 1974; Coomaraswamy 1956, 40). According to the tenets of Buddhism, these gods are no more than lay followers of the Buddha who were pious men during previous lives.

Although Buddhism is silent about what took place in the beginning, it does have a well-developed cosmology. According to this cosmology, world systems are destroyed and recreated in *kalpas* (cycles or great ages). The Buddhist accounts of what transpires within a *kalpa* are a transformation of Hindu myths, as can be seen from the following. According to canonical Buddhism, at the beginning of the *kalpa* there were Brahmas who lived on nectar and were able to fly through the air. Due to their greed they gradually lost the brightness of their bodies and the ability to pass through the air and they had to walk in darkness. At this time the sun, the oceans, Mount Meru,[1] and other great mountains and the continents came into being so that mankind would be able to live (LeMesurier and Panabokke 1880, 4–5).

The world system that exists during a *kalpa* has thirty-one planes of existence divided into three major worlds (*Kāma Loka, Rūpa Loka,* and *Arūpa Loka*). These, in turn, are subdivided into hells, animal worlds, worlds of humans, the world of the gods on top of the cosmic mountain, Mount Meru, and the higher Brahma heavens. All of these different forms of existence belong to *Laukika* (the world of sensation) as distinguished from *Lokottara* (the world of *Nirvāṇa*: Tambiah 1976, 9; see also R.F. Gombrich 1971, 153–213).

According to the Buddhist view, Mount Meru lies at the center of the universe on Trikūṭa and reaches an altitude of 84,000 *yōduns*.[2] High above the summit of Mount Meru are the heavens of the Brahma gods. Upon the summit of Meru resides Sakra, the king of the thirty-two gods. The palaces of the four great guardians of the world adorn the slopes of Meru. Below Meru on Trikūṭa is the world of the *asuras* (demons), and outside Trikūṭa is the world of the *nāgas* (serpents). Mount Meru is surrounded by seven annular seas which are in turn separated from each other by seven mountain ranges (Davy 1821, 141) or alternatively seven Kula Rocks (Rajavaliya 1900,

1).³ Beyond the last of these ranges lies an ocean containing the four continents, one at each of the cardinal directions. The continent known as Jambudvīpa, which contains India and Lanka, is located to the south of Meru. The cosmic Himālaya rises out of Jambudvipa, and on top of Himalaya sits Lake Anōtatta, the sacred lake of the Buddhists. The lake is surrounded by five great rocks, six other lakes and four rivers. The great rocks on Himalaya are Sudarṣana, Chitrakūṭa, Kālakūṭa, Gandhamādana, and Kailāsa. On Himalaya are the palaces of the *gandharva* gods (Rajavaliya 1900, 1–2). Around the ocean marking the edge of the universe lies a great mountain wall known as the Cakravāla rocks.⁴ This whole world system perishes at the end of a *kalpa* only to be recreated again during the succeeding *kalpa*.

This cosmology served as a diffuse narrative field from which certain elements were drawn to construct a narrative of the landscape of the gods. There were in turn several motifs in the narrative of the landscape of the gods which were of sufficient importance for several subnarratives to be constructed around each of them. The first of these was the cosmic Ocean of Milk.

The cosmic ocean, although conceived of slightly differently in Hindu and Buddhist traditions, remains an important symbol for both. Although it represents the endless cycle of the creation and destruction of the world it is primarily an allegory of creation and fertility.

In India and Lanka, where the monsoon was uncertain and crop failure due to drought all too common, water symbolized creation. This ecological characteristic had thus entered the philosophical system with water seen as the source of all existence, as that which contained the potentiality of existence in unbroken unity (Eliade 1973, 188). According to Hinduism, during the primeval situation there was no universe, only water and the starless night. The cosmic ocean contained all potentialities in a dormant state of undifferentiation. Visnu, the anthropomorphic embodiment of the fluid of life, floats on the ocean waiting to dream his great dream which is the universe. Visnu, the archetypal dreamer lies sometimes as the luminous cosmic giant Nārāyaṇa, sometimes as the beautiful god on the coils of Ananta, the abyssal serpent, whose name means unending (Zimmer 1974, 128–129; Campbell 1974, 7). Out of the navel of Narayana rises the cosmic tree, the tree of life which is the cosmic axis and the center of the universe.

In the later Puranic tradition the tree is replaced by the lotus from whose center the god Brahma was born (Eliade 1973, 190).⁵ Brahma in turn creates all the things in the universe, including the other gods. At the end of a *kalpa*, Brahma and everything else in the universe is dried up as Visnu pours his infinite energy into the sun; then the waters of the cosmic Ocean of Milk rise, and once again everything is absorbed into Visnu's dreamless sleep. The symbolism of Visnu in the cosmic ocean is one of the endless recreation and destruction of life. It also signifies that the universe is nothing other than illusion, the dream of Visnu, the great dreamer.

The myth of the cosmic ocean, however, is simply one aspect, although an extremely prominent one, of the whole myth of water as a creative agent. This myth of water incorporates the complete hydrologic cycle, the oceans, the lakes, rivers and rainfall. The tree of life, or the lotus in later myths, which rises out of Visnu's navel and serves as an *axis mundi* for the universe, is also conceived of as the cosmic mountain named Meru. It rises out of the cosmic Ocean of Milk to an altitude of 84,000 *yoganas* (*Culavamsa* 1953a, 5; *Sangaraja Vata* 1955, 112 v. 296; Ali 1973, 61–62). According to the *Puranas*, the great river Ganges flows with the same fluid as the cosmic Ocean of Milk. High up in the heavens the Āhās Gaṅgā, that "starry river" of milk which is seen as Mandākinī (the Milky Way), passes through the foot of Visnu at the pole star and falls on the top of Mount Meru (Ali 1973, 61–63; Zimmer 1974, 112–113; Stutley and Stutley 1984, 178). On top of the cosmic Himalaya or alternatively on top of Mount Meru lies Lake Anotatta, the most sacred of lakes in Buddhist literature.[6] Anotatta's waters contain *amṛita*, the potion of immortality that circulates through the Ocean of Milk and the heavenly Ganges (Mabbett 1983, 66).

Waters containing *amrita* possess the magical property of cleansing humans and making them fit for divine association. According to the *Jatakas* (1962, 50), just before her conception of the *bodhisattva* Queen Maya saw in a dream that she was taken to Lake Anotatta by the ladies of the four guardian gods and was bathed in its waters to cleanse her of human traits (Karunaratne 1978, 113–114). The Buddha himself took a meal on the shores of the lake before his visit to Lanka (*Mahavamsa* 1950, 3).

In the consecration of kings in Lanka, water symbolically drawn from Anotatta was used both to cleanse the future god-king and to ensure fertility in the kingdom (Fernando 1896, 127). According to a seventeenth-century Sinhalese text called the *Anōtatta Waruna* (1954, 289), at each of the cardinal directions the lake has a gate in the shape of an animal. The eastern gate is shaped like a lion's mouth.[7] To the south is the elephant's mouth, to the west the horse's mouth, and to the north the bull's mouth. The four streams then flow around the lake three times and at the eastern end of the lake become the Ahas Gaṅga, the sky river that drops into the ocean to the south.[8] It is *amrita*, the fluid of creation, then, that is in the cosmic Ocean of Milk at the time of creation and which circulates through the universe. It comes out of the heavens down onto the cosmic mountain at the center of the earth and flows back into the cosmic Ocean of Milk from whence it came. It is the rain and it is the rivers. It represents in mythic form the hydrologic cycle that produces the fertility of the earth.

There also exists a creation myth known as the churning of the Ocean of Milk.[9] Every *kalpa* is divided into fourteen *manvantaras*. In the sixth *manvantara* of the present Varāha *Kalpa* the *devas* (gods) and the *asuras* or *dānavas* (demons),[10] who were contending with each other for supremacy, negotiate a temporary truce in order to extract and share the *amrita* from the cosmic Ocean of Milk. All the gods lined up on one side of the ocean, all the *asuras* on the other, and they wrapped the king of Nagas, Vāsuki, around Mount Mandara and used him as a rope to churn the ocean. The great god Visnu assumed the form of a milk-white tortoise and placed himself under Mount Mandara to act as a pivot. As the gods and *asuras* churned, they produced milk, then butter, then wine, then poison which was swallowed by the Naga kings,[11] and finally *amrita*. Upon its emergence the *asuras* seized the *amrita*, but before they were able to drink it Visnu assumed the form a beautiful girl called Mohinī and held them spellbound. While they were bewitched by Mohini, Visnu snatched the *amrita* from their grasp and gave it to the gods. After drinking it, the gods fell upon the *asuras*, defeating them utterly and driving them back into the ocean.[12]

In addition to the *amrita* a series of auspicious objects emerged during the churning. The first was Surabhi, the white cow of abundance who granted wishes. She was followed by Vārunī, the goddess of wine, the celestial *pārijāta* tree that also granted wishes, the *apsarasas* (a group of heavenly nymphs), the moon, Airāvata the white elephant, and the white horse, both of whom were taken by Indra (Sakra), and finally the goddess Śrī, seated upon a lotus and holding a lotus flower, who was taken by Visnu as his consort.[13]

The churning of the Ocean of Milk, then, is one of the great symbols of fertility and creation in South Asian mythology. The cosmic ocean is the place where the beverage of the immortals and the symbol of everlasting fertility, *amrita*, is found. This substance flows throughout all things in the universe. According to the hymns of the *Rg Veda* it is in the waters,[14] it is likened to rain and to milk that flows from clouds or cows.[15] The post-Vedic mythology of the churning of the Ocean of Milk draws upon these early associations of *amrita* with rain clouds and cows.[16] In some of the Puranic texts Soma, the moon god, was seen as the receptacle of the *amrita*.[17] *Amrita* and *soma* are often conflated.[18] Like *amrita*, *soma* is also compared in the *Rg Veda* to rain or the milk from the heavenly cows which are the clouds (Stutley and Stutley 1984, 238). In the *Rg Veda*[19] *soma* which is considered to be an elixir rather than a god and is said to be "mountain born." There is a clear connection between this and the later claim in the *Mahābhārata* that the *amrita* in the cosmic ocean is derived from the sap of the trees growing on Mount Mandara which mingled with the waters during the churning of the ocean (Stutley and Stutley 1984, 12).

The second important motif in the narrative of the landscape of the gods around which a number of subnarratives are constructed is the cosmic mountain, Mount Meru. Throughout Indian Asia this mythical cosmic mountain at the center of the universe is thought to be the *axis mundi* joining heaven and earth. It serves as an allegory of natural and social stability and as such was one of the dominant political symbols in Indian Asia. But Meru, the cosmic mountain, also represents creation; for as Eliade (1959, 16) points out, the cosmic mountain is the navel at the center of the earth where the world first began.[20] Here we can see the conflation of time and space so that the spatial center represents the temporal beginning. The linkage of the cosmic mountain to creation is reinforced by the myth of Mount Meru rising out of the center of a lotus, itself a symbol of creation linked to water and earth (Dimmitt and Van Buitenen 1978, 27).

The symbolism of both the creative powers of the cosmic waters and the stability of the cosmic mountain are further conjoined in the myth of the celestial Ganges visible in the sky as the Milky Way flowing down out of the sky onto Meru's summit and down its sides into the cosmic Ocean of Milk at its foot (Ali 1973, 61–63). The symbolism of centrality is reinforced by the fact that the sun and the moon circle Meru (*Sūriya Sāntiya* 1954, 20)[21] and high above it lies the Pole Star through which the cosmic axis passes. Mount Meru in particular, and mountains generally, are liminal places, where one can pass from one cosmic zone to another; as such, they are the realm of gods (Eliade 1973, 99–100). Actually Mount Meru is not a single mountain but a central peak surrounded by four buttress mountains marking the compass points. Standing as it does equidistant from the cardinal directions, it is the center of the world. According to the *Puranas*, Brahma's city is located on the top of Mount Meru, while the city of Indra (Sakra) occupies the eastern peak of Meru, Mount Mandara (Dimmitt and Van Buitenen 1978, 52 53).

It is common to find Meru and Mandara conflated in Buddhist texts in India, Lanka, and throughout Southeast Asia (L. De Silva 1978, 243; Mabbett 1983, 71). Such a conflation tends to focus emphasis upon Indra, the king of the gods who was assimilated to Buddhism as Sakra. For example, according to the *Samyutta Nikaya* (1917, 279), the lowest of the *deva* worlds is located on the top of Mount Meru and Sakra is the king of this world. He rules here over the thirty-two gods.

A thick forest of silk cotton trees covers Meru's slopes and it is here that *garuḍas*, fierce, mythical birds who serve as the vehicles for the god Visnu, live (*Samyutta Nikaya*, 1917, 288). According to Davy (1821, 141–143),

Kandyans thought that Meru occupied a liminal position below the lowest heaven yet above the world of humans. Mount Meru was thought to be cylindrical (Ali 1973, 48),[22] five-colored, and to lie half-submerged in the cosmic ocean. On its slopes are the four Yogandara Rocks upon which the four guardian gods have palaces to protect the approach to Meru's summit (D'Alwis 1858–1859, 22).

At the foot of the mountain lies the world of the *asuras* (demons) who were banished from the mountain top by Sakra and are constantly at war with the gods in their attempts to reach the summit (D'Alwis 1858–1859, 21).[23] Beneath the ocean which surrounds Meru is the Naga world inhabited by serpents.

Another subnarrative of the narrative of "The world of the gods" is that of the city of Sakra, which was an allegorical representation of power. Upon the square top of Mount Mandara, the eastern peak of Mount Meru, sits Amarāvatī,[24] the city of Sakra, dominated by his palace Vejayanta, his audience hall, Sudharma, with octagonal pillars, and Nandana, his royal park, containing the wish-fulfilling tree, the white elephant, horse, and cow that he obtained during the churning of the Ocean of Milk.[25] He is attended by *gandharvas*, the guardians of the East who wear white robes and ride white horses and who both act as recorders in his audience hall and bring him reports from the world of humans (C.M.A. De Silva 1963–1865, 166–167). Sakra, as we saw in chapter 3, is not only the king of the gods, but a Buddhist monarch as well, whose duty it is to look after the interests of the Buddha. As such, upon the Buddha's death he received the relics of the Buddha upon a golden throne and worshipped a tooth relic of the Buddha in his city on top of Mount Mandara (Geiger 1960, 177, 213). Sakra had also agreed to fulfill his duty towards Buddhism on earth by using his powers to protect Buddhism in Lanka. This syncretic view of Sakra as the king of the gods who is also a righteous Buddhist monarch provided a model for Kandyan kings to emulate. As we shall see, this ideal was supplemented with narratives of the hero-kings and their royal cities, which also served as models. These landscapes of the *cakravartis*, the hero-kings, provided a kind of secondary, or derivative model, in that they themselves were also based on the narratives of the king of the gods.

The narratives of the landscapes of the hero-kings

As Wheatley (1971; 1977) has pointed out, the myth of Mount Meru became a paradigm for the spatial organization of state, capital, and temple in much of Southast Asia. Terrestrial space was structured in the image of celestial space. Many royal cities were explicitly built to represent the cosmos in miniatur-

Concretizing the Sakran discourse

ized forms, with the central part of the city representing the celestial city of the gods, high upon the cosmic mountain. These cities were built as a square or rectangle and fixed at the cardinal directions. The square form of the city was actually conceptualized as lying within a *maṇḍala*, a circular cosmic diagram fixed at the four cardinal directions and anchored by a fifth point in its center (Tucci 1971, 49).[26]

By paralleling the sacred shape of the *mandala*, these cities were transformed into microcosms of the cosmos. The king, by situating his palace at the center of this *mandala*, occupied the center of the universe, and the summit of Mount Meru, and hence maintained the liminal status of a god on earth. By occupying this position at the center of the cosmos, he became a *cakravarti* who could control the world through the magical power of parallelism.

The belief in the causal efficacy of parallelism was an important concept which structured the general, cultural Kandyan world view and as such was not seriously contested by any of the groups in the society. This was a theory of causation based on the idea that some of the characteristics and distinctive powers of one entity could be transferred to another entity if it was similar in form. This notion of causation based on resemblance or homology has been termed 'sympathetic magic." Eliade (1959) claims that the basis of much ritual lies in the faithful paralleling by the worshiper of an act thought to have been performed by the gods in *illo tempore*.[27]

In a similar fashion the theme of the cosmic waters flowing in a great hydrologic cycle between the Ocean of Milk and the heavenly Ganges was drawn upon time and again by kings who wished to associate themselves with the creative powers of the universe, and to draw upon the power of a landscape metaphor for the abundance which they believed that their rule would bring to the kingdom. The religious texts were transformed into landscape texts. Just as the religious texts had a clear narrative structure, so capital cities also became derivative texts with the same narrative structure. For a king to have a proper capital, then, he had to give it a proper textual foundation. There were, however, many texts from which to choose and multiple interpretations of what the landscape transformation of a given text should be like; consequently not all cities looked alike. In chapter 6 I will show how the subnarratives concerning Mount Meru, Sakra's heaven, and the cosmic ocean were encoded into the landscape of Kandy. First, however, I will discuss the incorporation of these narratives into urban design more generally.

According to the older Pali literature and the *Jatakas*, during the time of the Buddha in India the ideal shape of a capital was a square or rectangle which was divided by two main streets into quarters, symbolizing the four quarters of the universe. These cities typically had four main gates facing the quarters of the town (Geiger 1960, 53; Gunatilaka 1875, 41–42). According to the *Kautiliya Arthasastra* (1972), during the third century B.C. Indian royal cities were also square and were divided into four quarters by two main streets running east–west and north–south. Gates were located at the cardinal directions. The king's palace was either located in the center or in the eastern quarter of the city and faced either east or north. The *Kautiliya Arthasastra* (1972) places the palace to the north of center and assigns the eastern quarter to members of the royal caste. The merchant caste resided in the southern quarter, the artisans to the west, the priests to the north and untouchables outside the city. Cemeteries were also located outside the city (Hocart 1928a, 86–87; 1970, 353). Under Buddhism in India the northern quarter was reserved for Buddhist monks (Hocart 1928b, 88).

Capitals such as Pataliputra were surrounded by a moat and administered by a thirty-two-member council (Drekmeier 1962, 169). This provides strong evidence that by the third century B.C. royal capitals were modeled on the city of the king of the gods and his thirty-two lesser gods upon Mount Meru. Furthermore, the moat may not only have served defensive purposes, but also may have represented the annular cosmic ocean.[28]

Subsequently, throughout Lanka, Burma, Cambodia, Thailand, Laos, Indonesia, and parts of India, the model of the cosmos centered upon Mount Meru was adopted for capital cities (Fritz 1986; Mus 1937; Heine-Geldern 1942; Geertz 1980; 1983b; Shorto 1963; Tambiah 1976; Wheatley 1971; 1983).

As Heine-Geldern (1942) in his now classic article on conceptions of state and kingship in Southeast Asia writes, there was a persistent attempt to symbolically reduce the universe, the "macrocosmos," to the royal capital, the "microcosmos." In Hinduized states throughout the region, Meru, the cosmic axis, was centered on the temple of a god. In Theravada Buddhist nations such as Lanka, Cambodia, Burma, and Thailand, the cosmic axis was centered on a relic of the Buddha or on the palace of the king, the representative of Sakra, the king of the gods. The royal capital was thought of not as a mere city but, as Geertz (1980) has pointed out with reference to the Balinese Negara, as an "exemplary center," a microcosm of the universe and a paradigm of order for the kingdom.

In fourteenth-century Sukhodaya (Thailand) the capital followed a cosmological layout. The city was surrounded by three earthen ramparts and had four gates at the cardinal directions. At the center of the city lay the palace/temple complex containing important religious relics (Tambiah 1976, 86–87). The Mon, Pyu, Burmese, and Shan in what is today Burma made their capitals conform where possible to a square plan as prescribed by the *Kautiliya Arthasastra*. These cities had twelve gates connected by straight roads forming four quarters of four blocks each (Shorto 1963, 577).

Concretizing the Sakran discourse

Perhaps the outstanding example of cosmic modeling was the Angkor complex in Cambodia. On the top of the Bakheng complex in the center of the Angkor was the main pyramidal shrine surrounded by four smaller shrines symbolizing Mount Meru's buttress mountains. There were 109 shrines on the complex representing the polar axis, and the four phases of the moon multiplied by the twenty-seven mansions, thus concretizing the cosmic cycle. These tower shrines were arranged in such a fashion that a person approaching from the cardinal directions could see only thirty-three of them, representing the thirty-three gods on Mount Meru (Filliozat 1954, referenced in Mabbett 1983, 82; Mus 1937).

In the twelfth century King Jayavarman VII's capital, Angkor Thom, contained the central shrine palace complex, the Bayon, modeled upon Mount Mandara, at the central point between the gateways at the cardinal directions. The city was surrounded by a rectangular rampart and a moat which was clearly meant to represent the Ocean of Milk. This moat was referred to in a contemporary inscription as "the holy sea of victory (*Jayasindhu*) which in its measureless depth attained the serpent world" (Mus 1937, 69). The balustrades of the bridge leading across this moat consisted of carved stone figures of gods and *asuras* holding an enormous nine-headed serpent. The symbolism here was clear. The bridge over the moat represented the gods and *asuras* churning the Ocean of Milk (Mus 1937, 65–75; Heine-Geldern 1942, 15–30). The sea of victory referred to in the inscription alluded to the victory of the gods over the *asuras* and the ensuing fertility which the victory produced. Throughout the countryside, Jayavarman built a series of temples complete with representations of Lake Anotatta whose water was a powerful apotropaion (Wheatley 1971, 438). The landscape, therefore, spoke allegorically of that victory of good over evil in this capital, and of the recreation of the primordial creative act in this place at the center of the universe. The capital, and by extension the king who rules there, is given a cosmic identity.

After the decline of Buddhism in India, such cosmic modeling became less pronounced there. Although there was evidence of the use of cosmic models in fourteenth century Vijayanagara, it was not nearly as strongly developed as in Southeast Asia (Fritz 1986). Cosmic modeling was, however, still clearly visible over the centuries in Banaras as well as in eighteenth-century Jaipur, and sixteenth- and seventeenth-century Madurai (Eck 1982; 1987, 5; Fritz 1986; H.B. Reynolds 1987).

The early capitals of Lanka, Anuradhapura and Polonnaruva, had extensive contacts with both South Indian and Southeast Asian kingdoms. The links with South India are extensively documented from the fourth century B.C. in the *Mahavamsa* (1950) and *Culavamsa* (1953a; 1953b). There was also contact with Buddhists in the north east of India in the eleventh century (Paranavitana 1928, 51). In addition, Anuradhapura had links with Java in the eighth century A.D. (De Casparis 1961). As a result of these contacts the Javanese built an Abhayagiri monastery patterned upon one by the same name in Anuradhapura. From the twelfth to the fourteenth centuries there were also extensive ties with Indonesia (Evers 1972, 15), and from the twelfth century on, religious intercourse with Thailand (Van Lohuizen De Leeuw 1978, 139; Paranavitana 1932; Pieris and Crosby 1945; Tambiah 1976, 90–98; Malalgoda 1976, 62–63), Cambodia (Panditha 1954–1955, 127), and Burma (Arasaratnam 1963, 69; Van Gollenesse [1751] 1974, 17–18, 48; R.F. Gombrich 1971, 34; Shorto 1963, 574).

Fully elaborated cosmic cities modeled upon the cities of the gods were rare, however, during the Anuradhapura period in Lanka, for Theravada Buddhist orthodoxy repudiated such models at the time (Obeyesekere 1984, 340). Anuradhapura, the first of the great capitals of Lanka, although it did not match the cosmological modeling of a number of Southeast Asian capitals, did incorporate elements of the religious narrative. For example, the city was divided by streets running in north–south and east–west directions into four sections representing the four quarters of the universe (Geiger 1960, 54; Hocart 1924–1928d, 150–151). Although the city was not a true square, it was conceived of as such, for example the *Thūpavaṃsa* (1947) erroneously claims that the eastern, western, northern, and southern gates were all equidistant from one another. The king's palace and the Temple of the Tooth Relic were adjacent to each other in the eastern part of the city and the monasteries lay outside of the city proper, one to the north and the other to the south (Hocart 1924–1928d, 150–151).[29] Wickremaratne (1987) argues that Anuradhapura was in fact a cosmic city with two cosmic axes. The first was the palace/Tooth Temple complex in the city proper and the second was the sacred bo tree grown from a shoot taken from the tree under which the Buddha was enlightened in Bodhgaya, India. The bo tree in Anuradhapura was located in the Mahāmēgha park on the outskirts of the city. Wickremaratne goes on to argue that plowing of the sacred *sima* (furrow) around the city proper and the park, united both axes within the sacred space of the city. Therefore, in these respects at least, the layout of the city corresponded to that of a cosmic city.

The *Mahavamsa* (1950) and *Culavamsa* (1953a) also conceptualize Anuradhapura as a cosmic city. A great park named Nandana after the park of Sakra in the Tavatimsa heaven was laid out at the southern edge of the city (*Mahavamsa* 1950, 77). Allusions to the capital being on the cosmic axis, which is also the cosmic mountain, are found frequently in the chronicles. For example, it is said that when the monk Mahinda came to preach the *dhamma* for the first time in Lanka, the gods were summoned from high above Mount

Concretizing the Sakran discourse

Meru and the *nagas* from below the cosmic mountain (*Mahavamsa* 1950, 94). Similarly, when the branch of the bo tree was brought from Bodhgaya it was placed in the Mahamegha park at the east gate of the city where a bo tree was said to have been planted during the times of the three previous Buddhas who had visited Lanka (*Mahavamsa* 1950, 99–100, 131). As the bo tree under which the Buddha was enlightened was a cosmic axis, this spot in Anuradhapura is considered a perennial axis.

King Dutthagamani (161–137 B.C.) engaged in explicit cosmic modeling when he said to the monks in Mahamegha Park (*Mahavamsa* 1950, 183) "I will build for you a *pasada* [building with cells for monks] like to a palace of the gods. Send to a celestial palace and make me a drawing of it." The *Mahavama* further states that several monks went to the heaven and returned with such a drawing which the king reproduced in the park. The god Sakra was said to have commanded the divine architect, Viśvakarma, to build bricks so that King Dutthagamani could build the great *dagoba* in the city (*Mahavamsa* 1950, 187). In this way, the gods were implicated in the construction of the city of Anuradhapura.

Furthermore, Anuradhapura was compared in numerous places in the chronicles to the city of the gods (*Culavamsa* 1953a, 19, 46, 167). There were also direct references to the palace of the god Sakra. It was said that Sena II (853–887 A.D.) had the Lōhapāsāda (the Brazen Palace) restored "so that it resembled the Vejayanta palace [of Sakra]" and Kassapa IV (898–914 A.D.) "had *maṇḍapas* [halls] built resembling Vejayanta, painted in different colours" (*Culavamsa* 1953a, 153, 165).

It is important to note that although there was some cosmic modeling in Anuradhapura, it consisted of temples and monuments in honor of the religion rather than palaces for the glorification of the king that were modeled after the city of the gods. This conforms to the tenets of Theravada Buddhism, which during this period did not sanction the devotion of great expense to sacral kingship.

The theme of cosmic waters also formed an important component of urban texts in Lanka. In addition to their symbolic value, ponds and canals were useful as irrigation facilities for the benefit of the people. In this way the kings could engage in cosmic modeling while still adhering to the tenets of Theravada Buddhism. A early as the beginning of the fourth century B.C., King Pandukabhaya (c. 394–307 B.C.) built and enlarged a number of ponds in and around Anuradhapura. The king "had the pond deepened and abundantly filled with water, and since he had taken water there from, when victorious (for his consecration), they called it Jayavapi (pond of victory)" (*Mahavamsa* 1950, 74).[30] Although as I have mentioned, ponds served practical purposes for irrigation and drinking, I will focus on their symbolic significance. By naming a pond "Anotatta" or "Ocean of Milk" it became symbolically transformed by means of the magic of parallelism and thus acquired some of the characteristics of its mythic original. A capital which possessed one of these ponds thereby captured some of the fertility and cosmic power of creation. Water from such ponds was used in consecration because through this ceremony a king was prepared for divine association and transformed from a mere mortal into a higher liminal form. He was being reborn or recreated through the medium of ritual; projected back into the primordial time of the gods.[31] It is revealing that King Pandukabhaya should name his consecration pond "Jayavapi" or "pond of victory" for this, I believe, refers to the churning of the Ocean of Milk and the victory of the gods over the demons at the time of creation. According to the *Mahavamsa* (1950, 79–80), the Indian emperor Asoka sent a number of ritual items for the consecration of King Devanampiyatissa, the first Buddhist Lankan king, including water from Lake Anotatta and water from the Ganges. From that time forward, water from Lake Anotatta was always used for consecrations in ancient Lanka (Fernando 1896, 125–130). As J.M. Seneviratne (1918) points out, however, the water "from Lake Anotatta" that was used in consecrations was probably drawn from a pond in Anuradhapura. According to the *Pūjāvaliya* (Gunasekara 1895, 24), King Mahāsena (A.D. 334–362):

> engaged the services of demons; caused to be constructed [the reservoir] Miṇihiri Veva; dammed up the Karagaṇgā to supply water to Minihiri Veva; excavated [the canal] Talavatu Ela, tracing the marks indicated by the gods; supplied water thereby to cultivate 20,000 fields; provided for a regular supply of alms to the priesthood in Denānakaya; caused to be constructed by employing the labour of men and demons, seventeen large tanks. . . .

Here we can clearly see the cosmic link between practical irrigation projects and the gods.

Perhaps the clearest example of a cosmic city in early Lanka was built by one of the great villains of Sinhalese history, the parricide Kassapa I (A.D. 478–496). He ruled from a palace, built on top of Sigiri rock approximately thirty-eight miles to the southeast of Anuradhapura. He engaged in cosmic imagery, comparing his palace to that of the god Kuvera upon Kailasa mountain (*Culavamsa* 1953a, 42–45). He also constructed the Sigiri Vava (reservoir) which Paranavitana (1950, 150) believes was meant to represent Lake Anotatta.[32]

By the eleventh century, under the influence of Mahayana Buddhist ideas, the kings of Lanka increasingly came to see themselves as *bodhisattvas* and like Sakra in their divinity. Consequently, the great King Parakramabahu I

Concretizing the Sakran discourse

(A.D. 1153–1186) added even more cosmic symbolism to the lanscape of his capital than most of the kings of the earlier Anuradhapura period (see B.L. Smith 1987).

While still a prince, Parakramabahu constructed a cosmic city known as Paṇḍuvas Nuwara which was a representation of the universe in miniature. According to Paranavitana (1972, 131), at the center of this city he had constructed a square structure representing Mount Meru which was encircled by a series of brick ridges and depressions of white clay corresponding to the circular mountains and cosmic oceans surrounding Mount Meru. Paranavitana (1972, 132) argues that Parakramabahu probably used such a microcosmic representation of the macrocosmos to magically reinforce his claims to be a *cakravarti*. On the outskirts of this city he dammed up and greatly enlarged the Paṇḍavapi reservoir and renamed it the Parākkamasamudda (the Sea of Parakramabahu). On an island in the middle of the reservoir he built, on the summit of a rock, a *dagoba* "that showed forth the beauty of Kailasa mountain. In its center he built a royal pleasure house, three stories high and very beautiful, which was a habitation for a fulness of worldly joys" (*Culavamsa* 1953a, 280).[33] According to Obeyesekere (1984, 341), it is likely that the king thought of this particular reservoir as either the Ocean of Milk or as Lake Anotatta.

After a series of wars of succession, Prince Parakramabahu defeated his rivals for the kingship of Lanka and "entered the fair city of Pulatthinagara [Polonnaruva] even as the king of the gods (entered) the city of the gods after his victory in the battle with the Asuras" (*Culavamsa* 1953a, 346). In this passage we can clearly see that the capital was considered to be a heaven of the gods on Meru and therefore linked both to the Ocean of Milk at Meru's foot and Lake Anotatta on its summit. Upon capturing Polonnaruva, King Parakramabahu set about rebuilding it and making it once again a fit capital for a king (Law 1954–1955).

As the *Culavamsa* (1953b, 8–14) reveals, the king modeled his new capital on that of Sakra. The city was a walled rectangle with streets running north–south and east–west, and divided into two by a wall. The southern half was larger and contained the king's elevated enclosure and his island park. The king' palace within the enclosure faced east. To the immediate north of the enclosure stood a collection of temples including a Temple of the Tooth. On the west side stood the king's pleasure garden and to the north lay the majority of the temples of the gods (Hocart 1924–1928d, 151–152).[34] Around the city he built three great walls each narrower than the other as prescribed by the *Kautiliya Arthasastra* (*Culavamsa* 1953b, 6). Such walls represent, I would argue, the annular mountain range around the cosmic mountain.

His palace, the chronicle claimed (*Culavamsa* 1953b, 7–8) was named

Vejayanta after Sakra's palace on Mount Meru and was seven stories high with 1,000 chambers and hundreds of pillars of different hues. The height of the palace's splendor was reached in the royal sleeping apartment which had clusters of pearls suspended at the four corners which are described as reflecting moonlight like the divine Ganges river and networks of golden bells which sounded like the five mythical musical instruments. Here the symbolism of the city of Sakra on Mount Meru is clear, for the divine Ganges circles the city of Sakra on Meru and in his city are musicians who play the five instruments.

Parakramabahu erected fourteen gates around the city, each named after a mythical figure (*Culavamsa* 1953b, 20). He named his park Nandana after the park of the god Sakra in the Tavatimsa heaven (*Culavamsa* 1953b, 12). Among the reservoirs and ponds that he built in and around the capital one pond was named Nandāpokkharaṇī and was modeled on a pond in "the divine garden of Nandana" in Sakra's paradise, while another which was named "Anantapokkharaṇī had stones whose layers resembled the coils of Ananta (the serpent king)." (*Culavamsa* 1953b, 14–15). Ananta, which means "endless" or "infinite", is another name for the serpent Śeṣa who remains at the end of a *kalpa* when all else disintegrates. It is this serpent who floats on the cosmic Ocean of Milk cradling the sleeping Visnu waiting for the "dream of the universe" to begin anew (Stutley and Stutley 1984, 12).

Whereas these two ponds appear to have been largely decorative in function, he also built large reservoirs for irrigation. For example, he constructed a great reservoir called the Parakramasamudra or Sea of Parakrama which formed the western boundary of his city, mirroring the great Ocean of Milk which lay at the foot of the cosmic mountain.[35] It was described in the *Culavamsa* (1953b, 117–118) in the following terms:

> To put away the sufferings of famine from living creatures that most excellent of men had many tanks and canals made in divers places. By damming up the Karanganga by a great barrier between the hills and bringing its mighty flood of waters hither by means of a vast canal called Ākāsagaṅgā, the Ruler created that king of reservoirs continually filled with water and known by the name of Parakkamasamudda in which there was an island resplendent with a superb royal palace and which was like to a second ocean.

Whereas this reservoir was unquestionably of practical significance in irrigating dry lands, as the monks who wrote the *Culavamsa* emphasized, it would also appear to have cosmic significance. The canal which brought water to the reservoir was called the Akasaganga (Ahas Ganga) which, as was noted earlier, was the heavenly Ganges. The reservoir itself is called a second ocean, which presumably refers to the cosmic Ocean of Milk into which the Ahas Ganga falls. "The king also had a canal constructed, called Gambhīra (the deep), which started at the flood-escape called Makara of the Parakkamasamudda" (*Culavamsa* 1953b, 120). The "deep" usually designates the endless depths of the cosmic ocean while the Makara is the *vāhana* (vehicle) of the goddess Ganga and stands for the river Ganges (Mudiyanse 1959, 52).[36] Thus, through metonymy, the canal and reservoir systems were symbolically transformed into the whole hydrologic process of the universe in microcosm. Although there were in fact earlier instances, as Obeyesekere (1984, 341) points out, "it may have been Parakramabahu I's unique achievement to have combined cosmic symbolism with the more practical agricultural orientation of his predecessors: a cosmic ocean that is also an irrigation work, thus appeasing Theravada orthodoxy."

From the archaeological remains and the accounts of the *Culavamsa* it appears that Parakramabahu undertook a massive building program in Polonnaruva. He appears to have gone to greater lengths to mirror the city of the gods than had been attempted in Anuradhapura, and to have devoted great attention to the construction of his palace. The goal of his building program was, in the words of the *Culavamsa* (1953b, 20), to "make the aforetime small town of Pulatthinagara [Polonnaruva] which had suffered by many wars, splendidly adorned as the city of the Tavatimsa gods." He was probably able to do this because by the twelfth century the notion of a god-king was more firmly entrenched in Lanka than it had been during the Anuradhapura period. He did, however manage to maintain the balance referred to in the last chapter between the Asokan and Sakran discourses on kingship by building religious structures as well as palaces and by building irrigation facilities that served also to symbolize the Cosmic Ocean.

Approximately a century later King Vijayabahu IV (A.D. 1271–1273) acted in much the same manner by restoring the city of Polonnaruva, which had again fallen upon hard times. "And the Ruler restored superb Pulatthinagara as it had been aforetime, surrounded by a moat, deep as the sea, with a fine chain of walls like to the Cakkavala mountains" (*Culavamsa* 1953b, 191). Here one finds the symbolism of the capital of Polonnaruva as a microcosm of the whole world surrounded by the deep ocean and the Cakravala mountains that mark the outermost boundary of the universe.

When the Sinhalese kings were driven out of Polonnaruva by South Indian invaders in the thirteenth century and were forced to relocate their capitals further south and west, they adopted an even more fully elaborated South Indian conception of divine kingship (Obeyesekere 1984, 342; Derrett 1956, 139). Obeyesekere (1984, 342) astutely observes that this movement of Sinhalese power to the southwest had an impact upon the kings' use of reservoirs for symbolic purposes. Reservoirs which had such practical importance for agriculture in the dry north of Lanka served little practical purpose in the wet southwest. This did not restrain kings who wished to glorify their cities with cosmic symbolism from digging ponds, but it made their projects less easily justified as they were no longer able to demand labor for such large-scale symbolic projects under the guise of public works.[37]

For the later kingdoms in the wet zone, highly textualized urban landscapes continued to be an integral part of the ideology of the god-king. The urge to create divine landscapes was tempered, however by the political and economic realities facing these kingdoms. Because the wet zone was politically unstable and could not produce as much agricultural surplus as did the irrigation agriculture in the dry zone, these kingdoms were less able to bear the cost of monumental city building. Although a number of capitals arose in the wet zone between the fall of Polonnaruva in the thirteenth century and the rise of Kandy in the fifteenth (see Hocart 1924–1928d), it was Anuradhapura and Polonnaruva which Lankan history extolled as the seats of power of the hero-kings who had ruled during the golden age. Although by the fifteenth century these two cities were in ruins, their glories were recounted in the great chronicles of Lanka, the *Mahavamsa* and the *Culavamsa*. These written accounts and the landscape texts read in their ruins, along with Indian texts on capitals such as the *Kautiliya Arthasastra* and *Maimataya*, provided the Kandyans with narrative descriptions of the cities of the *cakravartis*, which were emulated in their own capital. Thus, the landscape of the city of Kandy was to become a highly intertextual portrait of the glory of Lankan kingship.

5

The Kandyan Landscape, 1312–1815

This is the science of laying out a town that fame, riches and plenty will result; if you know not how to build a town thus, evil will befall both king and town. (*Maimātaya n.d., v.115*)

Over a five-hundred-year period the landscape of Kandy has been built by the citizens, destroyed by foreign armies, and rebuilt yet again. While our most complete picture is of the landscape of the early nineteenth century, nevertheless it appears to be a transformation and elaboration of earlier landscapes. In its spatial layout and architectural features Kandy, it would appear, had always encoded the narratives of kingship. Its landscape was designed to be read as a testimony of the kings' responsibility as the guardians of Buddhism and to impress the people of the kingdom with the legitimacy and power of their rulers. Most importantly, however, the symbolic layout of the city and the pervasive religious motifs were metonyms for the power and celestial splendor of the gods, and they implicated the ruler as a liminal figure with both human and divine characteristics. Although this aspect of the logic and narrative structure of the earlier landscapes of Kandy was retained in the nineteenth century, certain narrative elements were accentuated while others were neglected.

According to the *Asgiriye Talpata* (1969, 6, v.21), General Sirivardhana, a nephew of Paṇḍita Parākramabāhu IV (A.D. 1302–1326) of Karuṇēgala, founded the monastery of Asgiri in the year 1312 at the site of the former city of Katupulu. He named the new city Seṅkaḍagala Sirivardhanapura, a century and a half later this city would become the capital of the Kandyan Kingdom. Evidence of the city's existence at this time is also found in an early-fourteenth-century manuscript entitled *Pradahāna Nuvaraval*, which lists it as one of the principal cities of the central highlands (Parker 1909, 354).

During the fourteenth century, long before the city gained its political importance, it enjoyed a reputation as a seat of the god Natha (Paranavitana 1943: 307). The Ampiṭiya Rock Inscription, written during the reign of Vikrama Bāhu III (A.D. 1347–1375), dedicates the village of Ampitiya on the outskirts of Kandy to the "God of Senkadagala" (*Epigraphia Zeylanica* 1943a, 271). The connection between Natha and the city is made explicit in the Sagama rock inscription of Bhuvanaikabāhu V (A.D. 1360–1391) which refers to "Lord Natha of Senkadagala and the God of the Nā tree" (*Epigraphia Zeylanica* 1943b, 310).[1] The Gedige shrine to Natha which still stands in Kandy was built in the South Indian Vijayanagara style in the fourteenth century. Recent archaeological research on the southwestern corner of these temple grounds has exposed the foundation of a bo-tree shrine which also dates from the fourteenth century (Prematilleke 1986, 11). For the fourteenth century, then, we know little about the city other than that it was associated with a shrine of the god Natha and was the site of the Asgiri monastery.

Although the city of Kandy rose to prominence in the fifteenth century we also have scant information about the landscape of the city at that time. In 1474 a general named Vikramabahu declared his independence from King Bhuvanekabahu VI of Jayavardhanapura and made Kandy his capital (D'Oyly 1929: i). One of his first architectural achievements in the new capital was the building of a palace for his mother and a shrine room on pillars (*Asgiriye Talpata* 1969, 7, vv.29–30). He later constructed the Adahana Maḷuva Gedige shrine in the Dravidian style at the Asgiri monastery in 1474–1475 over the ashes of his mother (*Epigraphia Zeylanica*, 1943c, 9; Mudiyanse 1959, 60).

From the sixteenth century on more information on the city of Kandy is available. King Vīravikrama came to power in Kandy in 1542 and procured the Tooth Relic of the Buddha. The acquisition of this relic resulted in a set of important building projects.

> The fair relic of the Prince of the wise he brought to a piece of land charmingly situated not far from the royal palace. Then he built a *cetiya* [*dagoba*] and near to it a two-storey house for the Uposatha ceremony, as well as round about the town eighty-six dwellings for the community [of monks] furnished with a roof of brick and so forth, made the *bhikkhus* take up their abode here and there, granted them maintenance and heard preached the true doctrine of the Victor. (*Culavamsa* 1953b, 220–221)

Viravikrama, then, was the first king to build a Temple of the Tooth in Kandy. He followed the textually recorded precedent of the kings of Anuradhapura and Polonnaruva by building the Tooth Temple adjacent to his palace (Geiger 1960, 215, 54). He also had an inscription cut in the Natha Devale in 1543 (*Epigraphia Zeylanica* 1943d, 27–34).[2] In 1546 Viravikrama, in order to strengthen his position against King Mayadunne in the south, wooed the Portuguese by offering to convert to Christianity. As evidence of his good faith, he took the extraordinary step of converting one of the temples in the city into a Christian church. It is not known whether Viravikrama had actually intended to convert, for the Kandyans became rebellious at the rumor causing him to deny any such intention (O.M. De Silva 1967, 40). According to De Queyroz ([1687] 1930, 258), however, the church known to the Portuguese as "Our Lady of Conception" was nevertheless built in 1547.

Vimala Dharma Suriya ascended to the throne in Kandy in 1592 and within two years the Portuguese under Lopez de Souza attacked the capital. As the king abandoned the city to the Portuguese he set it ablaze, destroying half of the city (De Queyroz [1687] 1930, 482). Upon recapturing the city he began the laborious process of rebuilding.

> He surrounded the whole of the vast city with a massive wall on the heights of which he had placed at intervals eighteen tower structures. . . . He had the Tooth Relic which had been brought to Labujagama in the province of Saparagamu fetched (thence) and in order to venerate it day by day in his own fair town and to dedicate a ritual to it, the wise (prince) had a two-storeyed, superb relic temple erected on an exquisitely beautiful piece of ground in the neighborhood of the royal palace. Here he placed the Tooth and in lasting devotion brought offerings to it. *(Culavamsa 1953b, 228)*

In the year 1596 the king had a beautiful building erected for the monkhood at Getembe on the outskirts of Kandy (*Culavamsa* 1953b, 229). By the turn of the seventeenth century Kandy had become a fine city, befitting the capital of a king. The building program of Vimala Dharma was capped by the construction of a new palace on the site of the old one which was, presumably, burned in 1594. The labor of Portuguese prisoners was used to build it, which accounts for its European character, noted by Dutch emissaries when they arrived in Kandy several years later (Tennent 1859, 195).

It was from this time that we have the first detailed description of the city of Kandy, thanks to contemporary Portuguese accounts compiled eighty years later by De Queyroz ([1687] 1930) and the diary and map of the Dutch embassy of Spilberger in 1602 (P.E. Pieris 1913, 363–370). The following is an excerpt from De Queyroz's ([1687] 1930, 60, 59) account of the city in 1597:

> The Metropolis has well-built houses and streets, cleaned and adorned. The buildings are of masonry, thatched with leaves of bamboo and rattan, . . . though the Pagodes and the Palace of the King, they say, were covered with copper, silver and gold. In the city there will be 2,500 inhabitants, because they are not obliged to live there except the Captains whom they called Araches and Modeliares, and even those who govern Provinces or arrayals reside in other places. The greatest

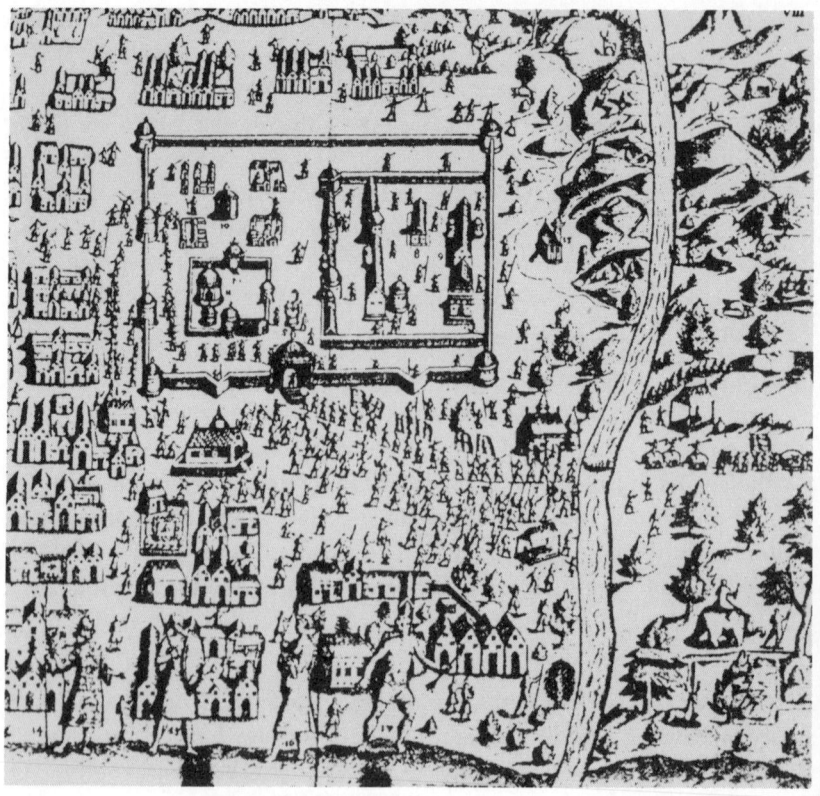

2 Kandy in 1602 (taken from P.E. Pieris 1913)

part of the other inhabitants are merchants, Moors and Parauz from the coast of India, who sell their goods, have a large street, which serves them as a fair or *vazar* [bazaar] as they call it there . . .

The walls of the King's Palace are a little less than a half league in circuit, making a turn over the top of a hill the foot of which is washed by the River, and besides the enclosure of stone, there is another of ditches. The houses of the King are many but very low, and the apartments in which he dwells, below the average. Near the Palace there is a Pagode, which they look upon as a fine building, and it has some appearance of being good, besides being better lighted than the others, because, unlike the others, it has two skylights which let into it the light by means of which, under an arch of the altar, can be seen Demons whom that heathendom venerates as gods . . . They call it *Daladaz Guey*, which means "house of the tooth", because it is on the very altar under seven golden caskets, each inside the other, the tooth

The Kandyan landscape, 1312–1815

of a buffalo, holding it for certain that it is of Buddum . . . Within the precincts of the Palace there is an enclosure which occupies it almost entirely, and within are two other Pagodes, dark and ugly.

Ambassador Spilberger's map of 1602 [see figure 2], which is not drawn to scale, shows the city very much as De Queyroz describes it. The palace/temple complex lies in the eastern part of the city, separated by high walls from the houses and shops of the nobles and traders that lie to the west. The palace/temple complex consists of a large walled rectangle divided into two squares, one containing the palace of the king and the Tooth Temple and the other two temples to the gods. The eastern location and square and rectangular shapes of these enclosures show them to be modeled on the narratives of the cities of the *cakravartis* and of the gods. The map shows two temples within the small square and one within the large rectangle.

The Englishman Robert Knox (1681, 150), who was in Kandy half a century later, noted that there were three temples represented at the great religious festival known as the Asala Perahera: Pattini, Dēvatā Baṇḍāra, and Kataragama. Since we know that the temple of Natha was standing in Kandy during Knox's time, there must have been four temples at that time. It is not clear, however, exactly when the fourth temple was built. De Queyroz ([1687] 1930, 614) claims that four sumptuous temples were destroyed in 1611, but one of these was probably the Temple of the Tooth. It is likely, therefore, that there were three temples within the eastern section of the city in 1602, as there are today.

It would appear almost certain from Spilberger's map that one of the temples in the small square was Natha Devale. If the major temples were the same four in 1602 as they were half a century later – and while we can not assume that they necessarily were, it seems likely – then the Pattini Devale was probably located in the small square next to Natha Devale and Devata Bandara Devale was located within the large rectangle to the north of the small square. If this is the case then they would have occupied the same places that they occupy to this day. If Kataragama Devale, which Knox mentioned in the 1670s, existed in 1602, it is possible that it was located outside of the palace/temple complex in the western part of the city as it is today.

It appears from the map of the city in 1602 that in overall form the city was little changed by the early nineteenth century when the last king of Kandy was deposed. It is also possible, as I have suggestetd, that the location of the major temples was also the same. The map shows two ramparts surrounding the palace, one of earth and the other of stone. The ditch mentioned by De Queyroz is not shown. Whereas these ramparts and ditches undoubtedly served as an important line of defence, the Kandyans regularly abandoned the capital when attacked by the Portuguese. Thus, it is likely that they were also important symbols of the mountain chains and oceans which surround the city of the king of the gods on the top of Mount Meru.

Ambassador Spilberger's map of 1602 also shows a *kuṇḍasāle* (pleasure house) surrounded by water in a marshy area to the east of the palace. The *kundasale* was reputed to contain the treasures of the king (P.E. Pieris 1913, 320). There is no indication, however, as to what the symbolic significance of this body of water was. If the king did in fact keep treasure there, then one would be led to think of the symbolism of Kuvera's treasure kept at the bottom of the ocean (Godakumbura n.d., 20), of the treasures such as *amrita* and the wishing tree that were churned from the Ocean of Milk, and of the great relic treasure of the Buddha's tooth guarded under the seas in the *naga* realm (*Mahavamsa* 1950, 213–215), or of the treasure in Lake Anotatta guarded by the Naga king.

Throughout the early years of the seventeenth century the Portuguese launched attacks against the Kandyan Kingdom. In 1602 some Malay slaves of the Portuguese General Pero Lopez de Souza who were being held prisoner in Kandy escaped, but not before setting fire to the king's munitions. The ensuing explosion brought down a portion of the palace and its surrounding rampart (De Queyroz [1687] 1930, 565). In 1603 de Azevedo attacked the forts guarding the mountain approaches to Kandy and took brief possession of the city. He was forced to retreat, however, due to the revolt of his Sinhalese militiamen.

The Portuguese then shifted to a policy of weakening Kandy by conducting devastating raids on Kandyan territory twice a year during harvest time. They also blockaded the eastern coast of the island to weaken the kingdom before a final decisive campaign was launched against the capital (C.R. De Silva 1972, 13). In 1611 General de Azevedo attacked and captured the city of Kandy which according to De Queyroz' description ([1687] 1930, 614) was "large, and in those times one of goodly buildings, and it was put to the sword and fire with the other villages of that Kingdom to drive terror into those people."

While the Portuguese were fighting their way toward Kandy, the Kandyans removed the Tooth Relic and other valuables from the city, leaving only "the Royal Palaces standing which were formerly most beautiful and storied, with many Pagodes and four of them the most sumptuous that ever were seen. All this was set on fire" (De Queyroz [1687] 1930, 614). Contemporary Sinhalese accounts confirm these events. The *Culavamsa* (1953b, 231–231) states that the Portuguese destroyed towns and that King Sēnarat removed the Tooth Relic and his family from the capital. The *Parangi Haṭane* (P.E. Pieris 1913,

415–417), a contemporary Kandyan account, portrays the city and its destruction by Azevedo in more poetic terms:

> 'Twere an endless task for Ananta himself with his 1,000 tongues to recount the glories of proud Siriwardhana Pura.
> Stately halls, the abode of wealth, proud in their storied height, and countless lawns where lovely Bo trees grow, bedeck the city.
> Crowded stores of merchandise delight the hearts of passersby;
> Like mountains the raging elephants tramp, and the horses fleet as the fleeting clouds;
> While above in the gleaming palaces appear the lovely damsels as they sport, divine in form;
> As if created by Sekraya [Sakra] for the protection of the faith of the Muni [Buddha], is our mighty host.
> Ceaselessly the waves of the great sandy river lisp in their course, a circlet of pearls around a maiden's neck.
> From the lofty towers and the mighty palace gates the gilded spires flash forth their rays.
> Pleasant waters cool the wearied man, sweet as the lake of Anotat.
> From the great fane of the Sacred Tooth the flags with their pearls and tinkling bells rustle in the breeze, as in the abode of the God himself.
> Skilled in the arts of war, with hearts eager for the fray there stands the army, our protecting host, a very band of Asuras.
> Now the host of Portugal rose in its pride, with the throng that clove to the fort of Colombo.
> "Let us go," they urged "and war; let us collect our brave hosts for now we shall win the mountain realm."
> And thus they went and built the fort at Balane and raged in havoc through the country round.
> And many a sacred shrine and palace proud and the very temple of the Sacred Tooth were consumed in the devouring flame.
> While many a fertile land of fruit and flower, mango and plantain, jak and arecanut, betel and coconut, were ravaged by the destroying host.
> Our gentle herds of kine were slain to fill the maw of these devouring ogres, and many a wanton deed was wrought.
> As when long ago the cruel Demalas [Tamils] did land and sack our city Anura pura.
> And our King could no longer abide in his city and had no strength for war;

But with his family, his jewels of gold and his gems, his slaves and records and treasure chests.
King Senerat sought refuge in the Pattu of the Veddahs, for his glory was dimmed and his merit had failed;
And the heart of man melted as wax before the flame of the Parangi foe.

Such verses cannot, of course be taken as literal descriptions of the city for there is much stylized praise here. Rather it tells us how the city was idealized and theoretically conceived of, not only as the capital of a *cakravarti*, but also as a transformation of the city of Sakra, king of the gods. First the wealth and greatness of the city is extolled; it is then compared to the city of Sakra; finally it is described as a projection of cosmic space. It is 'as if created by Sekraya [Sakra]," its waters are "as the lake of Anotat" in Sakra's heaven, and the Temple of the Tooth is like that "in the abode of God himself." The city is also projected back in time by being compared to the greatest city in Lankan history, Anuradhapura. Such poetry therefore, although it fails to give specific information about the city, shows us that it was thought of as in a direct line with the city of Sakra and of the earlier capitals in Lanka.

The *Maga Salakuṇa* (1612–1629, 214), written sometime between 1612 and 1629, describes a pilgrim's view of the city as he approaches from the north east. He sees the temples and the palace, presumably rebuilt after 1611, and mentions both a rampart and a moat around the city, but fails to describe its location. It is fair to assume that this is the same rampart and ditch described by the Dutch and Portuguese at the beginning of the century.

Portuguese attacks on Kandyan territory continued until 1620, after which a period of peace ensued until 1628. King Senarat used this period to consolidate his control over the kingdom (C.R. De Silva 1972, 17, 55, 77). The final years of Senarat's reign were again punctuated by warfare against the Portuguese. In 1629 Kandy was burned by the Portuguese under General Constantine De Sa (*Maga Salakuna* 1947, 215). The following year, however, De Sa's army was destroyed.

In 1638 the Portuguese, this time under the leadership of General De Mello, attacked Kandy once again, and the new king, Rajā Siṇha II burned the city before abandoning it to the invaders (De Queyroz, [1687] 1930, 804). The Kandyans, however, claimed that it was the Portuguese who set fire to the "temple of the god Gaṇesh, the monasteries of the monks, and the Tooth Temple" (*Rajāsiṇha Haṭana* 1966, 4, v.23). The Kandyans later retook the city and massacred the retreating Portuguese.

Raja Sinha II gradually rebuilt the city. Feeling more secure against

The Kandyan landscape, 1312–1815

Portuguese attack, he built a palace that was more elegant and substantial than that of his predecessor (C.R. De Silva 1981, 206). The palace, with its "large, shining doors with finials made of gold" (*Rajasinha Hatana* 1966, 2, v.7), was built in the eastern part of the city in which Knox noted it was customary to locate palaces. The city also had at this time a great earthen rampart twenty feet high which stretched between the hills on the southern part of the city (Hocart 1924–1928d, 153). We also know from Knox (1681, 150) that in addition to the older Natha Devale there were three other *devala*: Kataragama, Pattini, and Devata Bandara.

The Kandyans continued to attach great symbolic importance to canals or moats. According to Knox's contemporary account, the king was a great builder of ponds and canals. Knox (1681, 83) writes disapprovingly that Raja Sinha employed large numbers of citizens to dig in order to allow "the water to run into the pond, and elsewhere for his use in his Palace. Where he hath it running thro in many places unto little ponds made with Lime and Stone, and full of Fish." Knox (1681, 83) also claims that the people were forced to dig four or five miles of ditches in order to bring water to the palace. It is unclear why it should have required four or five miles of ditches to bring water to the pond and the palace when the Spilberger map of 1602 clearly shows that a stream flowed past the palace to the south. One would have to conclude either that Knox is wrong about the extent of the ditches or that the ditches were dug to bring water around the palace to the north thereby encircling the city with a moat in classic fashion.[3] There is reason to believe, as we shall see shortly, that a canal was dug to at least partially encircle the town. It is clear from the *Pujavaliya* (B. Gunasakara 1895, 24) that the canals were heavenly rivers or symbolic demarcations of the edge of the sacred cities just as the annular oceans demarcated the edge of the world. Thus we can safely assume that this canal flowing around Kandy was seen in terms of cosmic symbolism perhaps as the heavenly Ganges or an annular ocean.

Obeyesekere (1984, 345) argues that "the pond" referred to by Knox was Lake Bogambara which lay in the southwestern corner of the city, and that Raja Sinha II built it "either to beautify the city or, more likely, to serve as an earthly replica of a cosmic lake – either Sakra's pond, or Anotatta, near Meru in the cosmic Himalaya or the Milk Ocean." I would favor the view that Lake Bogambara was thought to be Lake Anotatta because an epic poem called the *Parangi Hatana* (P.E. Pieris 1913, 416) written during this time spoke of the water in the town of Kandy as "pleasant waters cool wearied man, sweet as the lake of Anotat." This interpretation can be strengthened by reference to another seventeenth century poem, the *Rajasinha Hatana* (1966, 2, v.8), which refers to "the Diyatilaka tank in the city which cools the body (and) is like the Anothatha lake in heaven." It could, of course, have been thought of as both Lake Anotatta and Sakra's pond, for the Sinhalese sometimes conflated the two (Obeyesekere 1984, 334). However, from the point of view of the argument I wish to construct it is not significant which of these cosmic bodies of water Lake Bogambara was thought to be, it is the fact that there were cosmic waters in the capital that is important.

Like Vimala Dharma Suriya I earlier in the century, Raja Sinha II was reputed to have placed some of his treasure "into a made Pond by the Palace in the City of Cande . . . Wherein are kept to this day two Alligators, so that none dare go into the water for fear of being devoured by them" (Knox 1681, 92). It is unclear whether or not this man-made pond near the palace was Lake Bogambara or Vimala Dharma Suriya's pond. It is also by no means certain that Raja Sinha II did in fact bury any treasure in the pond. If treasure was hidden there, then this would surely have been an ineffective stratagem, for if Know had heard of it then, presumably, so had many others in the kingdom, including the Potrtuguese through their spies. The pond could have been easily drained, as Knox (1681, 92) points out, and the treasure lost to the Portuguese on one of their frequent raids on Kandy. The traditional way of hiding treasure was to keep it in the king's treasury and remove it to safer parts of the kingdom when the city was threatened. There is little reason to think that Raja Sinha II, who was astute in other matters, would have risked his treasure so foolishly. There was, however, something to be gained by encouraging a rumor that the king's treasure was hidden in the pond. First of all, the Portuguese might in fact think that the treasure was there and waste time draining the pond during an invasion of Kandy. Second, and more importantly, the rumor of the treasure under the water further elaborated the landscape as an allegorical portrait of the city of the god-king.[4] By claiming to bury the treasure he was imitating the gods in mythic time (Eliade 1959). He was acting like Kuvera, the god of wealth, who buried his treasure at the bottom of the ocean (Godakumbure n.d., 20).

The crocodiles, which Knox noted were kept in the pond, also can be understood symbolically. This is not to deny the obvious role that these beasts played in discouraging Kandyans from exploring the pond for the alleged treasure. But the crocodile was thought of as the prototype of the *makara*, the mythical dragon who guards the entranceways to temples (Coomaraswamy 1931, 49). The *makara* which has a head like a crocodile is not only a cosmic guardian, but also a symbol of the essence of the waters and of fertility (Coomaraswarmy 1931, 47, 55). It was for this reason that in the typical *makara toraṇa* (dragon gateway) the two *makara* appear to spew out vegetation such as lotus blossoms, or pearls. The *makara*, as Coomaraswamy points out, is traditionally linked to pearls. This connection between the *makara* and wealth is highlighted by the fact that the *makara* is listed as one of the god Kuvera's nine treasures (Coomaraswamy 1931, 49).

Raja Sinha II, therefore, not only reproduced within his capital Lake Anotatta, and the heavenly Ganges, but also the cosmic ocean where Kuvera buried his treasure, guarded by the mythical *makara*. Capturing the essence of these mythical landscapes in his city, he demonstrated yet again that he was like a god.

After a major revolt by his nobles in 1664, he moved out of Kandy to the more secure Hanguranketa for a period of about twenty years and the city was sorely neglected (Knox 1681, 7–8). During the reign of Vimala Dharma Suriya II (1687–1707) a new three-storey Temple of the Tooth was erected on the site of the older one and in it was placed a reliquary made of gold and ornamented with nine kinds of precious stones (*Culavamsa* 1953b, 239). Recent archaeological excavation shows that a seventeenth-century audience hall stood next to the Tooth Temple where later ones have stood, but it is unclear when during the century it was constructed (Prematilleke 1986, 9).

King Narendra Sinha (1707–1739) initiated a number of building projects both within the city and suburbs of Kandy. While he retained the old palace in Kandy for ceremonial purposes such as the reception of ambassadors, for reasons that are unclear from the literature he built a new palace and royal garden for himself at Kundasale four miles to the south east of Kandy (*Culavamsa* 1953b, 242). He was known to the people as Kundasale Deyyo, the god of Kundasale (Dewaraja 1972, 20).

Dutch records show that throughout the 1720s the king constantly demanded presents of rare birds and animals for his royal garden (Bell 1915–1916, 119). The Dutch tried their best to comply and in fact went to considerable lengths to procure animals from their company's trading posts in India, Southeast Asia, and the Middle East (Van Gollenesse [1751] 1974, 8). The Dutch were, however, bemused when the Kandyans asked them to produce a *hamsa*, a mythical water bird whose image decorates the palaces in Kandy. The Dutch inquired as to what this bird looked like and were told by the Kandyans that it was tall and large. The Dutch concluded that the Kandyans desired an ostrich! (Bell 1915–1916, 123.) No record exists of whether an ostrich was ever delivered or, if so, what the Kandyans' reaction to it was.

It would appear that Narendra Sinha wished to have a palace garden like that of the kings of old and of the gods, with rare animals roaming the grounds and water birds in the ponds. Water birds in general and *hamsas* in particular were thought to be *apsarasas*, the handmaidens of Sakra, who were sometimes known to take the form of swan maidens swimming on lakes

(Coomaraswamy 1931, 33). Again one can see that the impulse to capture the heavens on earth was compelling.

Narendra Sinha also undertook some major building within the city limits. According to the *Culavama* (1953b, 242) the Temple of the Tooth had become so decayed that:

> The Lord of men had the beautiful [temple] rebuilt, two-storied, splendid; he provided it with a portal resplendent with all kinds of brilliant ornaments, made it so that with its stucco coating it ressembled a mountain of silver, provided it with a graceful roof and had thirty two *jatakas* [tales of the former lives of the Buddha] depicted in colored painting on the two walls of the courtyard.

He also enclosed the temple of Natha and the sacred bo tree next to the place:

> In the midst of the town he had erected round the great Bodhi tree, the cetiyas and the temple of Nathasura . . . enclosing them on all sides . . . a fine wall of stone, massive, lofty, brilliant in its coating of stucco, like a necklace of pearls adorning the necks of the ladies of the town and created thereby for himself an abundance of renown.
> (*Culavamsa* 1953b, 243)

Recent archaeological research (Prematilleke 1983, 7) indicates that there was more than one *dagoba* in the Natha Devale compound during Narendra Sinha's time. It would appear that the *dagoba* in the western part of the Natha Devale was either built or rebuilt by Narendra Sinha after 1729, for Lawrie (n.d., vol. 4) notes that when thieves broke it open in 1889 a Dutch coin bearing the date 1729 was found in among the relics.

Narendra Sinha enlisted the help of the Dutch, who controlled the coasts, to bring princesses from Madura in South India so that he could be properly consecrated as king. So many of the brides' relatives accompanied them that they formed a large foreign community in Kandy and exercised much influence on the court (Dewaraja 1972, 65, 71, 73). Narendra Sinha gave them a separate street (Kumaruppe Vīdiya) on which to live to the east of the palace. To calm the nobles and the *sangha* who felt that he was neglecting Buddhism, the king destroyed the Catholic church at Bogambara (Casie Chitty 1834, 57). It is possible that this was the same church that had been built by Viravikrama in the sixteenth century.

During the 1730 two Dutch embassies which made their way to Kandy provide us with some details of the city at that time. In March 1732 Captain John Wilhelm Schnee arrived in Kandy across the bridge at Bogambara and was ushered through the main gateway of the palace to be received by the king in his audience hall (P.E. Pieris 1909, 204–205). The great wall around

The Kandyan landscape, 1312–1815

Natha Devale was not mentioned and it is possible that it was not there at the time.

A map and a more detailed description of Kandy is provided by Heydt, who accompanied the Dutch ambassador Daniel Aggreen to the city in 1736 [see figure 3]. Heydt ([1744] 1952, 91) noted that "the streets are wide and straight; but the whole city lies at the foot of a hill, so that one must always go upwards to the Royal Palace." As we can see from the map, the city, which lies to the west of the palace as it did in the early seventeenth century, is composed of rectangular blocks of buildings. Heydt ([1744] 1952, 92–93) noted both the "fine white-painted wall' which surrounded Natha Devale, and the "thick wall made of hewn free-stone" through which he passed to enter the palace. Heydt's diagram of the palace shows a broad inner courtyard within the palace, in the central portion of which was an audience hall where the king received the ambassador. To the east of that was "a small towerlet resting on posts, which was visible both without and within the courtyard." It is unclear exactly what this towerlet signified.

Paranavitana (1954, G19) reports that his archaeological team working on the remains of the old (eighteenth-century) palace in Kandy, discovered a building facing the Natha Devale that

> seems originally to have been some kind of tower. It has considerable resemblance to the so-called mausoleum in Niṣṣaṃka Malla's palace at Polonnaruwa and judging from the sun and the moon which adorn it, was probably a representation of the cosmic mountain.

It is possible that the towerlet noted by Heydt was also a symbol of the cosmic mountain. Certainly such tower images were found in other capitals throughout Indian Asia (see Geertz 1980; Heine-Geldern 1942).

Within the palace complex to the south of the audience hall was the Temple of the Tooth which Heydt ([1744] 1952, 93) describes as a "long and high building, on the outside of which were painted all sorts of dragons and foliage in yellow and red colors, and which also is provided with an entrance."

Although Narendra Sinha rebuilt the Temple of the Tooth and surrounded the Natha Devale with a high wall, he allowed the palace buildings in Kandy to fall into disrepair. It would appear that he devoted his resources to constructing his new palace at Kundasale on the outskirts of the city. His successor Vijaya Rājasiṇha (1739–1747) moved back to the palace in Kandy, found it dilapidated and rebuilt it, adding on a two-storey gate building (*Culavamsa* 1953b, 252).

During the reign of Kirti Sri (1747–1782) many new buildings were constructed, not only in the city of Kandy but throughout the kingdom as well. In fact a substantial portion of the kingdom's revenues went into the building and repair of religious structures. This was part of the stratagem whereby the king built a power base among the people in various parts of the kingdom (Malalgoda 1976, 65). In 1748 Kirti Sri had the image of the god Visnu brought from Alutnuwara to Kandy. A temple for Visnu was built to the northwest of the palace where a temple for the local godling, Devata Bandara, had been (see figure 4). The image of Devata Bandara was removed to Alutnuwara and a small *devale* for a smaller image of Devata Bandara was built next to the new one for Visnu in Kandy (Winslow 1984, 280–281). Devata Bandara, who was also known as Dedimunda, remained in Kandy as Visnu's chief *adikar* and commander in chief.[5] The *Culavamsa* (1953b, 258–259) notes this move in passing by merely mentioning that "a sacrificial festival for the lotus-hewed patron god [Visnu] . . ." was held. The *Culavamsa* makes little of this move as the monks' interest lay in honoring the Buddha rather than the gods.

In the early 1750s the king converted his flower garden called Pūspārāma into the Malwatte Vihare (see figure 4) and had a building constructed for the monks (Coomaraswamy 1956, 12). According to the *Moratota Vata* (1798, 52, v.64) Kirti Sri also built the Pohoya gē at Malwatte.

In 1753 and again in 1756 he brought monks from Thailand to revive the Buddhist order in Lanka and gave them residence at Malwatte (Malalgoda 1976, 62–63). Malwatte and the older Asgiri Vihare were made the centers of ordination for the whole island and all other monasteries were subordinated to them (Malalgoda 1976, 67). In the early 1760s Kirti Sri enlarged the palace (K.M. De Silva 1981, 206). It is not certain whether this was completed when Pybus, the British envoy, arrived in Kandy in 1762. With the exception of some breastworks to the east of the palace, he found no fortifications either in or around the city (Pybus [1762] 1958, 28–29).

In 1765 the Dutch under General Van Eck captured Kandy. This expedition provides us with the best descriptions available of the palace and the city. Van Eck's map (see figure 4) shows the major public buildings in the same locations as they were in 1815. In the east there is the palace/Temple of the Tooth complex surrounded by a high wall. To the north of the palace is another temple which must be Visnu Devale, moved to Kandy seventeen years earlier. Immediately to the west of the palace is the walled complex, which the Dutch incorrectly labeled the king's garden, containing the sacred bo tree, the Natha Devale, and the two *dagobas* containing relics. Immediately to the west of this is a small unnamed temple, which must have been Pattini Devale as it was in existence a century earlier during Knox's time and is there today. To the west of this *devale* is another temple that one would have to assume was the Kataragama Devale, which we know was one of the

The Kandyan landscape, 1312–1815

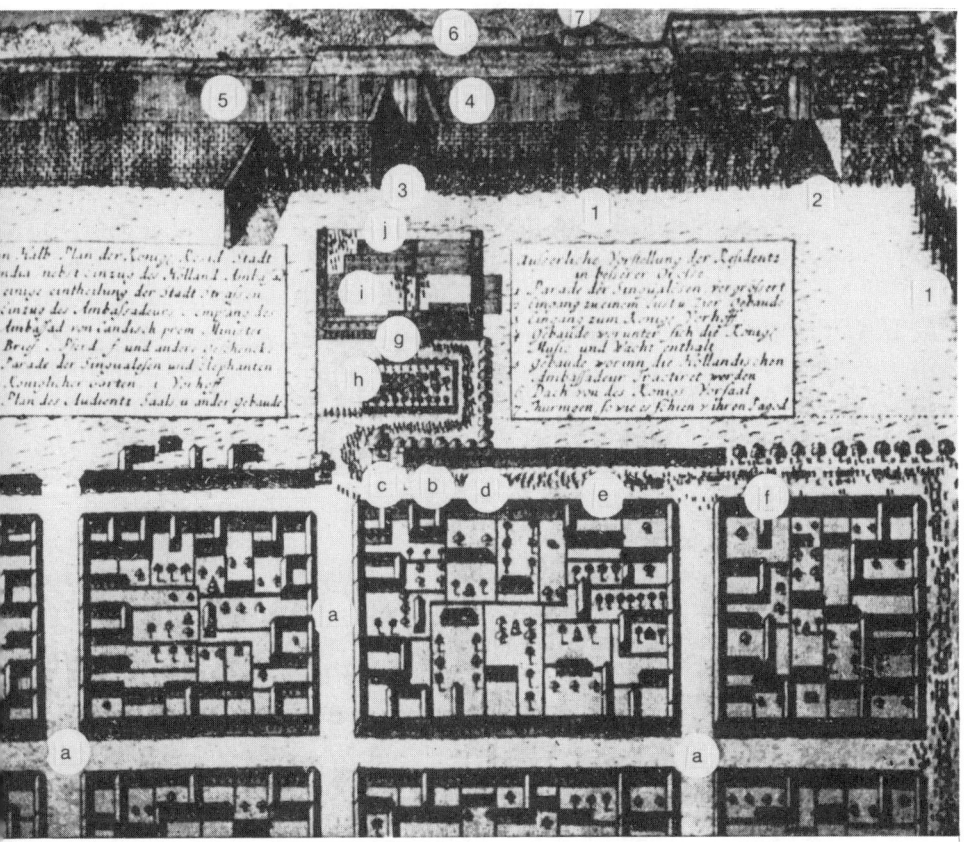

3 Kandy in 1736 (taken from Heydt [1744] 1952)
   a City streets
   b The ambassador's procession
   c Their reception by the first *adikar*
   d The letter to the king
   e Horses for the king
   f Other presents
   g Procession of Kandyans and elephants
   h Royal garden
   i Forecourt of palace
   j Audience hall and other palace buildings

1 Sinhalese soldiers armed with seven-foot spears and carrying torches
2 Entrance to the Temple of the Tooth
3 Entrance to the palace
4 Palace buildings
5 Palace buildings
6 Audience hall
7 Tower

four major *devala* in Kandy at the time and which stands today at that approximate location. As further evidence that this *devale* is in fact Kataragama, the *Siṇhala Upāsakajanalaṅkāraya* (n.d., 351), which described the city during Kirti Sri's time, describes Kataragama Devale as "like the moon in the middle of thousands of people." This would perfectly describe the temple in the densely crowded western portion of the city.

The whole southern flank of the town was protected by a line of batteries, just as it was during the seventeenth century. The *Kavmini Koṇḍola* (1905, 21, v.75), written during this period, also tells of "large walls that were seen in the city which are like the huge waves that surrounded the Ocean of Milk when the god Visnu stirred it [at the time of creation]." Eck has also produced a diagram of the palace/Tooth Temple complex (see figure 5). The complex was divided into a number of discrete areas. The rear half constituted the private area where the king, his wives, and the family of his brother lived. The front half was divided into thirds. In the northern third were the king's stores and in the central third was the reception area of the palace, at the center of which there stood the audience hall where the king sat in state. In the southern third was located the Temple of the Tooth. Each of these three sections had its own entrance and constituted a separate unit of the complex.

Kirti Sri's recent renovation to his palace obviously impressed the Dutch invaders who, according to one eye-witness (Buultjens [1765] 1899, 49), remarked to each other

> with great astonishment how it was possible for a black king to have such a palace. Shortly after it was inspected this castle was plundered and everything given up for booty. There was much treasure, consisting of gold, silver, precious stones, gold and silver cloths, velvets, silk stuffs, fine linen of all sorts in abundance. For three days the men did nothing else but roam and plunder so that everything had been ruined, both the walls and the doors, which were plated with silver, and now stripped of everything, it was a miserable spectacle.

A captain of the militia (Buultjens [1765] 1899, 56) summed up the destruction wrought by the Dutch as follows: "Candea has been captured and plundered and even the holiest temples and pagodas of the Candians and Sinhayes. Some of them, it is said, have been razed to the ground." The destruction of the city was confirmed by the Kandyans, who wrote: "Thereupon the hostile hosts, like cruel armies of Yakkhas [devils] forced their way into the town and destroyed the sacred books and everything else" (*Culavamsa* 1953b, 267).

In the end the palace was destroyed and Kirti Sri began construction of a more modest version (K.M. De Silva 1981, 206). The audience hall was badly

The Kandyan landscape, 1312–1815

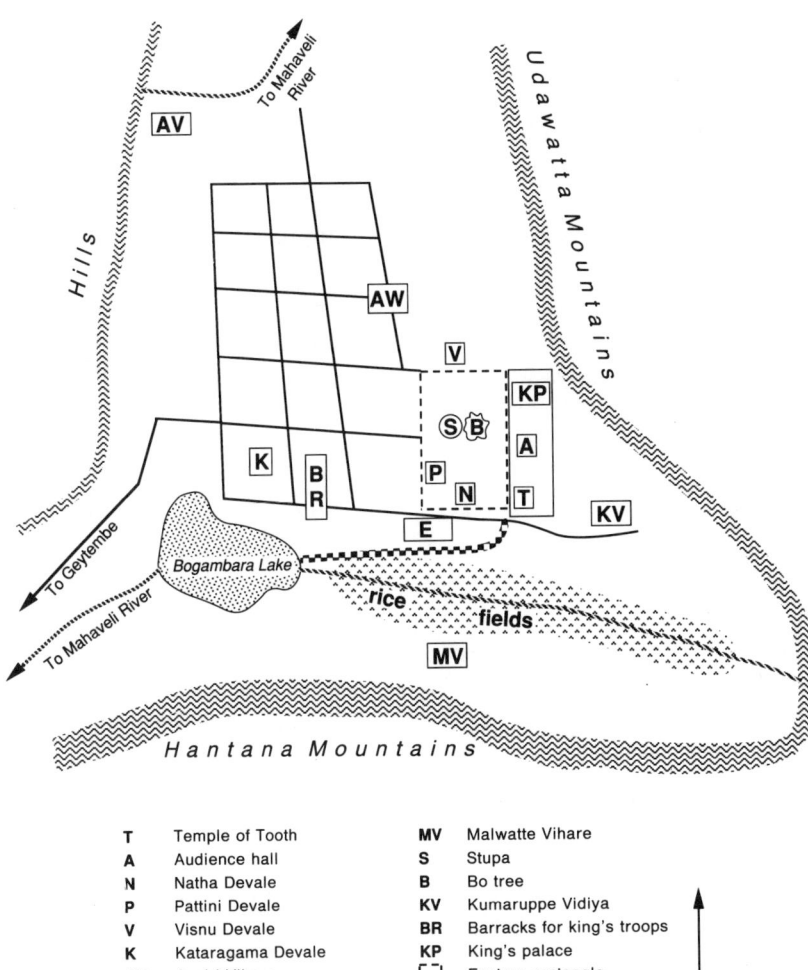

T	Temple of Tooth	MV	Malwatte Vihare
A	Audience hall	S	Stupa
N	Natha Devale	B	Bo tree
P	Pattini Devale	KV	Kumaruppe Vidiya
V	Visnu Devale	BR	Barracks for king's troops
K	Kataragama Devale	KP	King's palace
AV	Asgiri Vihare	⌐ ⌐ └ ┘	Eastern rectangle
AW	Adigar's Walawa	——	Roads
		⌇⌇⌇	Stream

4 Kandy in 1765 (adapted from a map by General Van Eck in the Kandy Museum)

damaged and also had to be repaired (Panawatta 1983, 17). The Temple of the Tooth must also have been largely destroyed for a *tuḍopata* (manuscript) of 1803 (Lawrie 1896, 472) noted that Kirti Sri "built the Dalada Temple in Kandy anew, which resembles another mansion of the gods." The *Sangaraja Vata* (1955, 108, v.266), written during Kirti Sri's reign, elaborates upon this description; "He built a two storey building for the sacred tooth and made paintings [of the *Jatakas*] on it. On the top of the building he placed two *kots* [finials] in gold."

In 1766 Pilima Talavve (the elder), the highest-ranking noble in the kingdom, built the Parana Vihāra at Asgiriya. Heretofore, the only building which existed at Asgiriya was the Gedige Vihara founded in the fourteenth century (Lawrie, 1896, 69, 72, 73). Kirti Sri also built many religious buildings such as the temples of Ampitiya, Gangārama and Degaldoruva on the outskirts of Kandy (*Sangaraja Vata* 1955, 108, vv.267–272; K.M. De Silva 1981, 207). He also erected a *vihara* in Kundasale (*Culavamsa* 1953b, 291) and built a royal garden at Pērādeṇiya, a suburb five miles to the south west of Kandy (D'Oyly 1929, 212). In 1774 the Meda Vāhala (middle palace) was built (Nanayakkara 1977, 19).

Although King Kirti Sri is primarily remembered as a great builder of religious buildings throughout the kingdom, he also, like the Sinhalese kings of old, constructed water works of symbolic significance. According to the *Sangaraja Vata* (1955, 106, v.255), he "built a tank like to the great ocean."[6] The image of cosmic waters in Kandy emerges clearly in poems written during his reign. The *Sinhala Upasakajanalankaraya* (n.d., 350), for example, describes the river Mahaveli Ganga which flows around the city as a deep moat surrounding the "exemplary city with the name Senkadagala Siriwardana [Kandy]." During the eighteenth century, and perhaps earlier, the river acted as an important symbolic barrier for the capital. It was conceived of as being like a circular ocean that separated one continent from the other.[7]

The *Kavmini Kondola* (1905, 6, v.22) written during Kirti Sri's reign, includes in its description of Kandy the statement that "From the middle of the city to the interior of the ocean flows the king of rivers." One would assume that this is an allusion to the Ganges flowing into the Ocean of Milk represented by canals within the city flowing into a lake such as Bogambara. Allusions to the cosmic waters continue (*Kavmini Kondola* 1905, 23, v.85) as the poet describes "White swans and amazing fish, frolicking in the water like the waves on the Ocean of Milk."

Shortly after he succeeded to the throne in 1782 Rājadhi began constructing a new audience hall on the site of the old one that had been damaged by the Dutch (Nanayakkara 1977, 13). He made few other changes to the

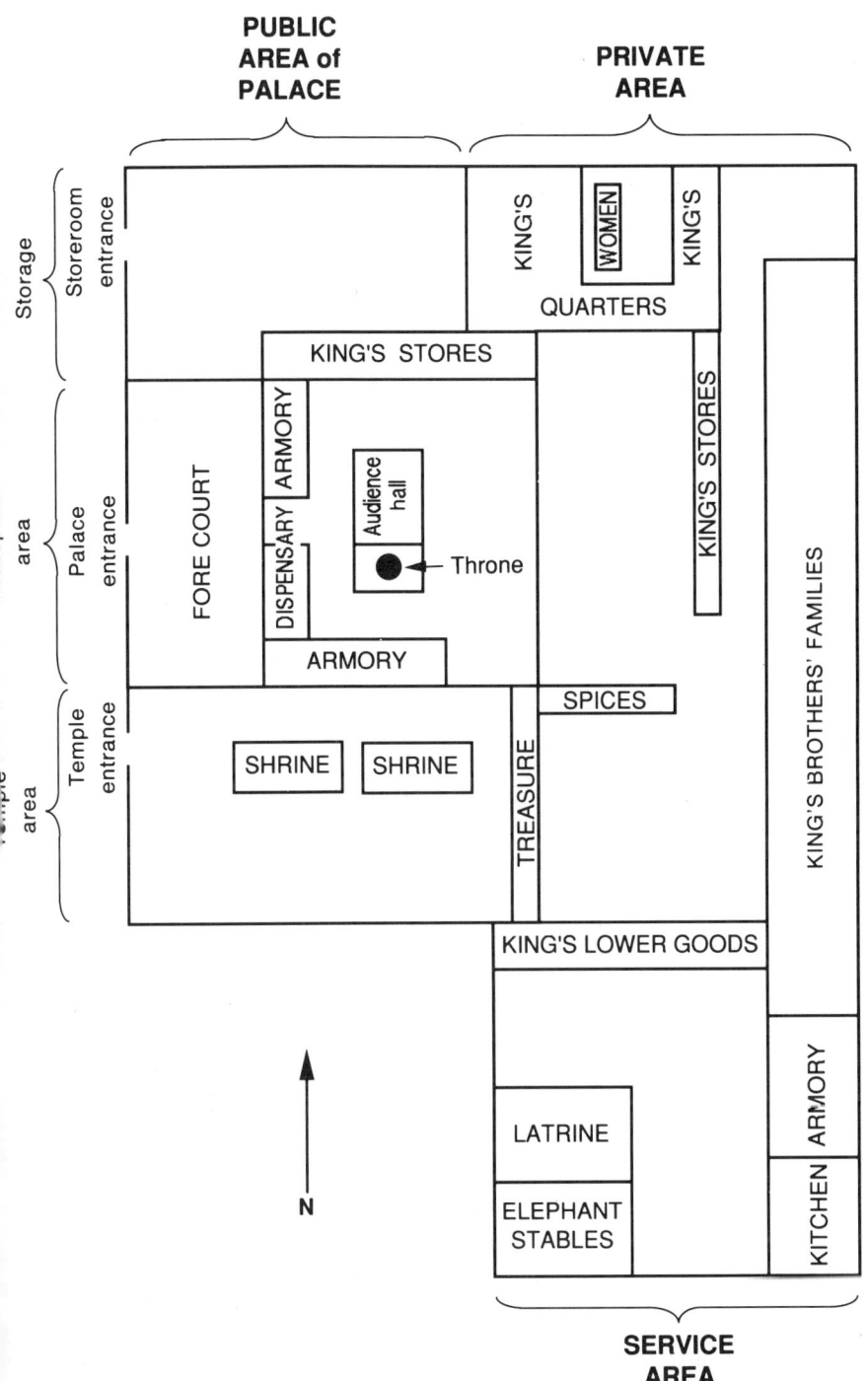

5 The palace/temple complex in 1765 (adapted from a map by General Van Eck in the Kandy Museum)

landscape of Kandy however, other than replacing the decaying Pohoya-ge which had been built by Kirti Sri in the Malwatte Vihare complex (*Moratota Vata* 1798, 52, v.64) and building a few *dagobas* and *vihara* on the outskirts of the city (*Rājaratnā Karaya* n.d., 59–64). The English ambassador, Boyd ([1782] 1973, 209), was impressed with the city when he saw it barely three weeks after the accession of Rajadhi. It was, he said, "of better appearance and more regularly built than any Indian town I had yet seen." Rajadhi, it would appear, was not a strong ruler; rather he was interested in the arts. He was, in the words of the *Culavamsa* (1953b, 301), "like the god of love." He resided in the garden at Peradeniya which Kirti Sri had constructed during 1790 and 1798. Apparently he marked out ten streets in that place and encouraged his ministers to reside there (Lawrie 1898, 719).

The last king of Kandy, Sri Vikrama Raja Sinha (1798–1815) was a great builder. Unlike Kirti Sri, however, he was much more interested in building palaces and ponds than in constructing religious buildings. The Asokan discourse on kingship emphasises the duty of a legitimate ruler to construct buildings for the good of the people, such as religious structures or reservoirs to irrigate rice paddies. The Sakran view assumes the value and efficacy of building palaces, ornamental parks and ponds to glorify the god-king and bring upon him the powers of the gods. Sri Vikrama clearly took this latter perspective to heart and during the final years of his reign undertook building projects of such grandiose scale that he thoroughly alienated the people.

Jonville's (1948, 17–18) narrative of the MacDowall embassy to Kandy in 1800 provides us with little new information about the city other than to mention that there were four thorn gates between the river crossing at Gannoruva and the city and that this road was thickly populated with dwellings. Percival (1803, 235) who also accompanied this embassy, mentions that the city is surrounded by a mud wall. In 1801 Pilima Talavve (the younger) who at that time was the first *adikar* carried on a family tradition by building a new temple called the Alut Vihāre at Asgiriye (Lawrie 1896, 74).

Two years later General MacDowall returned, this time at the head of an invading army of 3,000 men. The general found the city deserted and burning, for prior to his departure for Hanguranketa the king had ordered the torching of portions of the palace, the magazine, and most of the temples, so that the British would not desecrate them (C.O. 54/10 [1803a] 1973, 191). According to General MacDowall (C.O. 54/10 [1803b] 1973, 258)

> From the palace all articles of any value have been removed. The houses of the ministers have also been completely plundered and the scenes of ruin and devastation which are presented on all sides were accomplished before the British troops entered the city.

The Kandyan landscape, 1312–1815

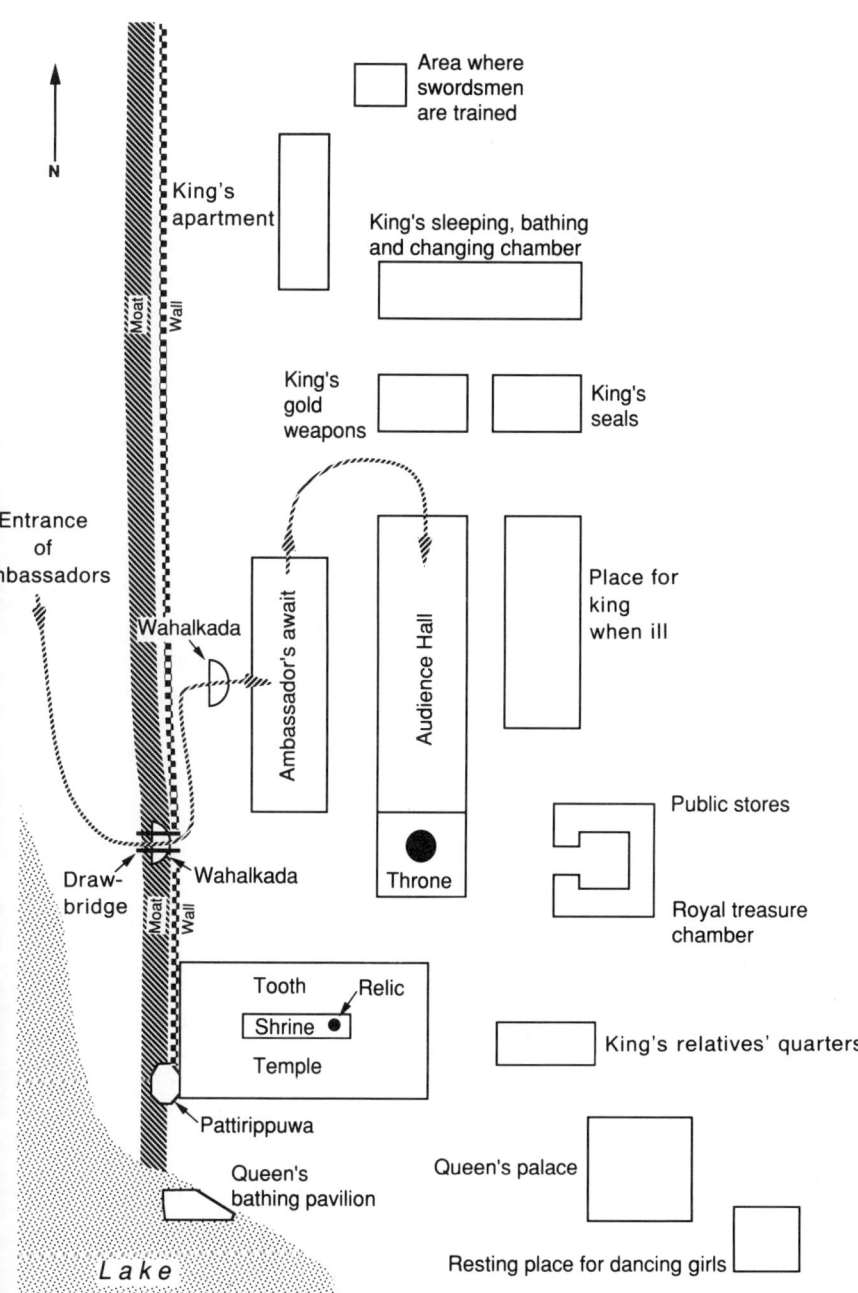

6 The palace/temple complex in 1815

As if the retreating Kandyans themselves had not done sufficient damage to the capital, the *vihare* in the royal gardens of Peradeniya was burned by the British (Nanayakkara 1977, 18). After occupying Kandy for several months the British garrison was captured and put to death. This represented a great triumph for the Kandyan king and, with the British reluctant to risk another invasion, there insued a period of uneasy peace. The king used this period to launch a great building program. According to Davy (1821, 133), from 1809 to 1812 there was continuous rebuilding, enlarging, and decorating of the city, the palace and the royal gardens. By October 1810 the renovation on the palace had been largely completed and a *pāṭṭirippuwa* (octagonal structure) where the king could address the populace had been added to the Temple of the Tooth (D'Oyly [1825] 1917, 29; see figures 6 and 7).

Later that year a trench was dug around the esplanade in front of the palace and a stone rampart was constructed with a canon on it. The old gateways into the palace and the Temple of the Tooth were replaced by a single, massive stone gateway leading both to the palace and the Tooth Temple. The entire complex was then surrounded by a wall and a moat. Subsequently, this moat and wall were extended to pass in front of the Visnu Devale at the northern edge of the sacred rectangle (D'Oyly [1825] 1917, 28–29, 47; see figure 8). Davy (1821, 365–366) described the renovated palace in the following terms:

> It looked towards the principal temples and rose above a handsome moat, the walls of which were pierced with triangular cavities for the purposes of illumination. At one extremity it was terminated by a hexagonal building of two stories called Pateripooa, in which the King, on great occasions, appeared to the people assembled in the square below. At the other extremity, it was bounded by the women's apartments, on the front of which the sun, moon, and stars (not out of gallantry but as insignia of royalty) were carved in stone, and in which, at public festivals, the king and his ladies stationed themselves to witness the processions. The intermediate space was occupied chiefly by the great entrance to the palace and by the temple (the Dalada Maligawa) a little to the rear. The entrance was by a drawbridge over the moat, through a massive archway, on one hand, up a flight of huge steps and through another archway to the hall of audience; and on the other hand, up another flight of steps to the temple and the hexagonal building.

Behind the palace rose the sacred forest of Udawattakellē and one of the king's royal gardens (Prematilleke 1983, 2). Work was begun on a rampart, presumably in the unprotected southwest portion of the city, made of "earth and stones and faced with *chunnam* [lime] and holes in it the size of two hands" (D'Oyly [1825] 1917, 38).

7 Sketch of the palace/temple complex in 1815 (taken from Davy 1821)

In the western portion of the city he added five new city blocks of shops and residences (*Ingrīsi Hatana* [c.1812] 1906, 27, vv.249, 253), while in Kumaruppe Vidyia in the eastern part of the city he greatly increased the number of residences for his Tamil relatives and courtiers (*Ahalepola Varnanava* n.d., 50, v.24). There were four guardhouse gates in the city in 1815 (Siebel 1955, 14–15).

Perhaps the greatest single piece of construction ever undertaken in the history of Kandy was the artificial lake built by Sri Vikrama. The site of this lake was initially a *deṇiya*, or low, marshy plot of land, that had subsequently been converted into paddy fields for the king (L.J.B. Turner 1918, 78). By the late eighteenth century, these fields belonged primarily to Natha Devale, Poya Malu Devale, and Malwatte Vihare. A stream which ran across the fields from east to west was called Tingola Kumbura, after a huge *tingul* bush growing between the Malwatte Vihare and the Daḷadā Māligāva (Temple of the Tooth; Karunatilake 1958, 132; Panawatta 1978, 17). King Sir Vikrama constructed a huge dam at the west end of this low ground trapping the waters of the Tingola Kumbura and forming a lake over two miles in circumference and forty-six feet in depth. From 1810 until 1812 between 2,000 and 3,000 men were forced to work on this dam and the hostility engendered by this massive project created serious political consequences for the king (D'Oyly [1825] 1917, 55, 89, 123).

In order to widen the lake further the king wished to remove the Malwatte Vihare from its location southeast of the city, but the monks dissuaded him from attempting what they pereceived as a rash act (Dewaraja 1972, 134). In spite of this, the creation of the lake seriously disrupted a large section of the city. Many houses and trees were removed from an area in the south west known as Kotugodolle (*Ahalepola Varnanava* n.d., 50, v.26). According to De Bussche (1815, 42) the lake was surrounded on three sides by a wall of stone and on the fourth side by Kotugodolle Mountain. The king used earth from the excavation of the lake to raise the level of the terrace within the Natha Devale (Prematilleke 1983, 7). It is likely that he also used this opportunity to build a similar wall around the adjacent Pattini Devale and raise its terrace with dirt to the same level.

In the center of the lake he constructed a rectangular island upon which a square *kundasale* [pleasure house] was built (D'Oyly [1825] 1917, 121). This is approximately the same location where an earlier *kundasale* had been noted by Ambassador Spilberger in 1602. This pleasure house was connected to the shore by means of a suspension bridge which could be folded up. The bridge apparently reached shore at the point where the queen's bathing pavilion jutted out into the lake. A wall and moat connected the bathing pavilion to the Tooth Temple and thereby separated the palace/temple complex from the rest of the city.

The Kandyan landscape, 1312–1815

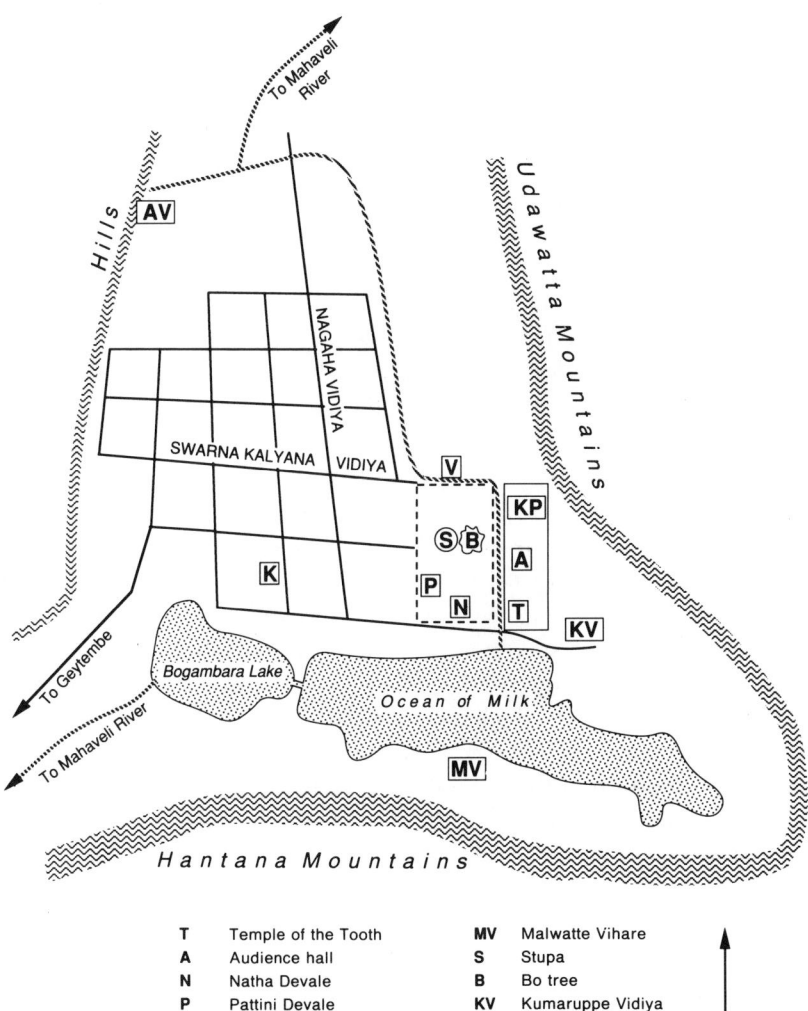

T	Temple of the Tooth	MV	Malwatte Vihare
A	Audience hall	S	Stupa
N	Natha Devale	B	Bo tree
P	Pattini Devale	KV	Kumaruppe Vidiya
V	Vishnu Devale	KP	King's palace
K	Kataragama Devale	⌐ ⌐	Eastern rectangle
AV	Asgiri Vihare	——	Roads
		⌇⌇⌇	Moats and streams

Nagaha Vidiya – N–S divide of city
Swarna Kalyana Vidiya – E–W divide of City

8 Kandy in 1815 (adapted from L.J.B. Turner 1918)

While Sri Vikrama's greatest building project unquestionably was the lake of Kandy completed in 1812 (D'Oyly [1825] 1917, 115), he constructed other water works in and around the city as well. He built a reservoir one and a half leagues outside Kandy and ordered a new paddy field to be constructed where the ceremony of cutting the new rice was to be held (D'Oyly [1825], 1917, 176; *Ahalepola Varnanava* n.d., 53, v.39). The movement of this ritual site, which the author of the *Ahalepola Varnanava* suggests was totally unnecessary, required the cutting of a canal through some difficult terrain (*Ahalepola Varnanava* n.d., 54, vv.40–41).[8]

Sri Vikrama also ordered a ditch to be cut around the perimeter of the city which renewed an older one with slight alterations (Dambuve Nayaka Unnanse [1857] 1956). One suspects that this earlier ditch, which Sri Vikrama modified, was that built by Raja Sinha II a century and a half before, which extended for four or five miles (Knox 1681, 83). According to Dambuve Nayaka Unnanse's evidence, the ditch was started approximately half a mile up the Ampitiya road to the west of Kandy and ran east, curving around the Udawattakelle forest past the palace of the king and Vishnu Devale, and thence north along Maha Devale Vidiya, and then to the west over to Asgiriya Vihare and a low area of ground known as Mahayiyava.

A map by G. Williams (1816), a soldier with the British force that took Kandy in 1815, shows this ditch running north along Udawattakelle but fails to show where it goes from there. Karunaratna (n.d., 25) believes that it eventually ended up in the Bora Veva, a small pond at Mahayiyava near Asgiriya.[9] It would appear that Sir Vikrama and Raja Sinha II before him were attempting to form a moat around the city, a synecdochal allusion to the annular ocean around Mount Meru.

Although over the centuries European attacks partially or wholly destroyed the city many times, each time it was rebuilt. While the landscape of the city varied in details over the centuries, it retained the same general configuration. This continuity represents one of the important tropes of which the text of the landscape is composed: recurrent narrative structure.

Having surveyed the evolution of the Kandyan landscape and elucidated the landscape narratives that form a part of the Sakran and Asokan discourses on kingship, we will now turn to a detailed examination of a fully developed Sakran landscape: Kandy during the final years of Sri Vikrama's reign. I will present the king's reading of this landscape in chapters 6 and 7, and then show in chapter 8 how there is no univalence, no one-to-one correspondence between a reading and a landscape text. Different individuals or groups with different goals and intentions, positioned within differing or even opposing discourses, produce different readings of the same landscape.

Part III

THE POLITICS OF LANDSCAPE INTERPRETATION IN EARLY-NINETEENTH-CENTURY KANDY

6

From discourse to landscape: a kingly reading

I speak thus [in images] because of the frailty of the intelligence of the tender children of men (*Lankavatara Sutra II*)

Topography and political aims interlocked and their interweaving was mirrored by visual evidence (*Krautheimer 1983, 5*)

The king's reading of the landscape

There have been a number of studies of kingship and ritual in eighteenth century Kandy (Hocart 1931; Seneviratne 1978a; 1978b; 1985; Dewaraja 1972; Obeyesekere 1984; Winslow 1984). Although these studies have suggested the importance of the urban landscape to the practice of kingship, none has analyzed it in detail. Attention has been focused primarily on the religious and political significance of the Temple of the Tooth and the Asala Perahara (Seneviratne 1978a; 1985; Hocart 1931).

In the last chapter I traced the development of the landscape of Kandy from 1312 to 1815. However, while I have only alluded to the symbolic significance of some of the landscape elements prior to 1800, I will "thicken" the description by offering a "reading" of the royal city of Kandy, its sacred and profane spaces, buildings, and architectural detail, which I suggest was the king's reading – one that he hoped the people and especially the nobles would accept. I will argue that this landscape is a text, written in the language of the concrete, and that it communicated the governing ideas of political and religious life. By tacking back and forth between the landscape text and various written works – religious scriptures, architectural manuals, political and historical texts as well as court poetry – I will attempt to reconstruct the king's reading: how it served to link the city of Kandy with an ideal landscape in order to legitimate his claims to political power.[1]

What do I imply when I say that this was the king's reading? First, it was not a personal reading, not the idiosyncratic reading of a particular king; rather it was a *kingly* reading generated by a particular model of kingship within a general discursive field on kingship which can be traced back through Sinhalese and Indian texts. Although the king could emphasize one model of kingship or the other, he could not stray outside the wider discursive field and remain effective. Second, it implies that there were other possible readings of the city, readings of the nobles or of the ordinary citizens. This chapter will focus on the kingly reading of the landscape, reserving the discussion of alternative and contestatory readings for chapter 8.

It would appear that the landscape of Kandy which Sri Vikrama inherited in 1798 represented in concrete form the history of a compromise between the Asokan and Sakran philosophies of kingship. After his defeat of the British in the early nineteenth century, Sri Vikrama undertook a re-creation of the landscape which spoke more forcefully of Sakran kingship. His building program was designed to reinforce his claims to Sakran kingship, while the buildings themselves provided a more fitting backdrop for his civic ceremonies.

There are two principal ways in which the landscape and the king's quest for political power were intertwined. The first was in his attempt to employ the magic of parallelism to strengthen his political power, in this case to create an homology between the landscape of Kandy and the landscapes of the cities of the gods, and thereby to partake of the power of the gods.

The second way was implicit in the first. The king attempted to stun his subjects with the sheer magnificence of his surroundings. This was not simply a form of elaborate impression management, however, as all concerned – the king as well as the nobles, citizens, and monks – also believed in the real causal efficacy of spatial parallels and the power of symbols. Nevertheless the king took a calculated risk in over-emphasizing the Sakran self-aggrandizement to the detriment of the *sangha* and the people's welfare. But for now our concern is with the role the landscape played in the effort of this king to portray himself as divine. To examine the precise manner in which the landscape was used to achieve this political goal we must return to the concepts outlined in chapter 2, including allegory, multiple media, synecdoche, and recurrence.

As I discussed above, the Sakran discourse is based on two principal intertwined narratives. I will refer to the first of these as "The world of the gods." This narrative can be in turn subdivided into three subnarratives. The first was the story of the cities of the gods, especially the city of Sakra. This served as the model of an ideal capital in which the king was omnipotent. The second was the story of the Ocean of Milk, with its reference to the creation of the world and the renewal of the world's fertility. This served as a reminder of the fertility which emanated from the capital of a righteous king. The third subnarrative was of the cosmic axis which located the capital at the center of the world, assured its stability and allowed it to serve as a conduit between the worlds of the humans and the gods. The principal motifs in this were Mount Meru and the cosmic tree.

The second principal narrative I refer to as "The world of the *cakravarti*."

It was also subdivided into three subnarratives. The first of these centered around the *cakravarti*'s control over the whole world, the second his control over his kingdom; while the third concerned the cities of the hero-kings of Lanka, especially Anuradhapura and Polonnaruva. All three of these subnarratives spoke of a mythic time when the power of kings was, in theory at least, far less circumscribed.

These narratives were expressed in multiple media. The first medium was concrete, and its representation was iconic. It included various landscape features such as walls, ponds, canals, architectural detail, and the spatial relation of structures within the landscape. The second medium was language and its representation was metonymic. Objects within the landscape were denominated just as they were in the world of the gods. It is important to note that such iconic and linguistic representation was similar, for both allegorically transformed myth into landscape.

The third medium was behavior and its representation was ritualistic. Here the king, his entourage, and the common people emulated the world of the gods or of the *cakravarti*. They reproduced the allegory in rituals acted out in the landscape, itself an allegorical representation of these narratives. Thus, repeatedly composed in these multiple media was a powerful statement about an allegedly powerful king. In this chapter I shall concentrate upon the iconic and linguistic media, saving a consideration of the behavioral medium for chapter 7.

The mechanisms by which the Sakran narratives were communicated included two important tropes. The first was synecdoche and the second recurrence. Synecdoche, as I stated above in chapter 2, is a metonymic device by which a single element out of a series or syntagmatic chain of interconnected elements is made to stand for the whole of which it is a part. The wholes in this case were composed of elements drawn from the divine order of existence and expressed in the world of humans. Within the context of Kandy, these synecdoches were elements of the above-mentioned narratives which stood for the whole narrative. These synecdoches were found in different media; for example, there was an iconic representation in the wave-shaped wall around the lake in Kandy which stood for the waves raised during the churning of the cosmic ocean at the time of creation. Others were linguistic, such as the metonymic reference to the king's palace as the palace of Sakra. Some were ritualistic, such as the king's ascent of the square coronation stone which represented his ascension to the square cities of the gods on the top of Mount Meru. These synecdoches will be discussed in this and the following chapter and a listing of the major ones, showing their location in the landscape, their medium, and the narratives and subnarratives to which they allude is provided in the appendix.

A second trope was recurrence. I will show how the two principial allegories outlined above were repeated time and time again in the landscape, both using different synecdoches within the same medium and using the same synecdoche within different media.

The myth of the founding of Kandy

There is no way of knowing whether the town of Kandy was founded in the manner suggested by the foundation myth; for our purposes its instrumentality and not its veracity is at issue. Its social function was allegorical; it told the inhabitants of Kandy a story about the founding of their city that elevated the city out of the realm of ordinary cities. As such it told a story not only about the city, but about its kings and its people. As we shall see, this myth derives from a larger tradition of foundation myths.

The *Rajavaliya* (1900, 10) a late-seventeenth-century Sinhalese document, describes the founding of the city of Kapilawastupura near Benares in northern India by the four sons of King Suta of the Tritīya Okkāka people. These princes were important to the Sinhalese for it was they who had founded the Sakya dynasty into which the Buddha was born. It was said that the four princes:

> roamed the forest, seeking a site in its midst to fell and clear, with a view to construct tanks and dams, making fields and gardens, and build a city. There they found Bodhisattva, who in his birth as the hermit Kapila, was practicing severe austerities at the foot of a tree in the vicinity of a lake in the midst of a forest. He, seeing the Princes walking through the forest, asked them, "Princes, what seek ye in this forest?" They replied that they had left their country and were in search of a site whereupon to build a city. On learning this the Bodhisattva examined the nature of the site eighty cubits upwards and eighty cubits downward and said, "Princes, if you would build a city, take the site of my *pansala*: when foxes chasing after hares come to this place, the hares turning back chase the foxes; when cobras chasing after rats and frogs come to this place, these turn round and pursue the cobras; and when tigers hunting deer come to my *pansala* premises, they chase the tigers. A person who will herafter live in this place will be kindly treated by the gods and Brahmas. Take, therefore, this *pansala* ground of mine; even if an army of Cakravarti should come [here] it would be defeated: therefore take ye this site and build a city: the only favor I ask is that ye call the city Kapila-wastu-pura, after my

From discourse to landscape: a kingly reading

name, when ye have completed the building of it." Accordingly, the four princes when they completed the city gave it the name of Kapilawastupura.

It is revealing to compare this myth of the founding of the capital of the clan of the Buddha to those of the founding of Kandy. According to one Kandyan legend, a brahmin named Senkanda who lived in a cave in Udawatta, the hill in the eastern part of Kandy, saw a cobra chasing a mongoose, a rare sight as cobras normally flee from mongooses. The old brahmin informed the king of Gampola, Vikrama Bahu IV (A.D. 1347–1375), of this strange event and the king, thinking it auspicious, decided to build a royal palace on the site (L.J.B. Turner 1918, 78). Other versions had a rabbit giving chase to some hunters or to a jackal. In all of the cases the king asked the sage what the sign meant and was told that this was victorious ground that the gods had ordained for the establishment of his kingdom. "You will be well protected in this place and instead of fleeing before thine enemies thou wilt turn and put them to flight" (A. Seneviratne 1983, 23–24). Although all of these legends differed in detail, the allegorical message that they conveyed was the same. All spoke of a weak kingdom that was insecure in the face of stronger enemies. The Kandyans in the mountain kingdom were the rabbits or cobras while their enemies the Sinhalese of the coastal kingdoms and the Europeans were the jackals and mongooses.

The foundation myth of Kandy justified the choice of its location in several different ways. First, it showed that it was a place chosen by the gods. As a place where the normal order of the mundane world was reversed it was liminal, an *axis mundi* where the worlds of humans and gods mingled and merged. Second, in this place that had received the favor of the gods, weakness prevailed over strength. This myth provided psychological solace to the threatened kingdom. Third, because the founding of Kandy was a transformation of the founding of the capital of the Buddha's clan, the Sakyas, the kings of Kandy, through the power of ritual duplication, laid claim to the heritage of the Buddha as well as to that of the *cakravarti*. Just as Gautama Sakya was a *bodhisattva* in his city, so the kings of Kandy were *bodhisattvas* in theirs. The ritual duplication was achieved through the foundation myth, and as we shall see it was routinely employed as the kings of Kandy quested for power.

The city as an allegorical landscape

The very form of the city suggests that the king conceived of it as a cosmic capital. Kandy was composed of two rectangles (see figure 8), the sacred shape of the cosmic cities of the gods (Mus 1937, 69; Gunatilaka 1975, 41–42; Volwahsen 1969, 44–46; Maimataya n.d.) and Kautiliya's description of a *cakravarti*'s capital (Hocart 1970, 353).² As such the very outline of the city was a powerful iconic synecdoche standing for the two central allegories that I have identified: "The world of the gods" and "The world of the *cakravarti*." But the city, as we have seen, was composed of several different parts and I will now interpret each in turn.

The western rectangle

The western rectangle was the location of both the residences of the nobles and the houses and shops of the common people. The city was divided into four quarters by two major streets running north–south and east–west (Keppitipola 1918; L.J.B. Turner 1918; see figure 8). Of these two streets, the one running east–west was the more important, for it divided the city into its two administrative units. The northeast and northwest quarters of the city were under the jurisdiction of the king's first *adikar*, while the southeast and southwest quarters were under the second *adikar* (D'Oyly 1929, 5; R. Pieris 1956, 19). Division of the city into two parts was metaphoric, as it mirrored the division of the kingdom itself between the first *adikar* who had responsibility for the north and east of the kingdom and the second *adikar* who had responsibility for the south and west (D'Oyly 1929, 6). Through the power of like numbers, the western rectangle stood for the kingdom as a whole.³ This parallelism was thought to be efficacious, extending the power of the *adikar* spatially.

The number four, and multiples of four, are highly symbolic throughout Indian Asia as they represent totality, the four cardinal directions which are synecdoches for the four quarters of the world (Rowland 1953a; Wheatley 1977; Zimmer 1974, 13; Hocart 1970, 63, 259; 1924–1928a; 1924–1928b; 1924–1928c; Shorto 1963). Hocart (1924–1928b, 177) believes that the typical kingdom in Lanka was conceived of as being, at least in theory, composed of four quarters. He quotes John Davy (1821) on the subject of the Tooth Relic of the Buddha in Kandy: "they who possess the relic have the right to rule the four kingdoms." In keeping with this practice we can see the recurrence of the number four within the city. For example, as I stated above, the city was divided into four quarters, there were four shrines to the gods in Kandy, four gates to the city (*Rajaratna Karaya*, n.d., 69), four great festivals (H.L. Seneviratne 1984, 6), and four ferries to bring people across the river into the city (D'Oyly 1929, 5). These many references to the four quarters served as recurrent synecdoches affording the king symbolic power over the kingdom and the world beyond. To have power over the four quarters is to be a world

From discourse to landscape: a kingly reading

ruler. Thus the number four occurring throughout the city in various media makes a clear reference to the narrative of "The world of the *cakravarti*." In other words, the city becomes a microcosm of the kingdom, the world, and beyond that the macrocosmos. It is, to use Eck's (1982, 284) term, a cosmopolis – a city that mirrors a world.

But this theme of the microcosmic reduction of the world and the kingdom also recurred in many other synecdoches. For example, as I pointed out earlier, in the late eighteenth and early nineteenth centuries the Kandyan kingdom was composed of twenty-one administrative units (see figure 1). These units appear to have been arrayed in the shape of a sacred cosmic diagram or *mandala* around the capital forming what Tambiah (1976, 102) has termed a "galactic polity." In the center was the city of Kandy surrounded by an inner circle of nine counties or *rata*. The outer ring was composed of twelve provinces or *disa*, which is the Pāli term for a direction point of the compass. The term for governor is *disava* – [*disa*+*va* (thing)]. The governors, therefore, were the lords of the compass points and in Kandy there were four major and eight minor *disavas*, mirroring in the bureaucracy the four and eight points of the compass (Hocart 1924–1928a, 106–107).

Until the reign of the last king of Kandy, the four quarters of the city were further subdivided by streets into sixteen squares constituting what one mid-eighteenth-century Kandyan text called a "properly divided street pattern" (*Sinhala Upasakajanalankaraya*, n.d., 357). According to the *Kautiliya Arthasastra*, which R.T. Clifford (1978, 44) notes was influential in the Kandyan court, this is the number of squares (4 × 4) into which a properly designed capital should be divided (Shorto 1963, 577).

Sri Vikrama, the last king, added two streets and extended three others. This increased the number of squares in the city to twenty-one and in the process made the western part of the city a more perfectly shaped rectangle. These additions have been interpreted as an attempt by an aesthetically minded king to beautify his capital (Davy 1821; Dewaraja 1972, 134). However, there are two reasons why these additions to the city can be better understood as a systematic attempt by the last king to reinforce his power.

First, by adding five squares to his city he raised their number to twenty-one, which is the number of administrative units in the kingdom. The kingdom, therefore, symbolically recurred within the city; the macrocosmos was reduced to the microcosmos. Second, there is strong evidence that the king was attempting a magical solution to the problems besetting his kingdom when he reshaped the city into a perfect rectangle. As a more faithful representation of the heavenly city of the gods it might, through the power of parallelism, partake of the potency of a heavenly city. The *Ingrisi Hatana* (1906, v.249), an early-nineteenth-century poem praising the king, confirms this interpretation: "After measuring the length and width of the city, he [the king] made it into a perfect square in order that the expenditure and income of the kingdom would also be equal." Furthermore, by assigning each province a square in the city, he was also able, through the metonymic power of the synecdoche, to bring the whole kingdom into the city. Thus he could magically control the kingdom by controlling the city. Because the city was a liminal place, the power of the gods manifest in the power of the king could be deployed against such irksome banalities as the kingdom's budget deficit.

The streets forming the borders of the twenty-one squares contained shops providing services for the king. Here also were the *valavvas*, the mansions of the governors of the twenty-one administrative units of the kingdom, where the families of the nobles were kept hostage as guarantors of their patriarch's loyalty (Hayley 1921, 49; Davy 1821, 146). Evidently, whatever power parallelism may have had to preserve his kingdom, the king was not above more practical precautions.

As tables 6.1 and 6.2 display, I found over twice the number of synecdoches in this part of the city standing for the narrative "The world of the *cakravarti*" as there were for the narrative "The world of gods." Similarly there were twice as many references to the first narrative as there were to the second. As table 6.1 demonstrates the greatest incidence of recurrence of synecdoche was found among those referring to the first and second subnarratives which emphasize control over the world and the kingdom. The majority of references to narratives in table 6.2 were to the Kataragama Devale in the western rectangle. This was not surprising as the western rectangle was the profane portion of the city which, in relation to the eastern rectangle of the city, stood as does the earth to the heavens. One final point that is striking about tables 6.1 and 6.2 is that the western rectangle contained only 10 out of 92 (just over 10 percent) of the synecdoches I discovered; 10 out of 101 (approximately 10 percent) of the references to narratives in table 6.1; 4 out of 157 (2 percent) of the synecdoches; and 5 out of 287 (just under 2 percent) references to narratives in table 6.2. This paucity demonstrate the low symbolic value of the western rectangle as compared to the eastern rectangle.

The eastern rectangle

To more fully understand the role of urban form in the legitimation of power one must be able to interpret the eastern rectangle, the so-called "sacred rectangle," the real locus of ritual power in the kingdom where the temples and the palace were located (see figure 8). Many royal cities in India were

From discourse to landscape: a kingly reading

Table 6.1

The recurrent narrative structure of the landscape
NARRATIVE: "THE WORLD OF THE *CAKRAVARTI*"

Location	Number of synecdoches	Number of references to narrative	Number of references to subnarrative (A)	Number of references to subnarrative (B)	Number of references to subnarrative (C)
Eastern rectangle	3	3	1	0	2
Palace	22	25	10	0	15
Audience hall	4	6	3	0	3
Temple	26	30	15	0	15
Visnu	9	9	8	0	1
Natha	1	1	1	0	0
Pattini	1	1	1	0	0
Center	3	3	0	0	3
Total	69	78	39	0	39
Western rectangle	10	10	4	4	2
Kataragama	0	0	0	0	0
Total	10	10	4	4	2
Lake	7	7	4	0	3
Canals	1	1	0	0	1
Totals	8	8	4	0	4
Provinces	5	5	3	2	0
Total recurrence in landscape	92	101	50	6	45

Note. The narrative "The world of the *cakravarti*" is composed of three subnarratives:
(A) Control over the whole world through reproduction of centrality and cardinal directions.
(B) Control over the kingdom through microcosmic reproduction.
(C) Reproduction of the cities of the Sinhalese hero-kings.

Table 6.2

The recurrent narrative structure of the landscape

NARRATIVE: "THE WORLD OF THE GODS"

Location	Number of synecdoches	Number of references to narrative	Number of references to subnarrative (A)	Number of references to subnarrative (B)	Number of references to subnarrative (C)
Eastern					
rectangle	1	2	1	0	1
Palace	36	57	21	18	18
Audience hall	10	21	10	3	8
Temple	56	103	44	26	33
Visnu	17	41	16	10	15
Natha	6	14	5	2	7
Pattini	5	10	5	0	5
Center	5	6	4	0	2
Total	136	254	106	59	89
Western					
rectangle	1	1	1	0	0
Kataragama	3	4	3	0	1
Total	4	5	4	0	1
Lake	15	22	1	15	6
Canals and rivers	2	6	2	2	2
Total	17	28	3	17	8
Total recurrence in landscape	157	287	113	76	98

Note. The narrative "The world of the gods" is composed of three subnarratives:
(A) The cities of the gods, especially Sakra's city.
(B) The Ocean of Milk, fertility and creation.
(C) The cosmic axis, especially the cosmic mountain and the cosmic tree.

composed of two rectangles, the first for the palace and the temples and the second for the citizens (Ananthalwar and Rao 1921, 178–179).

One way to unlock the mythic structure of a landscape, the hermeneutic circle of landscape and myth, is to begin with one element of the landscape and securely anchor it through synecdoche to a set of narratives. Having done this one can then move on to relate that landscape element to other elements of the landscape. These can be explained in turn through synecdoches that refer back to the initial narratives. This process entails simultaneous reconstruction of a landscape text and a myth system, with a constant tacking back and forth between elements of each.

Although the major features of the landscape remain the same today, in the description that follows I will use the past tense. While there is evidence in contemporary reports, paintings, and maps that the architecture and layout of the town was as I describe it, there is no evidence of what the frescoes on the walls inside the Temple of the Tooth Relic were like during the reign of Sri Vikrama or whether they were as they are today. My description of these frescoes is based on my own observations of the temple. Whereas the paintings may have changed, there is reason to assume that the symbols would be essentially the same, as their purpose was to reconfirm the same sets of religious narratives found in the architecture and spatial configurations of buildings, streets, and monuments.

The lake as the cosmic ocean

As a point of entry into the circle of landscape and narrative I have chosen a landscape element that is unambiguously allegorical. I will first uncover the synecdoches which link it to the narrative and then proceed outward in the field of other landscape elements to those whose allegorical connections are perhaps less obvious, that is, those which require a more indirect method of decoding. The lake in Kandy, which lay to the south of the sacred rectangle, was an unambiguous element. By its very name "Kiri Muhuda", the Ocean of Milk, it was linguistically secured to the narrative "The world of the gods."

However, before continuing it is important to pause and enquire as to the purpose of this lake. Clearly this large lake served no agricultural purpose; in fact some paddy fields were removed from production when it was dug. Furthermore, the capital was well watered by the Tingol Kumbura Stream, the various channels that had been cut by prior kings, and by Bogambara Lake within the western limits of the city. Why then was the lake constructed? Although, as I have said, the answer that most historians give is that Sri Vikrama was an aesthete, who constructed the lake in order to beautify the capital, and Obeyesekere has suggested that the king was engaging in cosmic symbolism, we might wish to take Obeyesekere's hunch one step further. As I have stated above, throughout the eighteenth century the Nayakkar dynasty greatly elaborated court ritual.

During this period the court became increasingly Hinduizied and kings strove to portray themselves as gods (Obeyesekere 1984, 7, 343). Sri Vikrama's building program must be seen in this context. He wished to show his subjects that he was a god like Sakra, a *cakravarti* and a future Buddha. This was to be accomplished largely through ritual and environmental symbolism. His capital already had the lake called Bogambara which was a representation of the mythical Lake Anotatta. What it lacked was the much larger body of water, the cosmic Ocean of Milk. Sri Vikrama accomplished this with the lake that he named the Kiri Muhuda, the Ocean of Milk. He now had symbolically reproduced within his capital both Anotatta, the mountain lake near the center of the world, and Kiri Muhuda, the cosmic ocean which surrounds Mount Meru. In doing so he captured the universe; he had reduced the macrocosm to the microcosm. How better to symbolize that he was a universal monarch? The island in the lake, with its white pleasure house, also acted as a powerful synecdoche for both the allegories of "The world of the *cakravarti*" and "The world of the Gods." It evoked the island parks of the great King Parakramabahu I of Polonnaruva, themselves evocations of the gardens, ponds, and pleasure houses of Sakra (*Culavamsa* 1953b, 13–14; Godage 1945, 57). Sri Vikrama had not, then, engaged in a frivolously aesthetic project; he had, through the power of metonymy, more firmly placed his capital, and by extension himself, at the center of the universe.

But let us now return to a consideration of the implications of naming the lake "The Ocean of Milk", the syntagmatic links between the lake and other elements in the landscape, and the power of this name to assemble disparate elements into an allegorical text or a landscape, that spoke of divine power. The name alluded to and embodied a greater complex of ideas just as its creator, the king, was the embodiment of divinity and all the glory associated with the gods.

As I discussed in chapter 4, the Ocean of Milk was the name given in the sacred texts to the cosmic ocean which lies at the foot of Mount Meru at the center of the universe. It forms one of the three subnarratives of the narrative "The world of the Gods," an important part of which is the churning of the Ocean of Milk. According to the *Visnu Purana* (1952), the Ocean of Milk was churned by the gods and demons with Vasuki, the cosmic serpent, wrapped around Mount Mandara, itself balanced on a tortoise that was Visnu incarnate. From this churning arose *soma*, the potion of immortality; the milk-white elephant, who became the mount of Sakra, the king of the gods;

From discourse to landscape: a kingly reading

the milk-white horse and milk-white cow, which Sakra also took as his own; and the *kapruka*, the gift-giving tree with the milky sap, which he took for his garden.

The presence of this artificial lake named the Ocean of Milk with its allegorical references reinforced the power of other linguistic, iconic, and behavioral synecdoches which also allegorically referred to the same subnarrative. For example, consider the color of the Ocean of Milk. White is held to be a "natural symbol" of fertility, symbolizing, in the South Asian tradition, both milk and semen.[4] Furthermore, it is the color associated with Sakra who, in addition to being the king of the gods, is the god of rain and hence of fertility (Geiger 1960, 179). White was therefore the official color used by the king of Kandy to symbolize his claim to be an incarnation of Sakra and a guarantor of fertility throughout the kingdom.

Like Sakra, the kings of Kandy possessed the gifts symbolizing fertility – the elephant, the horse, the cow, the tree – that arose out of the churning of the Ocean of Milk. The kings owned white, or light-colored state elephants (Heydt [1774] 1952, 92; Obeyesekere 1984, 525) and were known to have frequently requested European ambassadors to send white horses, which were unavailable locally (P.E. Pieris 1909, 203; R. Pieris 1956, 17). The kings also possessed small herds of sacred white cattle (Hayley 1921, 52; R. Pieris 1956, 17) and kept a *kapruka* in the Temple of the Tooth (Cumming 1893, 210). By naming the lake in Kandy the "Ocean of Milk", the last king simultaneously established a link between the lake and the world of the gods, and by extension between himself and Sakra. Furthermore, this act also vivified these other synecdoches evoking the subnarrative of the churning of the Ocean of Milk. Here, both iconically and linguistically, he possessed the Ocean of Milk itself. No longer did the people have only a white horse or white cattle to remind them of the churning. Now they had before their very eyes the Ocean of Milk itself. Collectively these synecdoches transformed the landscape into concrete evidence of the king's role as a god-like, creative agent.

However, as we saw in the last chapter, the lake was constructed with forced labor, and this building project imposed real hardships and provoked abiding resentment within the kingdom. In the eyes of the people, *rajakariya* (forced labor due the king) was legitimately due only when employed in building a "proper" capital for the king or for religious projects. In an attempt to mollify those who suspected that his excessive city building represented and sanctioned engrossment of regal power, the king apparently sought to define the lake construction as a religious project (Colebrook [1832] 1956, 196). This is apparent not only in the verbal associations which we have just outlined, but I will argue in the supplement of an important new component to the city's foundation myth, which L.J.B. Turner (1918) associates with the reign of Sri Vikrama.

According to this version of the foundation myth, King Vikrama Bahu IV of Gampola, having decided to found a new capital, sent an old man to search for an auspicious place (*jaya bhumi*). At the spot where the Temple of the Tooth was eventually located the old man saw a squirrel defeat a rat snake. Later others were sent to discover the meaning of this. They saw a frog defeat a rat snake on the same spot. When he was asked for the meaning of these two events, the king's *adikar* interpreted them as favorable portents and invited the king to examine the place himself. The king brought his astrologer, Hulaṇgomuwe Mulāchchāriya, who agreed that it was indeed an auspicious spot. The king remained unconvinced. He scanned the dubious terrain and asked, "Why should I leave Gampola for a place so surrounded by marshes and hills?" With this the king ordered his astrologer to consult the oracle for forty-eight hours. At the end of the two days the astrologer made his prediction. He ordered that the king's men begin digging at the *jaya bhumi* and said that they would first find milk-white clay, then a layer of sand and finally water. After the king's men had found these layers just as had been predicted, the astrologer asked for a pure-white cloth predicting that a milk-white tortoise would be found; as they dug in the mud the tortoise did indeed appear and was wrapped in the cloth. Delighted with the success of the predictions, the king ordered that a city be built around this lucky site. He intended to build his palace directly upon the *jaya bhumi*, but the astrologer said: "This is too good a place for a palace, it is a place for a temple." The king subsequently abandoned his capital at Gampola and moved to Kandy, building the town around a temple on the lucky spot. The white tortoise was given a small pool at the eastern end of what is now the Kandy Lake. This pool was called the Ocean of Milk (Kiri Muhuda) and the tortoise was served food from the king's kitchen. Later this land was converted into paddy fields for the king (L.J.B. Turner 1918, 78).

What is interesting about this foundation myth is that it took the basic myth, which we reviewed earlier, of the weak overcoming the strong in an auspicious site, and appended an alllusion to the subnarrative of the Ocean of Milk. This allusion to the Ocean of Milk, I would argue, is a rather desperate attempt by the last king to justify the construction of the lake by linking it to the founding of the city. The suggestion is that latent in that spot there was *always* an Ocean of Milk. It was for the last king and his subjects to realize this potentiality. If accepted, such a claim would, he hoped, extinguish the unrest. For who could object to fulfilling a plan laid by the gods?

From discourse to landscape: a kingly reading

We have seen how Sri Vikrama attempted to transform his lake into the Ocean of Milk though linguistic parallelism. A mundane landscape was made sacred through naming. But naming was not sufficient in and of itself. Names are used to establish a metonymic relation, a bridge across which meaning flows like electricity between two poles. But the poles are necessary. The positive pole in this case was the cosmic ocean in mythic time and the negative pole or ground was the lake in Kandy. By naming the lake in Kandy the Ocean of Milk, the connection was made and the symbolic charge flowed from mythic time to real time, from the ocean to the lake. Without the negative pole, the concrete synecdoche of the landscaped ground, the connection could not have been made, mythic time and place could not have been realized.

The language of walls

Names, either written or spoken are only one of the metonymic representations. Iconic representations may also establish a relationship of contiguity between realms because, as Mitchell (1986) points out, images can have a textual quality. My definition of an icon is broad and includes paintings, sculpture, walls, and the arrangements of buildings in space.

Consider, for example, the shape of the city: a rectangle, a geometric figure deeply imbedded within the Kandyan textual tradition, the shape of the city of the gods. In fact one could argue that such an image is closer to the world of the gods than is a name, for while the name is an arbitrary signifier the image is iconic, a "mirror," to use the Kandyan terminology, of what the city of the gods actually looked like. Yet for the Kandyans both the linguistic and the iconic provided a connection between the world of the gods and that of humans. It appears that neither words, images, nor abstract concepts such as symbolic numbers were granted a special privilege over the others. All were held to make the real world *like* the world of the gods; none was wholly transcendent; none transformed it *into* the world of the gods. It would appear that, for the Kandyan, achieving this liminal state of likeness was the closest that humans could approach to heaven while remaining in this world, and it is this liminality which parallelism through the use of synecdoche attempts to achieve.

Let us now turn to a consideration of how architectural elements in the landscape reinforced verbal imagery by linking the lake to the cosmic Ocean of Milk. A masonry wall known as the "wave swell wall" (Diyareli Bemma) ran along the eastern, northern and southern sides of the eastern rectangle, separating it on its southern side from the lake (see figure 9). The great undulating waves on the wall composed a powerful iconic synecdoche for the turbulence of the Ocean of Milk at the time of the churning by the gods and demons. They represented a time of ferment and of creation.

The wall had patterns incised in it which added many more references (see figure 10). Each wave on the wall had four triangular niches cut in it. Beneath each wave was a large circular niche and between each wave there was another triangular niche. Each of these shapes and the overall arrangement of these shapes can be seen as a synecdoche for the cosmic Ocean of Milk. In Buddhist iconography the triangle represents leaves in general and the leaf of the sacred bo tree (*Ficus religiosa*) in particular (Coomaraswamy 1956, 252). During the churning of the Ocean of Milk, the leaves of the trees on Mount Mandara were thought to have blended with the waters of the ocean to produce *amrita*, the elixir of life (Coomaraswamy 1931, 21). Thus I would argue that the triangular niches in the wave wall referred to primordial creativity and fertility associated with the churning of the Ocean of Milk.

Thus far I have analyzed the lake as a symbol of fertility, creativity, and primordial time. But the cosmic ocean also took part in the destruction of the three worlds at the end of the *kalpa* and this destructive power was symbolized by the wall around the lake in Kandy. This dialectical symbolism is typical of Indian thought, which is circular and oppositional rather than linear and cumulative, and it captures the endless cycle of creation and destruction which lies at the core of the Indian ontology. It could be argued that in addition the great waves and the triangles symbolized the awesome power of destruction of the Ocean of Milk; the same power of destruction which the king himself claimed to have over his subjects.

In Hindu iconography the triangle symbolizes Agni's fire (Aryan 1981, 51). Interestingly, there is a connection between the fig tree symbolized by the triangle in Buddhist iconography and the fire of Agni symbolized by a triangle in Hindu iconography. Both are called Vanaspati, lord of the jungle (Coomaraswamy 1972, 7–9). Furthermore, in *Maitrī Upaniṣad* (1975, IV, 1–4, VII, 11) the cosmic tree of life is conflated with the fiery cosmic pillar which arises out of the cosmic ocean. One might well ask why a symbol of fire was found in a wave wall which represented water. Again, we are confronted with the typically Indian logic of conjoining things which may appear to be opposites, for in Indian thought, both Hindu and Buddhist, there is a clear link between fire and water. The fire exists as the fire of destruction contained within the waters of creation.

O'Flaherty (1980, 213–237) has discussed the connection between fire and water and I have therefore drawn heavily upon her work in my analysis of the wave wall. In Raghavan on *Manu*, a commentary on the lawbook of Manu, fire and water are inextricably linked. "Fire is born of water, as is seen in the

9 Kandy Lake and the sacred rectangle (painted by O'Brian, c.1865)

10 The wave swell and cloud drift walls

case of lightning and the Mare's Fire."[5] Lightning as a kind of "natural" link between water and fire is understandable and I shall discuss it below in connection with the king's palace. What concerns us at the moment, however, is the Mare's Fire, or submarine fire as it is also known, for this is the fire of the doomsday at the end of the *kalpa*.

The submarine fire is called the Fire of Ūrva from the name of the sage whose anger was its source. Urva is a Vedic term which denotes the ocean and in particular that part of the ocean into which rivers flow, for the Mare's Fire arises at the confluence of the river and the ocean. The wave wall separating the city from the lake marked such a confluence, for it was there that the moat of the palace/temple complex joined the lake (see figure 9). According to the *Matsya Purana*,[6] the sage Urva had a son called Aurva:

> Aurva blazed so fiercely that he terrified the universe. He said, "Hunger binds me. I will eat the universe." He grew great, burning all creatures until Brahma said to Urva, "Restrain your son's fiery energy for the good of all people. I will give him a dwelling place and a food like Soma: he will dwell in the mouth of the mare in the ocean and he will

From discourse to landscape: a kingly reading

live upon an oblation of water. This water-eating fire will burn all creatures at the end of the Kali age." "So be it," said Urva and he threw the fire into the ocean.

This fire is also connected to the myth of the churning of the Ocean of Milk which we discussed earlier. The terrible poison which arose during the churning of the Ocean of Milk by the gods and the *asuras*, and which was drunk by Siva, the great destroyer, is simply another aspect of that destructive fire waiting to come forth from the cosmic ocean that contains the beginning and the end of all things. As noted earlier, the *nagas* are associated with waters in general and the cosmic ocean in particular. It is the fiery, poison breath of the *nagas* in their world under the ocean that causes disease.

It is worth noting that in another creation myth found in the *Siva Purana* (1970) Siva transformed himself into a flaming *lingam* (phallic column) which rose out of the Ocean of Milk. It is important to remember that the kings of the Nayakkar dynasty, although officially patrons of Buddhism, were secretly practicing Sivites (R.F. Gombrich 1971, 35). Sri Vikrama who constructed the wave wall was almost certainly a follower of Siva. But this Sivite symbol of fire was multivocal for it had been taken over at an early date by Buddhists who represented the Buddha as a pillar of fire (Aryan 1981, 24; Coomaraswamy, 1972). Precisely because of its multivocality this symbol was particularly useful to the king.[7]

The sun which in Buddhist cosmology is seen as the great destroyer at the end of the *kalpa* is also linked to the Mare's Fire in the bottom of the ocean. O'Flaherty (1980: 215) points out that in the *Siva Purana* (1970) the circle of the sun, surrounded by clouds in the rainy season is likened to the mare's head in the ocean. Similarly, it is thought that the sun's horses drive his chariot into the western ocean at night. In the *Rg Veda* (*Vedic Hymns* 1891; 1897) it is stated that the sun's chariot is pulled by seven bay mares, while the Lankan transformation of this myth states that seven suns cause the world to become desiccated at the end of a *kalpa*. The fire in the sun and the submarine Mare's Fire are interchangeable symbols. This is made clear in the *Matsya Purana*.[8]

> Visnu becomes the sun and dries up the ocean with his scorching rays . . . He goes down to Hell and drinks the water there, and then he sucks out the urine, blood and other moisture in the bodies of living creatures . . . He is the mare's head in the ocean of milk, the whirlpool fire that drinks the oblation made of water.

Let us return for a moment to the wave wall and more closely examine the triangular niches. As figure 10 reveals, there were four triangles on each wave. As I have said, the number four in Indian iconography stands for the four quarters of the universe, north, south, east, and west. Immediately below these four triangles at the base of each wave was found a circle with projections representing the four quarters. The circle is both the traditional symbol for water as well as the cyclical movement of time. Thus the circles were also the symbols of the waters of the great cycle of creation and destruction. Also according to Hocart 1924–1928a, 105) it was common to find a fifth mark below the other four in both Hindu and Buddhist iconography. This fifth one represented the sun and was thought to support the four directions. From the circle also is derived Soma, the moon, the wheel of law and the wheel of time (Aryan 1981, 43). The sun and moon refer back to the creation during the churning of the Ocean of Milk for Soma, the moon, was produced during the great churning and was the original source of *amrita*. The sun also represents destruction, for just as it lies as the submarine fire beneath the waves of the cosmic ocean, so it is set below the waves of the wall around the lake.

This leaves us with the two triangles between each wave to explain. According to the traditional canons of design, when two marks are added to the four directions, they fill out the compass by adding the zenith and nadir (Hocart 1924–1928a, 105). Although Hocart was speaking abstractly about numbers, it is clear that this symbolism could very well have applied to the wave wall in Kandy.

These six triangles together represented the fire that will incinerate every portion of the three worlds at the end of the *kalpa* and the circle represented both the sun and water, the submarine Mare's Fire and the water that blend into one as the fire consumes oblations of water.

For each wave, then, there were altogether seven marks, six triangles, and a circle. The number seven is highly symbolic for there are thought to be seven stars in the heavens forming the galaxy, seven mountain chains, seven oceans forming concentric rings around Mount Meru at the center of the world, seven sacred rivers, seven jewels of the *cakravarti*, and seven horses who pulled the chariot of Surya (Aryan 1981, 78).

Fire, then, is inextricably linked to water just as destruction is linked to creation. These pairs are also related to each other for the fire arises out of the water at the beginning of time as a flaming pillar of creation and arises once again at the end of a *kalpa* as the mare's head of destruction. Such allegories which were meant to teach the Kandyans about the circularity and unity of existence were encoded in the landscape in a simple and yet compelling fashion. A wall in the shape of waves, containing triangles and circles and surrounding a lake called the Ocean of Milk, transformed the allegory of the world of the gods into a landscape text and in the process helped to impress the allegory upon the everyday consciousness of the Kandyan citizen. As

From discourse to landscape: a kingly reading 107

tables 6.1 and 6.2 (pp.95-96) demonstrate, the lake is one of the most important transformations of the narratives into concrete form in the landscape. We can see this both in terms of numbers of synecdoches associated with it and with the number of allegorical references to the narrative.

As I have pointed out, the building of the lake was a political gamble for the king. Its construction alienated a large segment of the common people as well as members of the aristocracy. The king wished to deflect this criticism by asserting that this was a work of religious importance. We can see this message not only in the transformation of the myth of the founding of the city of Kandy, but in the recurrence of allegorical references associated with the lake. This recurrence was not merely a lesson in religion; it was a lesson in politics as well for it expressed the idea of a cosmic capital occupying a liminal position between heaven and earth.[9]

The eastern rectangle

As I have argued, it was the goal of the king to create a reduced version of the universe within the confines of the city; to mirror both the world of the gods and the cities of the *cakravartis*. We have already seen how the western rectangle of the city represented a reduced version of the Kandyan Kingdom and how the lake of Kandy represented the cosmic Ocean of Milk. What was missing from this microcosmos was Mount Meru, the central axis of the world upon which is located the city of the gods.

I will now turn to the eastern rectangle of the city, the location of the palace of the king, the Temple of the Tooth Relic of the Buddha, and the three temples to the gods, to show that it was the missing piece of this universe made small, the central cosmic mountain. As with the analysis of the Kandy Lake, I will show how this parallelism between the mythic cosmic mountain and the eastern rectangle of the city was accomplished through the use of both linguistic and iconic synecdoches.

First, let us examine the spatial relationship between the lake and the cosmic mountain. According to both the *Culavamsa* (1953a, 5) and the *Sangaraja Vata* (1955, 112, v.296), Mount Meru, the central cosmic mountain, arose out of the cosmic ocean. This relationship was expressed spatially in Kandy where the eastern rectangle was bordered on its southern side by the lake (see figure 8). Running along this border was the wave swell wall, symbolizing the waves of the cosmic ocean breaking against the flank of Mount Meru.

Next let us analyze in more detail the component parts of the eastern rectangle. First, I will review the geography of the cosmic mountain in the allegory of the World of the Gods that was outlined in chapter 3. According to the Puranic myths, Mount Meru has a central peak flanked by four buttress peaks which rise with it. The eastern peak of this Meru group is Mount Mandara and it is here that Sakra has his palace (Dimmitt and Van Buitenen 1978, 27, 28, 52). A Tooth Relic of the Buddha was removed to Sakra's palace on Mount Mandara where it was worshipped by the king of the gods (Geiger 1960, 213). Sakra's palace, thus, is on the eastern side of Mount Meru.

Let us now review the linguistic evidence for the parallelism between the eastern-square and Mount Meru. The *Culavamsa* (1953b, 276–277) and other eighteenth- and early-nineteenth-century texts (C.O. 54/44 [1812] 1984, no. 16; Bell and Gunasekara 1915–1916, 160–161; Bell 1904, 103; *Ingrisi Hatana* [*c*.1812] 1906, v.250) describe the kings of Kandy as being like Sakra, and the king's palace in Kandy as like Sakra's palace descended to earth. Similarly, the Temple of the Tooth was called a "divine palace descended from the world of the gods" (*Culavamsa* 1953b, 138, 182–184; *Sinhala Upasakajanalankaraya*, n.d., 350). There is also a reference in early-nineteenth-century Kandyan court poetry to Mount Mandara as the "royal splendor of prosperous Lanka" (*Kirala Sandēsaya* 1958, v.36). This "royal splendor", which the poem tells us came into the possession of King Sri Vikrama, is none other than the palace and the Relic in the Tooth Temple. Since Sakra's heaven is on Mount Mandara, these linguistic synecdoches situate the Kandyan palace and Tooth Temple there.

Further textual evidence linking the palace/temple complex in Kandy to Mount Mandara is found in the foundation myth of the city that I suggested was modified by Sri Vikrama to help alleviate unrest. It was here that the astrologer of King Vikrama Bahu IV (A.D. 1347–1375) found a milk-white tortoise and in this auspicious spot a temple and an adjoining palace were built, and the tortoise was then given a small pond named the Ocean of Milk at the eastern end of this marsh. The last king of Kandy subsequently flooded the whole marsh naming the resulting artificial lake the Ocean of Milk. We can find the connection between the white tortoise and Mount Mandara in Hindu mythology, for during the churning of the Ocean of Milk Visnu took the form of a white tortoise to act as a base upon which Mount Mandara pivoted to churn the Ocean of Milk. The Tooth Temple/palace complex, therefore, like Mount Mandara rose from the Ocean of Milk and rested upon a white tortoise. Here we see the ingenuity of Sri Vikrama's addition to the myth of the founding of Kandy, for not only did it justify his creation of the lake, it also reinforced the symbolism of the palace/temple complex as Mount Mandara.

The fact that the eastern portion of the eastern rectangle represented

From discourse to landscape: a kingly reading

Mount Mandara could be seen in the spatial positioning of the palace/temple complex. This complex was on the eastern side of the eastern rectangle just as Sakra's palace was on Mount Mandara, the eastern peak of Mount Meru. One could see it in the fact that the king's palace was attached to the Temple of the Tooth so that they formed a single, walled complex. Again, we have a parallel between the palace of Sakra containing a tooth relic on Mount Mandara and the palace/temple complex with its Tooth Relic in the eastern corner of the sacred square in Kandy.

H.L. Seneviratne (1978a, 2) has argued that both the spatial layout and the titles of functionaries of the place were identical to the spatial layout and titles of the functionaries of the Temple of the Tooth, suggesting an attempt by the king to mirror in his own palace the sanctity of the Temple of the Relic. While I would certainly agree with this interpretation, I would add the important point that in Kandy the term *maligawa* (palace) was given to both the Tooth Temple and the king's palace. I suggest that this is because the Temple of the Tooth can be seen as Sakra's palace on Mount Mandara, and that the parallels between the king's palace and Tooth Temple in Kandy imply that the two in fact constituted a single palace which mirrored the palace of Sakra on top of Mount Mandara.

One could also see the synecdoches representing Mount Mandara in the architecture itself. Let us first analyze the walls and the moat that separated the palace/temple complex from the rest of the eastern rectangle. Standing in the eastern rectangle and looking eastward, one saw a wave swell wall running the length of the palace/temple complex (see figure 7). This wall was identical to the wave swell wall separating the eastern rectangle from the lake in the south. Behind the wall was a moat which also ran the length of the complex and emptied into the lake. The wave swell wall and moat together can be considered a concretization in the landscape of a narrative in the *Vayu Purana* (Ali 1973, 100) about the celestial Ganges which flows off Mount Mandara into the cosmic ocean.

As I argued earlier, the fire motif in the wave swell wall symbolized the cosmic ocean as the locus of the Mare's Fire which consumed the world at the end of each *kalpa*. This fire was thought to be especially strong at the confluence of a river and the ocean (O'Flaherty 1980, 213–237); such a confluence was reproduced in Kandy where the moat flowed into the lake. Furthermore, the Ganges was thought of as an *axis mundi* connecting the three worlds – the fires of hell, the earth, and the heavens (Darian 1978, 69, 75). The triangle as a leaf also had symbolic significance, for not only is it a Buddhist symbol of the bo tree, itself a cosmic axis (Coomaraswamy 1972, 8–9; L. De Silva 1978, 248), but also, as mentioned earlier, it stands for the fiery cosmic pillar.

The symbolism of water was intimately connected with both Mount Mandara and the palace/Tooth Temple complex. For example, the word *manda* means water and since Mount Mandara was thought to scatter water it is called Mandara (Ali 1973, 41). Sakra who dwells here is the god of rain (L. De Silva 1980, 234) and his symbol is lightning, the fire that is born of water. Likewise the king of Kandy who dwelt in the palace was thought to produce rain, as was the Tooth Relic enclosed in the temple (L. De Silva 1980, 234). Both the king of Kandy and the Tooth Relic were also associated with lightning. Furthermore, the official in charge of the Tooth Relic was the *Diyawaḍana Nilame* which means "rain-making minister" (L. De Silva 1980, 234). Here once again we can see the recurrence of linguistic and iconic synecdoches standing for the subnarratives of the cosmic mountain, and the creative waters of the Ocean of Milk which flow in a hydrologic cycle through the three worlds.

On the eastern side of the moat rose the wall of the artificial terrace upon which was located the palace and the Tooth Temple. This wall was divided into two levels, the lower of which was a lotus wall. This represented the lotus which in Puranic mythology floats upon the Ocean of Milk. The next level of the wall had a series of pilasters embossed upon it, perhaps suggesting the 1,000 pillars of the palace of Sakra, or perhaps yet again symbolizing Mount Meru, as the conical pillar was a symbol of Meru for the Sinhalese. This wall, then, rested upon the lotus wall below which was the moat, in the same way that in the allegory Mount Meru rested upon the lotus sitting on the cosmic ocean.

This brings us to the top of the terrace from which the palace rose. The palace structure itself repeated the symbolism of the lower walls. At the base of the foundation of the palace was a second set of lotuses. On top of this was a series of niches in the form of a trefoil. The trefoil is the traditional symbol for Mount Meru in Hindu iconography (Aryan 1981, 15). These niches were interspersed with the symbols of the four quarters. On top of this was a third row of lotuses and above these lotuses was the entrance to the palace. The wall of the palace itself was embossed with pilasters apparently reaffirming the symbolism of Sakra's palace and Mount Meru.

Ascending from the level of the sacred square, a visitor would have risen past three lotus walls and two sets of Meru symbols before arriving at the pillared palace of Sakra on top of Mount Mandara. At the entrance to the palace were the sun and moon symbols. These symbols are conventionally thought to stand for the solar and lunar dynasties from which the kings of Kandy claimed to be descended. While not denying this interpretation, I suggest that the symbols were intentionaly multivalent, also representing the

From discourse to landscape: a kingly reading

sun and moon circling Mount Meru, for the symbols have this meaning when they are carved in a *dagoba*.[10]

The wave swell wall and moat passed the Temple of the Tooth on their way to the lake. The wall which rose up on the eastern side of the moat resembled a line of pillars resting upon a lotus. This wall was capped by a "cloud drift wall" known as the "Walakulu Bemma", which was also undulating but had niches shaped in the form of a trefoil (see figure 10). The celestial rampart displayed the Meru motif, again symbolizing the fact that the palace/temple complex is on the top of the cosmic mountain where the Tooth Relic was taken to Sakra's palace. It is possible that this cloud wall also served as a reminder of the Mēghagiri Vihara, the Rain Cloud Rock Monastery where the relic was first taken upon its arrival in Lanka in the fourth century A.D.

Sri Vikrama constructed a grand entrance to the palace/temple complex (figure 7). In order to enter the palace one crossed over the moonstone and passed two entrance stones with elephants on them. Elephants are symbols of Sakra, rain, the king, and the Buddha (O'Flaherty 1980, 258). On top of these entrance stones were four small conical structures at the four corners and one larger cone in the center, iconic representations of Mount Meru with its tall central peak and four outer peaks. Across the moat stretched a bridge with a very large "Meru gate" over it.[11] This gate had four openings facing the four cardinal directions and each face of the gate had four small indentations in the form of trefoil Meru symbols surrounding the large opening. Once again we can see the five peaks of the cosmic mountain reproduced in iconic form. Such gates, because they employed the symbolism of the four quarters, were thought to be at the center of the world. They were the entranceways to the cities of the gods, as well as to the cities of *cakravartis* and *bodhisattvas* (Rowland 1953a, 11, 16).

To the east of the Meru gate and the cloud drift wall was the Temple of the Tooth. Its walls were embossed with trefoil Meru symbols and its main entrance way had a large stone *makara torana* over the doorway. Sri Vikrama added a *pattirippuwa* (octagon tower) in the southwestern corner of the building. As an octagon it represented the eight directions of the compass and was thus considered the center of the world. From this liminal spot a *cakravarti* could dominate the world. There was an open courtyard in the center of the Temple of the Tooth and in it stood the two-storey shrine building whose base was in the form of a lotus. The Shrine of the Relic was the focus of ritual power in the city, for here lay the Relic of the Buddha, the palladium which legitimated kingship in Lanka. In this spot, according to the *Sulu Pūjāvaliya* (1913, 26), a mid-eighteenth-century account, was concentrated the power of the cosmos symbolized by the painting of the cosmos (the seven annular mountain and ocean rings around Mount Meru, the four continents and the heavens) on the walls of the shrine. These paintings have long since disappeared and may even have been effaced by the time Sri Vikrama acceded to the throne in 1798.

Today, and possibly during Sri Vikrama's time, the outer overhanging ceiling of the west wall is decorated with paintings of *hamsas* (mythical water birds), Sakra, King Kirti Sri who built the shrine, Natha flanked by the gods of the four directions, King Vimala Dharma Suriya – often thought to be the first king of an independent Kandy – and Maha Brahma. As there is no record of exactly what the wall paintings were like I can only assume that today's are similar. The inner overhanging ceiling is decorated with lotuses, pots of plenty and a horoscope. The western door to the shrine has a *makara torana* over it and is flanked by guardians.

The outer ceiling of the north side is decorated with paintings of lotuses, foliage, four *kiṇḍurā* (women with bird's bodies), Maha Brahma holding a pot, wrestlers, and people making offerings. The inner ceiling has lotuses, *nārilatā* (women with plant bodies), a sun, a horoscope, and a sign saying "Tavatimsa Heaven" under a painting of Sakra flanked by two women attendants, and other figurers. The north wall is decorated with sun and moon patterns surrounded by lions. The top of the door frame has a woman holding foliage. The sides of the door are flanked by guardians and the base is decorated with lions. The panels of the door itself are decorated with foliage, *hamsas*, birds in a tree, and women.

The outer ceiling of the east side is decorated with lotuses, pots, *narilata*, and *hamsas*. The inner ceiling is decorated with a sun, foliage, a *hamsa*, and a painting of Sakra surrounded by two gods on each side and three attendants on either side. Under this painting is a sign saying "Council of the Gods." The wall of the east side is decorated with suns and moons surrounded by lions, as is the north wall. There is no door on this side.

The south wall is decorated in a fashion similar to the other walls. The door has a stone frame showing a goddess or nymph seated among foliage. The panels of the door are decorated with *narilata*, boys holding foliage and birds in foliage. The posts around the whole shrine show worshippers making offerings, gods, and the creatures of the Tavatimsa heaven.

The textual allusions of the paintings on this building are repeatedly to the world of the gods, particularly of the Tavatimsa heaven whither Sakra took the Tooth Relic of the Buddha. One can see it not only in the iconic and linguistic synecdoches standing for Sakra and his heaven, but also in the mythical plants, animals, gods, goddesses, and nymphs of the Tavatimsa.

In a second-storey room at the eastern end of the shrine the Tooth Relic of

From discourse to landscape: a kingly reading 113

the Buddha lay as it does today enclosed within seven bejeweled *dagobas*, representing the seven mountains and oceans around Mount Meru. The relic sat on a silver table resting upon an eight-sided altar. The eight sides were believed to represent the cardinal directions. The relic, being at the center of the world, was thought to draw power directly from the heavenly plane. By inserting the Tooth of the Buddha in a *dagoba*, the person of the Buddha was given new form and made present in that place (Greenwald 1978, 29–30). The symbolism of fertility and the cosmic mountain was enhanced when the relic was displayed upon a silver table,[12] as this table itself was a syndecdoche for the cosmic ocean. On the silver table stood an octagonal cupola of silver and gold, supported by slender pillars. This stood for the cosmic mountain rising from the ocean.

In front of this were three small crystal *dagobas* resting upon square bases. The *dagobas* on either side displayed jeweled objects, while the larger central one contained a large golden lotus blossom in the heart of which rose the Tooth supported by a twist of gold wire. This again was a synecdoche for the subnarrative of the cosmic ocean, for at the beginning of creation a lotus was said to have risen out of the body of Visnu resting on the Cosmic Ocean. Out of the lotus arose Brahma who creates all things, just as out of the lotus in the shrine arose the Buddha in the form of his Tooth. Just as Brahma represented fertility so the Tooth did likewise, for it is able to produce rain.[13]

The king's audience hall sat on a raised terrace at the center of the palace/temple complex equidistant from the palace and the Shrine of the Relic (see figure 6). This positioning reflected the traditional Indian schema in which the audience hall is placed at the cosmic center (Inden 1978, 33). The audience hall was an open structure supported by twelve octagonal pillars, carved in the South Indian style, and mirroring the octagonal pillars in the audience hall of Sakra on Mount Mandara (J.P. Lewis 1912, 330; Godage 1945, 58). A *gaja lakśmi* (mythical beast) adorned the lintel of the hall (Karunaratne 1978: 115). The first seven pillars, which marked the area where visitors were received, represented the seven mountain rings around Mount Meru. The last five pillars marked the alcove where the king sat on his elevated throne (Jonville 1948, 15).

As I have suggested by these examples, the intertextual approach, the tacking back and forth between landscape text and allegories, allows us to develop an integrated reading of the landscape. This reading, which I call the king's reading, viewed the palace/temple complex as an earthly version of Mount Mandara where Sakra and the Tooth Relic of the Buddha dwell. By extension, I argue that the landscape proclaimed that the king was Sakra and also a *bodhisattva*, that he was a liminal being at the center of the world. This reading depended upon the identification of synecdoches that connect elements within the landscape to the allegories of power. The king's reading was perhaps more influential because of the repetition of the symbolism. As table 6.1 shows, the palace, temple, and audience hall accounted for 52 out of 92 (57 per cent) of the synecdoches I have found and 61 out of 101 (60 per cent) of the allegorical references to the narrative "The world of the *cakravarti*." For the narrative "The world of the gods" (see table 6.2) the figures are even higher: 102 out of 157 (65 per cent) of the synecdoches and 181 out of 287 (63 per cent) of the references. It is clear from these figures that the palace/temple complex was the major site of recurrence in the Kandyan landscape accounting for over 60 per cent of all the references to narratives that I was able to identify.

Thus far I have interpreted the eastern side of the eastern rectangle, but what of the other sides of the rectangle and the center? There were shrines to the gods on the northern, southern, and western sides of the rectangle as well. These shrines were thought of as the actual abodes of the gods in the capital (Obeyesekere 1984, 37).

To the north of the eastern rectangle lay the Visnu Devale, surrounded by a moat, a wave swell wall and a cloud drift wall, all synecdoches standing for the heavenly Ganges flowing down from Mount Meru (See figure 8). Post-Vedic mythology places Visnu's paradise, which is called Vaikunṭa, on the *northern* peak of Mount Meru (Stutley and Stutley 1984; 316; Hopkins 1915: 207). The *devale's* location, when considered in light of the fact that a road leading to it was at that time named Vaikunta Vidiya (L.J.B. Turner 1918), strongly suggests that the Visnu Devale was thought of as the northern peak of Mount Meru, which in turn lends credibility to my interpretation of the sacred square as Mount Meru. To the west of the Visnu Devale lay a small *devale* to Dedimunda (Devata Bandara), a godling who serves as Visnu's *adikar*, and commander in chief. Here we see the world of the gods mirroring the world of the king's court. This is an interesting reversal which reinforced the liminality of the city by further blurring the line between the world of the gods and the world of humans, for not only could the king emulate the gods, but the gods could also emulate the king.

At the southern edge of the eastern rectangle was the Devale of Natha, who was also thought to be the Maitreya (future Buddha) whose heavenly location according to the *Satara Dēvāla Devi Putwata* (1954, 158) is in the Tuṣita heaven above the Tavatimsa heaven on the top of Mount Meru. The *Sāriputra* specifies eight forms of the god Natha, one of which is Siva Natha. According to Paranavitana (1928, 60–62), some Buddhists believe that Natha is another name for Siva. Perera (1916, 19) also notes that "Natha is an impersonation of Siva Isvara" and cites as evidence a banner in the Natha Devale in Kandy showing Siva Natha seated bearing his (Siva's) weapon the

From discourse to landscape: a kingly reading 115

triśūla (trident) and in his two other hands a snake and a discus. As I have said above, there is strong evidence to suggest that the last kings of Kandy, although nominally Buddhist, were, in fact Sivites, who surreptitiously continued to worship Siva (R.F. Gombrich 1971, 35). Because Siva is thought to reside on top of Mount Meru (Dimmitt and Van Buitenen 1978, 28; *Samyutta Nikaya* 1917, 279–281), it can be argued that we have a series of synecdoches which symbolically place the Natha Devale on the top of Mount Meru.

At the western edge of the eastern rectangle was the Devale of Pattini who is a *bodhisattva* and therefore dwells in the Tusita heaven over Meru (Obeyesekere 1984, 59). She is also a manifestation of Pārvāti (Daughter of the Mountain), the consort of Siva who dwells on the top of Meru. Both Siva and Parvati (as Natha and Pattini) therefore were placed within the eastern rectangle. Here they sit together as if on the top of Mount Meru, as they do in some South Indian temples such as at twelfth-century Arunachaleshvara (Campbell 1974, 93). The temples of the four gods, thus, filled out the cardinal directions of the eastern rectangle and made it a complete replica of heaven on top of the cosmic mountain.

At the center of the eastern rectangle there was a bo tree grown from a shoot taken from the great bo tree in Anuradhapura which is said to have been taken from the tree in Gaya under which the Buddha was enlightened. The bo tree, for Buddhists, is a cosmic axis and as such partakes of the symbolism of Mount Meru (Coomaraswamy 1956, 32, 97; 1972, 7–9; L. De Silva 1978, 248). In the center was also found a *dagoba* containing the Bowl Relic of the Buddha which indicated that the Buddha was present in the structure (Greenwald 1978, 29–30). *Dagobas* are also symbolic of Mount Meru and are therefore thought to have a cosmic axis running through them (Mabbett 1983, 75–77; B.L. Smith, 1978a, 77–78). Furthermore, Sakra is reputed to have built a *dagoba* on the top of Mount Meru for a relic of the Buddha (Ariyapala 1956, 372).

In the northern portion of the eastern rectangle, to the south of the Visnu Devale and to the west of the palace, there was a place called the Dēva Sanhinde (Place of the Gods). There was a bell here, just as there is in an Indian temple, to summon a god. During the time of the kings, citizens could ring the bell if they felt an injustice had been committed and the king would sit in judgment in this place. It was believed that the king could do no wrong here, as he passed judgment in the presence of the gods in their shrines (Davy 1821, 322). Again, the parallel between the landscape and the sacred texts is striking, for according to the *Puranas* (Ali 1973, 47) the assembly of the gods was held on the northern side of Mount Meru.

There was a fourth major *devale* in Kandy, but it was located outside of the eastern rectangle in the profane western rectangle. I suggest that its location could also be explained by reference to the sacred texts. The god Kataragama (Skanda), to whom this temple was dedicated, is the son of Siva and he was banished by his father from the heavens to the world of mortals, to Kataragama in the south of Lanka (L. De Silva 1980, 167; Obeyesekere 1984, 471). He is considered the most human-like of the gods in Kandy for he is deeply involved in the affairs of the world. He abandoned his wife Dēvasena and took a mistress, Valli Ammā, who had been adopted by the Veddas, a tribal group in Lanka (Obeyesekere 1984, 60, 471). He is a powerful god, but a sinner, and therefore a resident of the world of humans (R.F. Gombrich 1971, 159). Thus the location of the Kataragama Devale in the profane western rectangle makes sense if urban form does indeed allegorize narrative. Just as Kataragama was cast out of heaven, so his *devale* was barred from the sacred eastern rectangle, the heaven on earth.

It is important to note that physical space in Hindu and Buddhist ritual is neither flat nor non-evaluative. It is symbolic, hierarchical and charged with moral value. H.L. Seneviratne (1978a, 21–22) has argued that the concepts of upper and lower were crucial in the Kandyan Kingdom. "This distinction is not merely physical, although 'upper' and 'lower' are often allocated appropriate elevations: it is moral and hierarchical." He points out that the palace had upper and lower sections; the Temple of the Tooth Relic had upper and lower shrines, as did the *devala* of the gods, and some political and religious units of the kingdom had upper and lower divisions. I argue that the city itself had this upper and lower quality, with the sacred eastern rectangle as the upper heaven and the profane western rectangle as the lower earth. This was concretized in the landscape through elevation as a type of landscape trope; the *devala* of Natha, Pattini, and Visnu, and the palace/temple complex were built on artificial terraces to place them above the rest of the city.

The cardinal directions also imbue space with a moral quality. The east, for example, is "higher" than the west in terms of ritual purity. It follows, then, that the further east in Kandy, the more morally elevated the spaces become. For example, to the east of the western rectangle was the eastern rectangle; in the eastern part of the eastern rectangle was the Temple of the Tooth; in the eastern part of the Temple of the Tooth was the Shrine of the Relic, and in the eastern part of the shrine was the relic itself. We can see then, that urban form in Kandy spoke of hierarchy, of power, and of the relationship between mere mortals and the god-king. The city as a whole represented the cosmos in miniature with the profane western rectangle inhabited by the citizens, symbolizing the earth and the eastern rectangle inhabited by the Buddha, the gods, and the king, symbolizing heaven.

From discourse to landscape: a kingly reading

The purity and power of the gods in heaven were captured in this mirror of the landscape of heaven. In the case of the Kandyan Kingdom we can see a nested hierarchy of declining purity moving from the heart of the city to the extremities of the kingdom. At the heart of the city lay the eastern rectangle. It came closest to mirroring the heaven of Sakra on Meru for it included Sakra's palace on Mount Mandara, the raised temples of the gods over Meru, and the cosmic Ocean of Milk at its foot. Just as Mount Meru towers above the world of *asuras* (demons) and humans at its base, so the temples and palace in the eastern rectangle stood above the western rectangle. Relative to the eastern rectangle, the western rectangle was not only physically lower, but represented the world of *asuras* and men in other ways as well. It was the location of the *devale* of Kataragama who was sent out of heaven to be among the humans and *asuras*. It mirrored the twenty-one provinces of the kingdom and was the location of shops, houses, and other secular buildings.

The city as a whole, however, including the western rectangle, was as a heaven to the kingdom as a whole. For, as we have seen, the city has been frequently referred to as the city of Sakra on the top of Mount Meru. The seventeenth-century *Parangi Hatana* (cited in P.E. Pieris 1914, 205 v.247) expresses this clearly:

> As the Asuras tried to scale Meru to reach the Sekraya's [Sakra's] city, so they [the Portuguese] began to climb Balanekanda [a mountain pass] to arrive at Senkadagala [Kandy], where is the center of our faith.

Similarly an early-nineteenth-century Kandyan report warned the English about the consequences they faced if they dared attack Kandy; "the gods of the four principal Pagodas called Hattara Devale had appeared to his Majesty in a dream and declared that if some enemies of the king came on top of the mountain within that week, they should be destroyed" (C.O. 54/10 [1803c] 1973). The city was Mount Meru to the kingdom. And yet, unlike the eastern rectangle which was completely pure, the city displayed a dual character. It was both heaven and earth, simultaneously symbolizing elements of each.

Finally, the kingdom was as Mount Meru to the lowland kingdoms controlled by the Europeans. It was Kande Uda Rata, the kingdom in the mountains, and it was conceived of as culturally and spiritually purer than the lowland kingdoms polluted by the subservience of their populations to European masters.

As should be clear from this discussion as well as from a comparison of tables 6.1 and 6.2, the dominant allegory for the eastern rectangle is "The world of the gods." There are twice as many synecdoches, with over three times as many references to this allegory as there are to the allegory "The world of the *cakravarti*." This does not, however, mean that the latter allegory is unimportant. For as we have seen in this chapter (and is tabulated in the appendix) this allegory was an important, if secondary, text within the landscape.

The whole basis of this kingly reading of the city was metaphoric and metonymic. Through the magic of parallelism, synecdochic elements in the landscape stand for and attract to themselves the power of the larger allegorical whole. These relationships which are established symbolically are highly complex. They are not only metaphorical in an especially efficacious way, but through the important religious concept of liminality they are metonymic or syntagmatic, for there is a kind of contiguity established between heavenly and earthly landscapes through such mechanisms as the cosmic axis. Also, important syntagmatic relationships were established through the spatial sequencing and juxtapositioning of iconic, linguistic, and behavioral symbols in the landscape. These relations of contiguity and similarity, along with relations of difference, such as sacred versus profane spaces, all joined to transform the landscape of Kandy into a highly complex, intertextual, and multivocal system of communication.

7

From landscape to civic ritual: a kingly reading

> Every action, gesture, speech of the ruler was an expression of ritual or symbolic significance, to be carefully observed and reported for its iconic reassurance of stability. The King's regalia, his dependents, his weapons, animals, coin, and personal surrogates and emissaries all carried with them the *mana* of their possessor. (Richards 1978, iii–iv)

Thus far I have described a landscape without people, a stage-set which spoke in the language of the concrete of a charismatic ruler, a Sakra among men, a *cakravarti* who rules from a heaven on earth, a liminal location, a cosmic axis at the center of the world. Let us now people this landscape by considering a number of civic rituals which demonstrate how this landscape was used in the production of charismatic rule.[1]

The creation of a god-king

In the Kandyan Kingdom, as elsewhere in South Asia, prosperity, the seasonal rains, the fertility of people, animals, and plants, and the maintenance of the social order were thought to depend upon a properly consecrated and wisely ruling monarch. Without a legitimate king, both the natural and social order would collapse and chaos would ensue. The period between the death of an old king and the installation of a new one was therefore a time fraught with danger (Richards 1978, iv). The ceremonies of removing a dead king and consecrating his successor were ceremonies of world renewal which invoked extensive cosmic symbolism.

During the Kandyan period, when a king died his successor was chosen by the *adikars*. In order to conform to popular Buddhist notions of elective kingship, however, the choice was made to appear as a choice of the people (Dewaraja 1972, 208). The future king was then bathed by the Diyavadhana Nilame (the lay leader of the Temple of the Tooth Relic), and dressed in regal robes. His first act as king was to worship the Tooth Relic and recite the *pan sil* (five precepts of lay life). Then, with guns booming, conches blaring and drums beating, he appeared at the balcony of the palace to announce the death of the old king and election of the new (Dolapihilla 1959, 10–11). Later the dead king's body, preceded by royal musicians, was carried to the cremation ground at Adahana Maluva to the north of the city. The body was set on a pyre in the form of seven steps, in the middle of which was a large hole filled with sandalwood, aloe wood, and fragrant spices. More wood and spices were piled up to the height of a man around the pyre. Above the pyre was a royal canopy in the form of a tower seven feet in height, made of costly gold cloth (see figure 11). The hole in the center of the pyre was filled with three pots of cinnamon oil and one of butter and then ignited. Half an hour after the oil had been lit, a relative of the deceased lit the wood around the pyre and the king was immolated (Valentijn 1978, 308).[2]

The symbolism of this event is readily interpretable in the light of the narrative structure recurrent in the landscape. The seven-stepped pyre topped by a seven-foot tower of golden cloth was a synecdoche referring to the suballegory of Mount Meru, the central mountain surrounded by the seven lesser mountain chains.[3] This earthly Meru is consumed by flames at the death of the king just as in the allegory Mount Meru is consumed by the cosmic fire at the end of a *kalpa*. In this way each reign is symbolically likened to one of the great ages of the world.

The cremation of kings in Kandy took twelve days. After the twelfth day the remains of the king were separated into ashes, bones, and melted jewelry and were placed in four new urns. A decorated loft was erected and a man dressed in white with a muffled mouth placed one of the pots on his head and ascended the loft. He was then carried by elephant or horse to Katugastota on the Mahaveli Ganga which flows around Kandy. Here he stepped into a boat and was launched into the river carrying the urn on his head and holding a sword in his hand. Arriving at mid-stream he cut the urn in half, spilling the contents into the river, and dived overboard never to return to the Kandy side of the river again. The horse or elephant were also carried over the river and set free (Davy 1821, 122; J.M. Seneviratne, 1916–1917, 121–22). This parallels the Indian tradition of placing ashes in the Ganges in order to allow the deceased to be carried heavenward, for the Ganges is the river which connects the three worlds. One is reminded here of the words of Indra to Yudhishthira and his brothers who wander in hell: "Here is the celestial Ganga, sacred and sanctifying the three worlds. Enter it and you will find your rightful place" (Darian 1978, 75). The other three pots of bones and jewels were treated as relics and were placed in a *dagoba* at the Adhahana Maluva (burial ground) as befitting a *cakravarti* and *bodhisattva*.

The old god-king had departed this world, as the Kandyans would say, and gone to heaven. His successor must become in turn a god-king. This was achieved through the ritual of consecration. This consecration ceremony was adapted from the traditional Indian *rājasūya* or *abhiṣēka*.[4] There were certain

11 The cremation of the prince (taken from Baldeus 1752)

preconditions, however, that had to be met before this ceremony could take place. According to the *Mahāvaṃsa Ṭīkā* (Fernando 1896, 126):

> he who wishes to be duly inaugurated as king should obtain for this purpose three *chanks* [sea shells] (golden and otherwise), water from the Ganges river, and a maiden of the Ksatriya race. He must himself be ripe for the ceremony [over 16 years of age] and be a *ksatriya* of noble lineage.'

The first two of these conditions were easy to fulfill, for decorated *chanks* were kept on hand, as was surrogate water from the Ganges, represented by water from the Mahaveli Ganga or perhaps from Anuradhapura, symbolizing the heavenly Ganges. The last three conditions were often more difficult to fulfill, in part because of the European presence in the lowlands. As I have indicated above, people who could claim *ksatriya* descent were few in Lanka. The European elimination of all the other kingdoms on the island meant that from the time of Vimala Dharma Suriya I (1592–1604), the Kandyan royal family was the only one on the island that could claim *ksatriya* blood (Dewaraja 1972, 27). From this time onward, *ksatriya* princesses had been procured from Southern India. Narendra Sinha (1707–1739) needed Dutch help to bring princesses from Madurai, for without a *ksatriya* maiden, consecration was impossible (Dewaraja 1972, 65).

When Narenda Sinha died without offspring, the crown passed to the South Indian brother of his wife, who claimed to be of *ksatriya* descent rather than to a member of the Sinhalese nobility who were *goyigama* (farmer caste).[5]

The inability to meet all of the conditions of consecration meant that there might be a hiatus between the time a prince assumed the throne and his consecration. During that time the ruler acted as a governor rather than as king (Hocart 1970, 137). For example, when Kirti Sri succeeded to the throne in 1747 he was under age. Although two years later a suitable princess arrived from South India, because of his age it was not until 1751 that he was consecrated (Van Gollenesse [1751] 1974, 17).

On the auspicious day chosen for the consecration, the king and his train emerged from the gate of the palace/temple complex and first marched northward to the Visnu Devale (Davy 1821, 122–123), for north is the direction in which a *cakravarti* must first march at the start of his reign. After receiving the blessing of Visnu,[6] who was himself a *bodhisattva*, head of the Buddhist pantheon and entrusted by Sakra to protect Buddhism in Lanka (A. Seneviratne 1983, 93; Bechert 1978, 5; Aluvihare 1952, 13), the king marched south to Natha Devale.

From landscape to civic ritual: a kingly reading 123

An *ola* (manuscript) in the possession of Madugalle Nayaka Unnanse of Poya Maulwa described the accession of Kirti Sri as follows (Codrington 1916–1917, 157):

> At the lucky hour when the *hora* was Sikura's, the lagna Kumbha, and the *nekata ma* at seven and a half *peyas* of the morning, being Thursday the third *tithiya* of the waning moon and the fifth *bhaga* of *Makara ravi* in the Saka year 1672 named Pramaduta, there took place the festival of tying on the golden sword, when the fortunate name of Kirttisiri Rajasinha had been assumed [by the King] with his face to the north west. On the occasion of this festival Kobbekaduwe Unavahanse wrote the fortunate name on the golden leaf and pronounced it, Mondaruwela the junior, Haluwadana Rala presented the brow fillet and Pilima Taluwuve, Haluwadana Rala presented the golden sword.

It is not entirely clear where in the grounds of the Natha Devale this ceremony took place. However, to the southwest of the bo tree there is a square stone slab mounted upon four small stone pillars which is generally thought to be the coronation stone (Prematilleke 1983, 5; Lawrie n.d., vol. 4). It is likely that the king stood here facing northwest, the direction of Indra, victory, heroism, success, and of the Maruts, storm gods who are the friends and allies of Indra, for they control the rain (Obeyesekere 1984, 336; Jayatilaka 1881, 151; Stutley and Stutley 1984, 165, 184). Here he received his sword, brow fillet, and name "given by the gods to the god on earth" (Vimalananda 1963, 333, cited in H.L. Seneviratne 1978a, 2). It was fitting that the king should receive his name and sword from the *bodhisattva* Natha (Paranavitana 1928, 59), for as a tenth-century slab inscription states (*Epigraphia Zeylanica* 1912, 243; cited in Evers 1972, 65): "none but the *bodhisattvas* would become kings of Sri Lanka."

The king then went to an adjacent circular pavilion used for the consecration ceremony (Prematilleke 1986, 11). According to a 1769 account of a Kandyan priest (Bertolacci 1817, 454–455):

> On the day of his installation the Royal Mandapa [pavilion] is beautifully decorated with all sorts of precious ornaments; within that Mandapa is erected another made of the branches of the *Udumbara* or *attika* tree; and in the center of this inner Mandapa is placed a seat of the wood of the same tree. The king, covered with jewels and invested with the insignia of royalty, wearing the sword, the pearl umbrella, the forehead band, the slippers and the chowrie made of the hair of the *semara's* tail, repairs to the above mentioned seat. A Royal virgin

adorned with costly ornaments and holding in her hand a sea chank filled with river water and opening to the right, then approaches the place where the king is seated and lifting up the chank with both hands, pours its contents upon the king's head.

A brahmin then repeated the virgin's action with a silver *chank*, followed by the principal queen who did the same with a golden *chank*. The king was then admonished to rule justly or his head would be split into seven pieces. In this ceremony the kings of Kandy repeated the traditional consecration ceremonies of the early kings of Lanka in Anuradhapura and Polonnaruva (see Fernando 1896; J.M. Seneviratne 1921–1922; Ariyapala 1956, 57–62).

Let us now examine the cosmic symbolism of this ceremony. The consecration of the king represented the first in a series of ritual beginnings (Heesterman 1978, 9). It was not simply a public act of affirmation, but a constitutive ritual whereby a man was transformed into a king (Inden 1978, 38), and, at the same time, transformed into a god (H.L. Seneviratne 1978a, 2). This act had particular significance in kingdoms such as Kandy for, due to a lack of hereditary rule, it was this ritual which imbued the human king with the charisma of the king of the gods thus making him a god-king (R. Pieris 1956, 11). The charisma of kingship was present in all the ritual objects used during the consecration; the right-turning *chank*, the sword, the forehead plate, slippers, the yak-tail chowrie, and the place where he was consecrated (Codrington 1909, 228; Gokhale 1966, 19).

The symbolic significance of the place is of particular interest to us. The pavilion was located at the center of the sacred rectangle next to the bo tree which, as I discussed above, places this spot of consecration at the cosmic axis, on the top of Mount Meru, in the world of the gods. As Heesterman (1957, 13) points out, the traditional consecration was based on the idea of ascension. In the rite of the mounting of the four quarters, the king symbolically ascended to the zenith. The king was thus raised above the earth at this spot which was called the "womb of sovereignty" (Hocart 1924–1928e, 117). Within the Indian tradition this pavilion is a synecdoche for the whole world, and the throne in the center of the hall is a synecdoche standing for the *axis mundi* from which the *cakravarti*, the world ruler, would arise (Inden 1978, 46). In Burma this consecration hall was thought of as Sakra's palace on top of mount Meru, royal power being derived from the mystical energy which welled up from the point of transcendence on Mount Meru (Mabbett 1983, 80, 83).

Within the Kandyan consecration hall was a second pavilion made of *udambara* wood and within this, at its center, was a consecration throne made of the same wood. Such a pavilion corresponded closely to that used in

From landscape to civic ritual: a kingly reading

the ancient Indian consecration (Inden 1978, 45, 66); even the variety of wood was the same. The choice of the wood of the fig tree (*udambara* – *Ficus glomerata*) was significant, not only because the fig is a cosmic axis and therefore symbolically situates the king on the cosmic mountain but also, according to the *Siva Purana*, because the waters of the heavenly Ganges flow "from the branches of an *udambara* tree" (Darian 1978, 189). The *udambara* is also associated with virility and creation (Coomaraswamy 1931, 21). Thus, we have at this place the symbolism of the heavenly Ganges coming down out of the *udambara* onto the king at the center of the world mountain. These waters of consecration are the waters of creation that flow from the heavens to the Ocean of Milk.

In ancient India the water poured over the head of the king was thought to be *soma* (Coomaraswamy 1931, 20–21); the Burmese claimed it came from the middle of the cosmic ocean (Shorto 1963, 589), while the Sinhalese in Anuradhapura considered it to be water from Lake Anotatta (J.M. Seneviratne 1918, 125). Foucher argues that for Buddhist kings this consecration ritual was also symbolic of the Buddha's birth when queen Maya was refreshed by elephants (Hocart 1924–1928f., 30). This interpretation is plausible, as it was at this ceremony that the king was reborn not only as a god, but also as a *bodhisattva*.

Davy (1821, 123) comments that immediately after his consecration Sri Vikrama first circled around the sacred square and then encircled the city in procession. The *Culavamsa* (1953b, 255–256) describes King Kirti Sri's circumambulation in more detail.

> The highly famed one had the whole town (of Sirivaddhana) [Kandy] cleansed and decorated with stuffs, triumphal arches and the like.
> Then he gathered together the whole of the inhabitants of Lanka completely in the fair, glorious town and moving along with royal magnificence, the Great King whose merit was now having its effect, marched round the town, his right side turned towards it, thus making known that the realm of Lanka bereft of its king had again a king.

H.L. Seneviratne (1978b, 180) comments that this type of circumambulation, with the right side facing an object, was both a traditional act of worship and sign of domination by force in Lanka. Ritual circumambulation of the capital by the new king was also practiced in parts of the Middle East, Cambodia, Thailand, and Burma (Saintyves 1923, 177–204; Coedes 1947, 98; Przyluski 1933, 320; Quaritch Wales 1931, 106–107; Heine-Geldern 1930, 58; cited in Wheatley 1971, 433). In the following section, I will discuss circumambulation as it pertains to the Asala Perahara.

Table 7.1

The recurrent narrative structure of the cremation and consecration

NARRATIVE "THE WORLD OF THE *CAKRAVARTI*"

Location	Number of synecdoches	Number of references to narrative	Number of references to subnarrative (A)	Number of references to subnarrative (B)	Number of references to subnarrative (C)
Cremation ground	3	3	0	0	3
Mahaveli River	1	1	0	0	1
Western rectangle	11	13	5	5	3
Eastern rectangle	4	6	2	1	3
Visnu	10	10	9	0	1
Natha	7	7	1	0	6
Center	14	19	5	0	14
Total recurrence in landscape	50	59	22	6	31

Note. The narrative "The world of the *cakravarti*" is composed of three subnarratives:
(A) Control over the whole world through rerproduction of centrality and cardinal directions.
(B) Control over kingdom through microcosmic reproduction.
(C) Reproduction of the cities of the Sinhalese hero-kings.

As table 7.1 demonstrates, I have identified 50 synecdoches making 59 references to the narrative, "The world of the *cakravarti*." The majority of these concern the consecration rather than the cremation of the king and they are concentrated around the eastern rectangle. The references to the subnarratives are equally divided between the subnarratives of the king's control over his kingdom and the world, and that of the reproduction of the cities of the hero-kings of Lanka. The fact that we find a greater emphasis in this ritual on the subnarrative of the hero-kings than we have seen in the landscape in general can be explained by the fact that it faithfully models the rituals which had been used in Anuradhapura and Polonnaruva.

As table 7.2 indicates, I have found 46 synecdoches making 94 references to

Table 7.2

The recurrent narrative structure of the cremation and consecration

NARRATIVE: "THE WORLD OF THE GODS"

Location	Number of synecdoches	Number of references to narrative	Number of references to subnarrative (A)	Number of references to subnarrative (B)	Number of references to subnarrative (C)
Cremation ground	2	4	2	0	2
Mahaveli river	1	3	1	1	1
Western rectangle	2	3	2	0	1
Eastern rectangle	2	4	2	0	2
Visnu	17	40	16	10	14
Natha	12	22	11	2	9
Center	10	18	9	2	7
Total recurrence in landscape	46	94	43	15	36

Note. The narrative "The world of the gods" is composed of three subnarratives:
(A) The cities of the gods, especially Sakra's city.
(B) The Ocean of Milk, fertility and creation.
(C) The cosmic axis, especially the cosmic mountain and the cosmic tree.

the narrative "The world of the gods." Of these 94, 79 referred either to the subnarratives of "The cities of the gods" or to "The cosmic mountain". The remaining 15 referred to fertility.

The message of this ritual is clear. There were at least 96 iconic, linguistic, and behavioral synecdoches, comprising 153 separate references to the narratives of "The world of the *cakravarti*" and "The world of the gods". These synecdoches, through their recurrence, impressed upon the people that the new king was a *cakravarti*. He was not only the lord of his kingdom, but of the world. The ritual also strongly highlighted the connection between the new king and the hero-kings of Anuradhapura and Polonnaruva. Finally, the greatest density of synecdochic references were to the city of Sakra on the top of Mount Meru. Here in no fewer than 79 instances the new king was related to the heaven of Sakra on Mount Meru.

Asala Perahara

The consecration ceremony which signaled the transformation of the man into a god-king also established important links between the world of the gods and the world of humans at a place held to be at the central axis of the earth. This coming together of gods and humans at the cosmic axis symbolized creation, renewal, and fertility for the whole kingdom. It was through the ritual mirroring of the world of the gods in the world of humans that order and fertility was ensured.

Although this link was established during a consecration, annual renewal was required. In these regenerative rituals the sacred power of kings was replenished, their mediation between the gods and their people was reaffirmed and prosperity was thereby assured (Stein 1984a, 303). Contact with the world of the gods was regulated through the periodicity of the official calendar (Tambiah 1976, 73). The most important regenerative festival in Kandy was the Asala Perahara (procession) held during the weeks preceding the full moon of Asala (July–August). The Asala full moon is an important date, for on this date the Buddha was conceived and on this same date he left his father's palace to seek salvation (Geiger 1960, 199). The date thus resonates with the significance of beginning and creation. The auspicious time to begin the festival was calculated by the temple astrologers (H.L. Seneviratne 1978a, 71) to ensure a proper flow of power between heaven and earth.

Peraharas of this sort were held in Anuradhapura and Polonnaruva by earlier kings of Lanka, and Knox mentions that one was held in Kandy in the seventeenth century. Until the mid eighteenth century, however, this was a festival of the gods. At that time King Kirti Sri decided to place the Relic of the Buddha in the position of honor in this festival (*Sangaraja Vata* 1955, 104, vv.238, 241; *Sulu Pujavaliya* 1913, 17), thereby symbolically reestablishing the primacy of Buddhism within the religious system (Malalgoda 1976, 64). The *perahara* itself was a procession or, more specifically, a circumambulation of the city of Kandy. Similar ritual processions, whose goal was to produce fertility and order within the kingdom, were also undertaken in India, China, and Southeast Asia (Fritz 1986, 46–49; Inden 1978, 55; Wheatley 1971, 433–434; Hocart 1924–1928a, 110; Geertz 1983b, 159).[7] Their purpose was twofold, for not only did they produce order in the kingdom through the power of ritual, but as Davy (1821, 176) wrote:

> the Perraherra had a more secret object: by obliging all chiefs, and the principal people of all the Dissavonies [provinces] and Ratties [counties] to appear before their sovereign in the capital at the same time, to take part in a pompous religious ceremony, besides tending to

From landscape to civic ritual: a kingly reading 129

excite national feeling and union, it had the effect of promoting loyalty, of keeping the ambitious in awe.

Of course it was not only the chiefs that came to Kandy for the *perahara*. Certainly many hundreds and perhaps thousands of peasants – retainers of the king, of the provincial lords, and of the *vihara* and *devala* were summoned to Kandy to fulfill their duty by participating in the procession. During the three weeks of the festival, the city was choked with people as peasants and nobles came from throughout the kingdom to participate in and be overawed by this splendid annual ritual in the city of the god-king.

As H.L. Seneviratne (1978a, 114) points out, it was not only fear of the king that compelled the nobles to attend this festival, but also the fear of divine retribution should they refuse "to attend the greatest festival in honor of such a mystically powerful object [as the Tooth Relic]." The Asala Perahara was essentially a ritual of control – control by the king over nature, his capital, and his kingdom. Such sweeping control was only possible with divine aid and intervention.

To efficaciously perform this ritual, the stage, which was the city itself, had to be properly set and carefully arranged. The arrangement which was thought to facilitate the ritual was as follows: the eastern rectangle, containing the palace, the Tooth Temple, the Natha, Visnu, and Pattini Devala, and the sacred bo tree, already, as we have seen, through the power of synecdoche, placed the capital at the center of the world on top of the cosmic mountain. However, it was necessary to strengthen this liminal linking at the time of the *perahara*. This was accomplished by reinforcing the symbolism of the cosmic axis through which divine power flows down to earth.

The *kapa* or ritual pole which was used in the *perahara* is just such a cosmic axis. The four *kapurāla* (priests) of the four *devala* in Kandy each chose a tree with milk-like sap for the *kapa*. A male tree, which is recognized by its uniform trunk size, was chosen (H.L. Seneviratne 1978a, 72–73). The symbolism here is clearly of fertility, milk and semen.[8] According to the *Maimataya* (Coomaraswamy 1956, 125), the tree which was chosen as the *magul kapa* (auspicious post) had the ground cleared around it and an *atamagala* diagram drawn around it. This magic diagram places eight auspicious objects at the eight points of the compass (Coomaraswamy 1956, 271–272). By locating the tree at the center of the eight compass points, it was symbolically converted into the *axis mundi*. At the north, south, east, and west corners of the diagram were placed full pots symbolizing fertility and sandalwood milk was sprinkled around, symbolizing the fertility of the Ocean of Milk.

A branch facing east, which is the most auspicious direction, was cut and divided into four two-foot sections, one for each *devale* (H.L. Seneviratne 1978a, 73). The branches were taken to the four *devala* in Kandy covered by a white cloth, reiterating the symbolism of milk. The *kapa* was then purified with milk and purifying powders, and was three times paraded around the *devale* before being planted in a special *kapa* house on the east side of the *devale*. Then the insignia of the god was paraded three times around the *devale* (H.L. Seneviratne 1978a, 74–75). The planting of the *kapa* marked the inauguration of the festival, as with this act an especially strong link along the cosmic axis was established. Each of the four *devala* in Kandy now had a cosmic axis connecting them to the three worlds. By circumambulating the *devale* with the *kapa* three times, the axis was extended through the three worlds, and by parading the insignia of the god around it three times, each of the four gods moved through the three worlds along this cosmic axis.

L. De Silva (1978) argues that the *kapa* was both the *kapruka* tree, which grants all wishes, that arose fom the churning of the Ocean of Milk, and the *indrakīla*, the post of Indra (Sakra). The *kapruka* symbolizes fertility while the *indrakila* represents Mount Mandara or Mount Meru, the stable cosmic axis. In fact both represent the cosmic axis in the form of the world tree and that cosmic mountain. The *indrakila* served to project the ceremony to the central point of the earth which is the cosmic mountain (L. De Silva 1978, 249; see also H.L. Seneviratne 1978a, 71).

The Asala Perahara is divided into three distinct phases: the Devala Perahara, the Kumbal Perahara, and the Randōli Perahara (Aluvihare 1964; H.L. Seneviratne 1978a, 82).[9] During the first phase, known as the Devala Perahara, the insignia of the gods were carried by the *kapurala* of each *devale* in circumambulation around their respective *devale* as described above. This, I have argued, established the connection between the world of the gods and the capital along the cosmic axis represented by the *kapa*. During the second phase, known as the Kumbal Perahara, the insignia of the gods of the four *devala* were added to the sacred relic casket representing the Tooth Relic, in procession (see figure 12). Not only was this the first time that all four *devala* joined the procession of the relic, it was also the first time that elephants and large numbers of retainers, drawn from villages controlled by the Temple of the Tooth and the four *devala*, marched in the procession.

The *perahara* in fact consisted of five separate *peraharas*. The first was that of the Tooth Relic, which had been placed at the head by Kirti Sri in 1747. The second was dedicated to Natha because he is the next Buddha. Third was Visnu's, who is next in line to be Buddha after Natha. Kataragama, Sakra's general, followed, as his assistance is needed in battle. The last section was for the goddess Pattini. Dressed in white, the Basnayāke Nilamē (lay head) of

12 The Asala Perahara (courtesy of the Kandy Museum)

each *devale* marched with his troop of elephants, torchbearers, spear and ritual umbrella carriers, drummers, and dancers.

During the first few nights, the Kumbal Perahara marched in procession around the sacred square. According to Coomaraswamy (1956, 38), the *perahara* circumambulated the sacred bo tree at the center of the square. The bo, as I have argued, was considered a cosmic axis at the center of the city and by circling it the *perahara* passed around the whole world, Mount Meru, and the heaven of the gods.

During the final stage of the *perahara*, named the Randoli Perahera, the procession left the sacred square and circumambulated the city (Coomaraswamy 1956, 38). Each night the *perahara* circummambulated a larger area, always circling the bo tree, but taking in more and more of the city. This final stage of the *perahara* was the most impressive and it is here that the king inserted himself into the proceedings. Davy (1821, 130) writes:

> The King, who before was a spectator merely of the ceremony, now took an active part in it, and during the five days that the Randoely-beyma lasted, regularly joined the evening procession in his golden chariot drawn by eight horses.

A Kandyan chief in 1834 described the role played by the king in the *perahara* in more detail (Perera 1916, 27).

> The king in rich dress came into the Pattrippo [octagonal tower] when the curtain was drawn aside, and as soon as the royal person was presented to public view the leader of the band of singers recited an invocation in verse which was immediately succeeded by instrumental music. This having ceased the two *adigars* and all the other chiefs presented themselves in view of the king, uttered aloud their prayers for the prosperity of their monarch and his empire and paid homage by prostrations . . . The procession being arranged and marshalled in the square, the king repaired to the Maligawa, and thence with his own hands the Karandoowe [reliquary] which he placed within the *ranhilligey* upon the elephant and thence proceeded on foot to the square, where he took his stand on a *haridagala* (a stone having the figure of the moon carved upon it) with a silver wand in his hand, and followed in the train of the procession after the randolee.

The king's actions here spoke of power. King Sri Vikrama built an octagonal *pattirippuwa* attached to the Temple of the Tooth for precisely such ritual displays. This eight-sided structure symbolized the eight directions, and the king who stood at the center of such a structure symbolically

From landscape to civic ritual: a kingly reading

controlled the whole of the world for he was considered equidistant from the cardinal direction points. It was the prerogative of the *cakravarti* to stand here (Gunatilaka 1975, 43). As the curtain opened in the *pattirippuwa*, the king was revealed to the populace as a god in a shrine. He was considered to be like to Sakra in his palace, like the ideal *cakravarti*, as well as like a future Buddha.

The king wore an eight-cornered hat in the center of which was a tree-shaped tassel fashioned out of gold (Coomaraswamy 1956, 32). The hat repeated the symbolism of the center, while the golden tree stood for both the wish granting tree from the Ocean of Milk and the world tree that is a cosmic axis. The *adikars*, who wore four-cornered hats (Coomaraswamy 1956, 33), represented the kings of the four quarters who paid homage to the *cakravarti* at the center of the world.

After making this dramatic appearance, the king then vanished into the Temple of the Tooth. Suddenly reappearing at the main gate, he placed the *dagoba*-shaped reliquary containing the Tooth Relic in a howdah similar to the vehicle of Sakra,[10] which rested on the back of the state elephant. Here the king mirrored the actions of Sakra, who keeps a Tooth Relic in his palace in the Tavatimsa heaven. The king subsequently reviewed the *perahara* from a ceremonial stone (see figure 13). This represented a throne and was marked with the figure of the moon, symbolizing both the lunar dynasty from which the kings of Kandy were thought to descend and the god Siva.

The various sections of the *perahara* passed the king in the following order. At the head of the procession came the vanguard which was composed of government officials (H.L. Seneviratne 1978a, 108–110; Aluvihare 1952, 10–14). First came an official who rode upon an elephant and carried the *lēkam miṭi* or state records of the kingdom. It is interesting to note that first in order of precedence among the king's departments was the keeper of the state records. This shows the great importance placed upon texts in the kingdom. Second came the Gajanayaka Nilame, a very high official in charge of the king's ceremonial elephants. He rode an elephant and carried a silver goad. The *nilame* was followed by the king's elephants, the insignia of his department, the officials of the department, their retainers, arms bearers, and drummers playing war drums. Next came representatives of the Kodituvakku department carrying their gun flag and followed by their retinue, drummers, and dancers.

The next twelve sections of the *perahara* represented the *disa* (twelve provinces) of the kingdom. At the head of each provincial section marched the *disava* (governor) followed by his retainers carrying the provincial flag and other insignia and by the officials, the arms bearers of the province, drummers, and dancers. After these twelve sections it was said that there followed "bamboos or images representing devils, covered with cloth" (Millava 1817, cited in H.L. Seneviratne 1978a, 109).

Next in procession were the representatives of the Tooth Temple followed by the state elephant, the Maligawa Tusker carrying the *perahara karaṇḍuva* (golden casket) containing the Tooth Relic. A canopy was held over the tusker while white cloths strewn with flowers were continually spread in its path. The tusker was followed by the Diyavadana Nilame (lay head of the Tooth Temple) and other functionaries, retinues, drummers and musicians. On either side of the tusker walked six monks from the Asgiriya and Malwatte monasteries.

The next four sections consisted of the representatives of the four *devala* in Kandy. The first section was composed of the representatives of the Natha Devale. The *kapurala* (chief priest) of the *devale* rode upon the chief elephant and carried the *ran āyudhaya* (the apparel and insignia) of the deity. He was followed by Basnayaka Nilame of the *devale* and his retinue of dancers, drummers, torchbearers, and attendants. This section was followed by the sections representing the Visnu, Kataragama, and Pattini Devala.

The next section of the procession consisted of the representatives of the nine inner *rata* (provinces) of the kingdom. Each had its *ratemahatmaya* (governor), insignia, flags, officials, retinue, and drummers and dancers. The final six sections of the *perahara* were composed of different departments of the central administration with their insignia, flags, retinues, and musicians.

At the end of the procession came the *randoli* (golden carriages of the consorts of the gods) containing the "lightning weapon ornaments" of the gods (Perera 1916, 27) and followed by the king, either on a white horse (P.E. Pieris 1956, 17) or in a "golden chariot drawn by eight horses" (Davy 1821, 130). Either way, the king was acting out the narrative of "The world of the gods," by imitating Sakra riding on the white charger who emerged from the Ocean of Milk or riding on the chariot of the gods drawn by the eight horses representing the directions of the compass.

After circumambulating the town, the *perahara* returned to the sacred rectangle and circled it three times before disbanding (H.L. Seneviratne 1978a, 88). The *perahara* was now over as the gods had passed through the three worlds and returned to their heavens.

The king, the representatives of his twenty-one provinces, his central administration, his soldiers, and retainers, the four gods, and the tooth relic had all circumambulated the capital. This act reaffirmed his control over the city, but also, through the power of parallelism, reaffirmed his control over his whole kingdom. It should be emphasized that this ritual act was not "merely symbolic" in our sense of the term. It was thought to be causally

13 Sri Vikrama and his courtiers (taken from Davy 1821)

efficacious as well. Circumambulation with the right side facing the city, was a ritual act that worked, by analogy, to maintain power over the capital and the wider kingdom that was magically reproduced within it through the power of like numbers. According to H.L. Seneviratne (1978a; 1984, 6), the *perahara* represented the symbolic reconquest of the kingdom through the symbolic capture of the capital. It is intriguing to note that this festival of conquest lasted twenty-one days, perhaps mirroring the twenty-one units of the kingdom temporally, as the landscape mirrored them spatially.

The *perahara* also symbolized fertility (H.L. Seneviratne 1978a, 111). The Tooth Relic was thought to produce light rain, "flower rains" as they are called, which explains why flowers were strewn in front of the Maligawa Tusker as it paraded through the streets of the city. The symbolism of fertility was reiterated by the *kapurala* of the four *devala* who went to the river at Geytembe Ferry and emptied out the water they had collected the previous year and refilled their golden pitchers with fresh water. This water was then restored to the *devala* where it would remain until the following year. The stored water symbolized the fertility that was safeguarded by the gods of the city (H.L. Seneviratne 1978a, 101–102). The god's lightning-weapon ornaments were used to cut circles in the water thereby controlling the waters through circumambulation in the same way as the city was controlled by the *perahara*.

Such a water-cutting ceremony is reminiscent of Indra's (Sakra's) victory over the demon Vṛta, who had blocked the waters of the world, and of Visnu's washing his sword in the river after his defeat of the Asuras (H.L. Seneviratne 1978a, 111). At this water-cutting ceremony the *kapa* were removed from the *devala* and thrown into the river, thus marking the end of the festival. Citizens then gathered them and these were planted in fields to ensure prosperity during the coming year (H.L. Seneviratne 1978a, 72).

Large numbers of elephants were used in the *perahara*. Throughout Indian Asia elephants were employed both in war and in state rituals. In the *perahara* they not only stood as living synecdoches for the military power that the king used to recapture his capital and kingdom, but also as magical forces capable of capturing rain. Elephants, with their great grey mass, resembled storm clouds and thus, through the magic of similarity, were thought to cause rain (*Kokila Sandesa* 1918–1919, 161, v.48). According to the myths of the time, in the past sacred elephants had been able to fly and Sakra's white elephant still flew from the earth up to his heaven (Zimmer 1974, 59; Davy 1821, 144). They were considered to be like "rain cloud[s] walking on the earth." Like decoys they could attract their fellows in the atmosphere (Zimmer 1974, 109). Of special value in attracting rain clouds were white elephants or those with light spots, for these were associated with the white elephant Airavata who

From landscape to civic ritual: a kingly reading 137

belonged to Sakra and who emerged from the churning of the Ocean of Milk (Zimmer 1974, 105).

The white elephant was not only a symbol of fertility, but of royalty and the Buddha as well (O'Flaherty 1980, 258). For example, the Buddha's mother, Maya, had a dream that a four-tusked white elephant descended from heaven, circled her three times and entered her womb (Campbell 1974, 243). It was said that the Bodhisattva descended from the heavens in the form of a white elephant and the Buddha in his last existence gave away his white state elephant in order to end a drought (Coomaraswamy 1972, 72; Zimmer 1974, 107).

In Thailand white elephants were kept by kings, at times they even acted as the kings' doubles (Pieris and Crosby 1945, 103; Hocart 1970, 91). Wars were fought over them as they were considered to have powers similar to relics (Andaya 1978, 7). Evidence that kings of Lanka did in fact own white elephants is found in statements by travellers such as Ibn Battuta who claimed that when he arrived in Lanka in 1344 he saw King Alagakkarara's white state elephant (Obeyesekere 1984, 525). Nearly four hundred years later the Dutch ambassador Aggreen wrote that he saw the king's "highly prized white elephant" at the entrance to the palace when he arrived in Kandy in 1736 (Heydt [1744] 1952, 92). The last king of Kandy apparently did not have a white elephant and was forced to content himself with a light spotted one. He claimed that a white elephant existed in the kingdom, but that since it was sacred to Sri Pade, the holy mountain in the south of the kingdom, it could not be caught (D'Oyly [1825] 1917, 52).

The *perahara*, therefore, was a ritual of kingly power. Through it the king's control over the capital, the kingdom and the productive forces of nature was reestablished annually before large numbers of citizens drawn from every part of the kingdom. The procession reaffirmed the power of the spatial symbolism of the city through which the power of the gods and the Buddha could be summoned.

Tables 7.3 and 7.4 summarize in quantitative form the narrative structure of the *perahara* as we have discussed it in this chapter. As a comparison of these two tables shows, once again the narrative "The world of the gods" is the dominant one. There are over twice as many synecdoches referring to it as to "The world of the *cakravarti*" and over three times as many separate references. As subnarratives A and C in table 7.4 demonstrate, over three-quarters of the references to the narrative of "The world of the gods" are to Sakra's heaven or to the cosmic mountain. This is understandable for the *perahara* is a ritual of control which emphasizes the link between the king and the king of the gods upon Mount Meru. That slightly less than a quarter of the references should be to the subnarrative "The Ocean of Milk, fertility and

Table 7.3

The recurrent narrative structure of the perahara

NARRATIVE: "THE WORLD OF THE *CAKRAVARTI*"

Location	Number of synecdoches	Number of references to narrative	Number of references to subnarrative (A)	Number of references to subnarrative (B)	Number of references to subnarrative (C)
Western rectangle	16	19	6	8	5
Kataragama	1	1	1	0	0
Eastern rectangle	9	12	3	4	5
Temple	28	32	17	0	15
Visnu	10	10	9	0	1
Natha	2	2	2	0	0
Pattini	2	2	2	0	0
Total recurrence in landscape	68	78	40	12	26

Note. The narrative "The world of the *cakravarti*" is composed of three subnarratives:
(A) Control over the whole world through reproduction of centrality and cardinal directions.
(B) Control over kingdom through microcosmic reproduction.
(C) Reproduction of the cities of the Sinhalese hero-kings.

creation" also makes sense, as the ritual has strong undertones of world renewal, as I discussed above. It is somewhat surprising that table 7.3 shows that less than one-sixth of the references are to the subnarrative "Control over the kingdom," as one of its purposes was to reassert actual political dominance over the kingdom. I would argue, however, that this control was achieved in part through the use of symbols of control over the whole world (see subnarrative A). Second in number were references to the cities of the hero-kings of Lanka, paradigms of political might. Perhaps, then, control over the kingdom could be as well or more powerfully symbolized by recurrent reference to "The world of the gods," "Control over the whole world," and reference to the "Hero cities of Lanka" than by direct reference to the kingdom itself.

Table 7.4

The recurrent narrative structure of the perahana

NARRATIVE: "THE WORLD OF THE GODS"

Location	Number of synecdoches	Number of references to narrative	Number of references to subnarrative (A)	Number of references to subnarrative (B)	Number of references to subnarrative (C)
Western rectangle	14	30	13	7	10
Kataragama	6	11	5	3	3
Eastern rectangle	15	33	14	7	12
Temple	59	110	47	27	36
Visnu	22	50	20	13	17
Natha	12	25	10	5	10
Pattini	11	21	10	3	8
River	3	8	3	3	2
Total recurrence in landscape	142	288	122	68	98

Note. The narrative "The world of the gods" is composed of three subnarratives:
(A) The cities of the gods, especially Sakra's city.
(B) The Ocean of Milk, fertility and creation.
(C) The cosmic axis, especially the cosmic mountain and the cosmic tree.

The reception of foreign embassies

The first European ambassador to visit Kandy was Nuno Alvarez Pereira, who arrived in the year 1542 (O.M. De Silva 1967, 6). He was followed over the next two and a half centuries by many Portuguese, Dutch, and English ambassadors, all of whom found the journey from the coast to the mountain top an arduous undertaking. The terrain was rough and steep and the paths were ill maintained and by Kandyan order were to remain so (see figure 14). These paths turned into quagmires during the rainy season making it nearly impossible to bring even relatively small artillery pieces up to Kandy. Road building was forbidden in order to protect the kingdom from invasion by foreign armies (Dewaraja 1972, 170). Kandyan officials often took embassies along the steepest possible routes in order to impress upon them the difficulty which an invading force would encounter should it try to reach the city. However, in addition to the desire to protect the capital, the king had a symbolic reason for making an ambassador's journey to the capital long and arduous.

Within the Indian tradition time as well as space is highly charged with symbolic meaning. The Kandyans ritualized time and space in a highly nuanced fashion. Just as it is not without symbolic meaning that many pilgrimage sites in South Asia are inaccessible, so it was thought that Kandy would acquire symbolic elevation by being difficult to reach. Thus the trip to the capital was designed as a difficult ritual passage for European ambassadors to impress upon them the moral elevation of the king. In addition to the natural challenges imposed by the terrain, an ambassador suffered the many delaying tactics of the king. In order to see the god-king, therefore, an ambassador not only had to overcome space, but much time as well.

Ambassadors set their own pace while in European-held territory along the coast, but once they entered the Kandyan Kingdom both their route and their rate of progress was dictated by the king. One of the slowest journeys to Kandy was an early one made by the Dutch ambassador, Schnee, in 1731–1732. It took his embassy three months to reach Kandy from Colombo because the king kept halting him along the way (P.E. Pieris 1909). His return journey, on the other hand, unimpeded by the king, took a mere six days.[11] General MacDowall's embassy in 1800 set out from Colombo with 1,000 men and six cannon, a show of force meant to intimidate the king.[12] They crossed the river into Kandyan territory at Sitavaca (see Figure 1), the traditional entry point into the kingdom and were met by the *adikar* and several thousand Kandyan troops (Percival 1803, 380). The embassy then camped on the Kandyan side of the river in buildings especially built to receive embassies. Once they were settled, the *adikar* arrived for the presentation of letters.

Jonville (1948, 2–3), who along with Percival accompanied General MacDowall as part of his embassy, writes that Governor North's letter to the king was treated with the greatest reverence since it bore the king's name. An *appuhāmi* (gentleman-in-waiting) of the highest caste bore the letter on a silver tray resting on his head. The letter had been wrapped in four layers of white muslin and placed in a bag of gold tissue. A large piece of gold cloth was then draped over the tray so that only the lower part of the *appuhami*'s body was visible. Four *appuhamis* carried a white linen canopy ornamented with a fringe over the letter bearer. In this fashion the letter was carried from the border of the kingdom to the palace. This ritual replicated the symbolism of the cosmic axis surrounded by the lords of the four quarters. In addition the letter was provided with an escort of twenty-four *lascarins* (native militia) and four *sepoys* (native troops in British employ). This adds up to thirty-three

14 The Kandyan Mountains (painted by O'Brian, c.1865)

attendants accompanying the letter, signifiying, I would argue, Sakra and his thirty-two gods in the Tavatimsa heaven.

In addition to the letter, the MacDowall embassy took along with them thirty-two cases of presents (P.E. Pieris 1945b, 12). One can only assume that the British had been made aware of the cosmic implications of this number. The presents were wrapped in a "huge amount of rags and straw" (Jonville 1948, 4) for the greater the train, the more grand the king was made to appear in the eyes of his subjects (see figure 15). The cases and the bamboo poles used to carry them were by order of the king covered in white linen which had to be changed two or three times during the trip (Jonville 1948, 4). Included in the cases were presents of rose water, fine muslins, and a betel dish with ornaments of solid gold which belonged to Tippoo Sultan, the South Indian monarch recently deposed by the British. In addition to the thirty-two cases was "an elegant state coach drawn by six horses" (Percival 1803, 384).[13]

Jonville (1948, 3) described a house for the ambassador at one of the official stopping places as follows:

> This house is a sort of cloister. A court of from 15 to 20 paces square is surrounded by little cells, eight feet long by ten broad, their only opening a very small door. The walls are of mud coated with bright whitewash outside and hung with white linen inside. In the center of the court is the little house for the letter. The two cells nearest to the door are reserved for the presents which His Excellency the Governor is sending to the King.

The little house at the center of the square was about six feet square and at the center of this building was "a little stage shaped like an altar and draped in white" where the letter sat (Jonville 1948, 3). Here again we can see the symbolism of the square, the perfect shape, with the letter resting on a shrine at this cosmic center like an offering to a god, placed at the cosmic axis where it could pass between the worlds. The letter was serenaded by trumpets and drums for a quarter of an hour at five each morning and six each night from the day it entered the kingdom until the day of the audience (Jonville 1948, 3, 6). Along the route, *disavas* and elephants came to do honor to the letter.

The Andrews' embassies (J.P. Lewis 1917, 64) to Kandy in 1795 and 1796 approached from Trincomalee in the northeast. Yet they found the same type of camps which had square resthouses with a central room for the letter and presents for the king. Andrews noted that the resthouses had four doors, one at each of the cardinal directions.[14] He (J.P. Lewis 1917, 180) also noted that:

> It is observable that these halting places improve in excellence as we advance towards Candia, which is no doubt intended as descriptive in

15 An ambassador's procession to the court (taken from Baledus 1752)

some degree of those rays which issue from its great King, and diffuse in a proportionate degree their luster around him, of which luster, all is no doubt supposed to partake.

All embassies had to stay at the resthouse at Gannoruva across the river from Kandy, even if they arrived from Trincomalee in the northeast.[15] According to Andrews (J.P. Lewis, 1917, 83) the resthouse at Gannoruva where embassies waited for permission to cross the Mahaveli Ganga before entering the royal city was a larger and more permanent version of the resthouses along the route. Boyd ([1782] 1973, 196) described this building as a square within a square. The inner square which was large, contained a central building for the letter, presents for the king, and sufficient space for five hundred men.

Jonville and others, who apparently did not understand the symbolism of centrality and Sakra's heaven were bemused by the attention lavished upon this message to the king. They failed to understand that as the embassy and the letter made the arduous climb up the mountains to Kandy it also symbolically ascended the cosmic axis to Sakra's heaven on Mount Mandara.

Ambassadors usually had to wait for days at the rest house at Gannoruva before being allowed to cross the river into the city. Ambassador Schnee in 1732 was made to wait five weeks to receive permission (P.E. Pieris 1909). Then, when it pleased the king to see the ambassador and when an auspicious time had been chosen by the astrologers, the ambassador was informed that the king would receive him.[16] He and his retinue were then allowed to cross the Mahaveli Ganga which flowed around Kandy just as the Celestial Ganges flows around Mount Meru and enter the city of heaven. The crossing always took place at the bo tree at Geytembe a village on the Kandy side of the river (Raven-Hart 1956, 171). This was undoubtedly because the bo tree served as a cosmic axis and point of entry to the heavenly city of the god-king.

The audiences with the king were held after midnight and the ambassadors were led into the city in their barefeet, often in ankle-deep mud during the monsoon season, for on the Kandy side of the river only the king was permitted to ride on an elephant, a horse, or in a palanquin. Similarly, only he was allowed to wear shoes (D'Oyly [1825] 1917, 7). It should be noted that although these rules were important in theory, they were bent slightly for several ambassadors. For example, in 1782 Ambassador Boyd ([1782] 1973, 207) claiming to be ill was permitted to be carried in a *dooley* (an uncovered chair) to within a mile of the city, as was Andrews in 1795 (J.P. Lewis 1917, 93) and Pybus ([1762] 1958, 61) in 1762. However, none were allowed to use a covered palanquin as this was reserved exclusively for the king; and none were allowed to be carried within the city itself as marked by the Kathoupelele gate a half mile from the palace. Similarly Pybus ([1762] 1958, 55) was allowed to wear his shoes until he entered the palace whereas Boyd ([1782] 1973, 212) was even allowed to keep shoes on in the audience hall in the presence of the king as a "special dispensation."

The ritual for bringing an ambassador into the city was as follows: the second minister of the king would bring him across the river at the Gannoruva ferry and take him to the edge of the sacred rectangle (the heaven on earth). Here the first minister would take over and lead him into the palace of the god-king.

Two days after his arrival at Gannoruva, General MacDowall was received by the king. The announcement that there was to be an audience that night was received by the ambassador at four-thirty in the afternoon. At eight-thirty the ambassador and his entourage arrived at the river and by nine in the evening the last of the presents for the king had been carried across. Once safely across the river the ambassador walked hand in hand with the second *adikar* towards the city which lay several miles to the northeast. The ambassador was attended by his staff, gentlemen belonging to the embassy and escorted by an English subaltern and fifty *sepoys*. The road to Kandy was lighted by a multitude of Kandyans holding great blazing torches (Jonville 1948, 14; P.E. Pieris 1945b, 14; Percival 1803, 404).

Although writers such as Jonville and Percival do not provide us with further details of this passing over the river into Kandy, the Andrews' embassy of 1795 does. It is safe to assume that the MacDowall embassy of 1800 was received in a like manner for:

> every incident connected with the ceremony, which according to invariable custom took place at night, was regulated by a ritual almost ecclesiastical in its elaboration, devised to impress foreign representatives with the greatness of the Ruler whom they were privileged to behold. (P.E. Pieris 1945b, 14)

Andrews carried the letter to the king over his head as he crossed the river. Once safely across, he marched with several courtiers behind the presents, but in front of the letter, along a road lined by several hundred Kandyans bearing torches, flags, pikes, bows and arrows, and muskets. This procession moved along for four miles until they reached the city proper (J.P. Lewis 1917, 92–93). Like Andrews, as MacDowall marched towards the city he passed four thick hedges containing gates made of interwoven thorns each guarded by twenty Malays. At eleven-twenty at night, nearly three hours after leaving the resthouse, they arrived at Kathoupelele, the fifth and largest thorn gate which marked the entrance to the city, a little over a half a mile from the king's palace. This last entrance to the city was further protected by an earthen rampart and breastwork upon which artillery was mounted. This gate also was guarded by Malay troops in the employ of the king. MacDowall and his party halted here for a short time until astrologers informed them that the time was auspicious and allowed them to proceed into the city proper (Jonville 1948, 14; P.E. Pieris 1945b, 14; Percival 1803, 404; J.P. Lewis 1917, 7–8). The route into the city was decorated with flowers and greenery and was lined with elephants, heavily armed soldiers bearing torches, and throngs of curious citizens who had come to enjoy the pageantry and glimpse the foreigners. Andrews in 1795 estimated that as many as two thousand troops lined the streets of Kandy and that as his embassy moved progressively nearer the city they were met by successively higher gradations of aristocracy (J.P. Lewis 1917, 93–94).[17] Again one would assume that the same applied for the MacDowall embassy five years later.

MacDowall's party halted at a spot approximately two hundred yards from the palace where they were provided with dinner. At midnight they once again moved forward to the sacred bo tree that lay at the center of the sacred rectangle fifty yards from the palace. Once again, as at the river entrance to Kandy, they had come to a bo tree which served as a liminal point, a cosmic axis which, I would argue, allowed them to enter into the sacred rectangle and palace which was a heaven on earth.

Here at the bo tree they were met by the first *adikar* who was to guide them into the palace. At the foot of the bo tree stood six huge elephants. It was at this spot where earlier ambassadors Aggreen (Heydt [1744] 1952, 92) in 1736 and Boyd ([1782] 1973, 210) in 1782 saw the pure-white state elephant emblematic of Sakra and used whenever possible by kings throughout Indian Asia. Apparently the Kandyans rather lamely explained to Jonville (1948, 14) the absence of this auspicious animal saying "the king has no white elephants, which is an animal of the gods alone; but he has some with large flesh-coloured patches on their heads which sometimes are so large and numerous that the trunk appears white."

As MacDowall entered Kandy in 1800 he passed through seven boundary markers. He first crossed the river at the bo tree at Geytembe; he then passed five guard gates of thorns the last of which was the Kathoupelele gate marking the entrance to the city at which he had to wait for an auspicious time to enter the city; next he entered the sacred rectangle where he was forced to wait at the sacred bo tree for the king's permission to enter the palace (Jonville 1948, 9–18; J.P. Lewis 1917, 7–8). I argue that the number seven here is highly symbolic for it represents the seven mountain rings around Mount Meru and the seven levels of heaven.

The closer the ambassador moved to the palace/temple complex in the

From landscape to civic ritual: a kingly reading 147

center, the higher were the ranks of the aristocracy whom he passed and the higher was the official that conducted him. Horizontal space on the ground was symbolically converted into vertical space; thus physical space was converted into moral space.

Upon the arrival of the first *adikar*, the ambassador and his retinue proceeded to enter the palace/temple complex to have an audience with the god-king. The ambassador was led past the wave swell wall and through the ceremonial great gate containing "Meru stones" the allegorical representation of "the gateway to the universe." The last king had rebuilt this gate so that it had portals facing the four quarters and symbolizing the center of the world. Such gates also symbolized the entrance to the city of the Buddha and the *cakravarti* (Rowland 1953a, 11, 16). It is interesting that the palace in official terminology was metonymically referred to as the "Great Gate" (*Maha Vahala*) and even more significant that the king himself was called the "Great Gate" (D'Oyly [1825] 1917, 95). This linguistic synecdoche evoked a visual image of the liminality of the king who like a four-portaled ceremonial gate constituted a signifier for the world center, the passage between earth and heaven.

The ambassador next climbed up steps past the cloud drift wall, the "celestial rampart" of the palace with its Meru symbols. He had entered the palace of the king of the gods and climbed to the top of the cosmic mountain at the center of the earth. He had entered into the heaven of the god Sakra. He then emerged onto a terrace courtyard and climbed another set of steps through yet another gate into an upper terrace upon which was located the audience hall with octagonal pillars similar to those of Sakra's audience hall on Mount Mandara (Godage 1945, 58).

This audience hall was located at the center of the palace/temple complex, equidistant from the palace and the shrine of the relic. Recent excavation (Prematilleke 1983; 1986, 6–9) has revealed that the audience hall was raised above the upper terrace and therefore an ambassador would have had to climb still more steps at its northern end. Here he waited in a lower portion of the hall to be beckoned into the throne room where he was received by the king seated majestically on a elevated lion throne.

Thus from the entrance to the palace the ambassador had ascended seven allegorical levels before seeing the king. He had risen past the wave swell wall, the Meru gate, the cloud drift wall, the lower terrace, the upper terrace, the lower audience hall, and finally into the throne room. As Andrews entered the throne room, six white curtains were slowly raised leaving a single thin gauze curtain covering an arch leading to an alcove at the far end of the hall. "This for a few seconds gave a dim view of his Majesty, which on its removal blazed forth in greatest splendour" (J.P. Lewis 1917, 12–13). The embassies of

Schnee in 1731–1732 (P.E. Pieris 1909, 205), Pybus in 1762 (Pybus [1762] 1958, 56), and MacDowall in 1800 (Jonville 1948, 15) also remarked that there were seven sets of curtains that were slowly raised in the audience hall as the ambassadors approached the king. For the third time since entering Kandy, the ambassador symbolically passed the seven mountain rings around Mount Meru on his climb towards Sakra's palace. The curtains also would have informed the audience that they were viewing a god in a shrine, for both in Hindu and Buddhist worship, images of the gods have curtains in front of them.

As the ambassador entered the hall "the King uttered some words; the tone of his voice conveyed unusual sensations; it seemed to issue as from some concavity, and was not attended by any motion on his part" (J.P. Lewis 1917, 13). The walls of the hall were draped in curtains like the shrines of gods and the hall's octagonal pillars were wrapped in white cloth. The hall was lit by large white candles scented with cinnamon oil (J.P. Lewis 1917, 14; Boyd [1782] 1973, 213). Members of the king's honor guard were dressed in white and held golden weapons (Jonville 1948, 14) as did the guards in Sakra's audience hall (C.M.A. De Silva 1963–1965, 166–167). Next to the alcove stood guards dressed in white holding images of the sun and the moon (J.P. Lewis 1917, 14). All of these attendants had strips of white cloth bound around their mouths so that their breath would not pollute the god-king. When the last curtain was raised the nobles of the court prostrated themselves and the ambassador bowed.[18]

The partition separating the alcove where the king sat from the rest of the audience hall was decorated with four immense mirrors and gold and silver ornaments. A gold-and-silver sun and moon hung over the entrance to the alcove. (J.P. Lewis 1917, 15). The throne, which was elevated upon a three-foot stage, stood five feet tall in the back and was covered in sheet gold. The arms of the throne were in the form of golden lions and on the inside of the back was a large golden sun. On either side was a female deity, perhaps the wife of Visnu (Pearson 1933–1934, 382).[19]

The recurrent sun-and-moon patterns which we have seen in the audience hall symbolized the solar and lunar origins of the kings. It was thought that the kings had the substance of the sun and the moon in their bodies and like the sun and the moon were intimately involved in the regulation of the day, month and year (Inden 1978, 35). The sun and moon also represented the planets circling Mount Meru; in Indian tradition the audience hall which traditionally lay to the east of the palace is depicted as a microcosmic synecdoche standing for the universe centered on Mount Meru. The throne in the audience hall was traditionally conceived to lie at the cosmic axis (Inden 1978, 33). Over the throne was a canopy of white-and-gold cloth symbolizing the firmament.

From landscape to civic ritual: a kingly reading

Inside the king's alcove two women fanned the king with yak-tailed whisks, traditionally symbols both of gods and kings (J.P. Lewis 1917, 17). The king was seated on the throne "his chest covered with a kind of gilt cuirass, over which were several gold chains set with gems." He wore brocade clothes with white muslin over the sleeves and shoulder plates of gold from which hung coloured stones in a fringe. On his head he wore "a crown of solid gold" which "seemed of quadrangular form, from each part of which issued a prong ornamented with precious stones – to the right and left of the center were also two" (Jonville 1948, 15; J.P. Lewis 1917, 16, 99).[20] In fact this "crown" was not solid gold as Lewis thought, but the traditional four-cornered Kandyan hat embroidered with gold, pearls, and gems. The gems at each corner symbolized the four cardinal directions which the king controlled. In the center of the hat was a spray of gems and pearls (Nevill 1887, 4–5) which represented the *kapruka*, the wish-granting tree in Sakra's heaven and the cosmic tree at the center of the world. This hat, then, was a synecdoche for the control which the king professed to exert from his palace at the center of the world.[21]

When the seventh curtain had risen and the nobles had completed nine prostrations, the king commanded his nobles to invite the ambassador to approach the lion throne. The ambassador was moved three paces forward, all the while holding the letter of introduction on a silver charger over his head like an offering to a god, and was stopped by the nobles, who performed a fresh set of prostrations, while the ambassador was asked to drop to his knees. Two more times the ambassador was commanded to advance then stop to perform prostrations. The nobles likewise advanced prostrating themselves at intervals crying out "May your Puissant Majesty live as long as the Sun and the Moon." To which the king replied "That is right and shall be" (Jonville 1948, 15).

The second *adikar* then took his place outside the king's alcove, while the first *adikar* sat within the alcove where he could address the king in a whisper (Jonville 1948, 16).[22] When the ambassador reached the throne, the king himself removed the letter from the tray over the ambassador's head and handed it to the first *adikar*. The ambassador then withdrew, bowing all the way to the center of the hall where, with the king's permission, he sat on a carpet. The interaction between the ambassador and the king was of a highly ritualized nature. Jonville (1948, 16) describes it as follows:

> When everything had been arranged the King summoned the Second Adikare by name, who prostrated himself ejaculating "May heaven crown your Majesty with prosperity." The Adikare after prostrating said "Dessauve" and he replied "Adikare" whereupon the Adikare intoned the King's question. The Dessauve repeated his words in a low

voice to the English interpreter who repeated them to the Ambassador. Then the Ambassador asked through the interpreters, the Dessauve and the Adikare, for the King's permission to reply. The King gave his consent, which was conveyed by the same circuitous route, and on receiving it he replied "The Governor is very well' which was conveyed to his Majesty with the same ceremony.

According to Andrews, it took between twenty and thirty minutes for a question to be answered (J.P. Lewis 1917, 19). All conversations with the king were conducted in a special vocabulary reserved for the court (Dewaraja 1972, 212). Few questions were asked during these audiences and they were of a purely ceremonial nature. Andrews (J.P. Lewis 1917, 97) was told that:

> my conversation must not exceed enquiries after the health of His Majesty and praying his gracious favor to accept of a few presents which had been sent by the government of Madras: all matters beyond that were to be made to the Prime Ministers and through them to the King.[23]

After making these polite inquiries the ambassador withdrew, bowing, and the seven curtains were drawn behind him. Again his actions were allegorical as he symbolically moved past the seven mountain rings surrounding the throne at the center of the world.

After this ceremony the ambassadors were taken to an adjacent pavilion in the palace to eat a meal of "patisseries, *kitul*, sugar, *betel*, *areca* and bananas." Jonville (1948, 16–17) allowed that the ambassador's party "sat and looked at" this food but were not inclined to eat it, while the king spent an hour inspecting the ambassador's presents in another part of the palace. Finally the ambassador was escorted by a palace official to the bo tree in the sacred rectangle. The *adikar* then accompanied them to the Kathoupelele gate which marked the boundary of the city. There they were permitted to get into *dooleys* (sedan chairs) and in the company of a *disava* ride back to their resthouse across the river.[24]

What was the impact of the audience upon those who witnessed it? For the Kandyans, the audience served as the most visible assertion that their king was a god on earth. It was, as Stein (1984, 321) points out, through public rituals that the divinity of South Asian monarchs was realized. The last king wrapped himself in the mystery of the gods. "Offences against the King were more than breaches of human law, they were transgressions against a religious cult. To touch his person was sacrilege" (P.E. Pieris 1945a, 1). The Kandyans even went so far as to secretly burn charcoal in braziers behind curtains in the hall in order to reduce oxygen, thereby making ambassadors and others feel faint in the presence of the "god-king" (Sirr 1850, 227).

Table 7.5

The recurrent narrative structure of the embassy

NARRATIVE: "THE WORLD OF THE *CAKRAVARTI*"

Location	Number of synecdoches	Number of references to narrative	Number of references to subnarrative (A)	Number of references to subnarrative (B)	Number of references to subnarrative (C)
Center	1	1	1	0	0
Palace	23	27	11	0	16
Audience hall	6	8	3	0	5
Total recurrence in landscape	30	36	15	0	21

Note. The narrative "The world of the *cakravarti*" is composed of three subnarratives:
(A) Control over the whole world through reproduction of centrality and cardinal directions.
(B) Control over kingdom through microcosmic reproduction.
(C) Reproduction of the cities of the Sinhalese hero-kings.

This highly complex, allegorical ritual had a high cost for the king, however. Increasingly, as the king sat isolated in solitary splendor, the nobles controlled the "affairs of state in a manner most profitable to them" (Dewaraja 1972, 220). They had very real material interests in encouraging the elaboration of ritual for they knew full well that "the slave of etiquette and ceremonial cannot be the master of his dignitaries, so his power passes to them" (Hocart 1970, 152).

The recurrent narrative structure of the embassy is very similar to that of the other rituals that we have examined. Once again as we can see by comparing tables 7.5 and 7.6, the narrative "The world of the gods" accounts for over twice as many synecdoches and over three times as many references as does the narrative "The world of the *cakravarti*." In table 7.5 the references are nearly equally divided between the subnarrative of "Control over the world" and the "Hero-cities". There are no references to the subnarrative "Control over the kingdom". The issue of control over the kingdom was not in question during this ritual; rather the king was attempting to display, through metonymy and the efficacy of recurrence, his status as a *cakravarti* who ruled over a city which approximated in splendor

152 *The politics of Kandyan landscape interpretation*

Table 7.6

The recurrent narrative structure of the embassy

NARRATIVE: "THE WORLD OF THE GODS"

Location	Number of synecdoches	Number of references to narrative	Number of references to subnarrative (A)	Number of references to subnarrative (B)	Number of references to subnarrative (C)
Outside city	19	27	17	1	9
Center	2	3	1	0	2
Palace	42	68	27	19	22
Audience hall	17	33	17	6	10
Total recurrence in landscape	80	131	62	26	43

Note. The narrative "The world of the gods" is composed of three subnarratives:
(A) The cities of the gods, especially Sakra's city.
(B) The Ocean of Milk, fertility and creation.
(C) The cosmic axis, especially the cosmic mountain and the cosmic tree.

and righteousness to those of the hero-kings of Lanka. In table 7.6, five-sixths of the references are to the subnarratives of "Sakra's heaven" or "The cosmic mountain". The other one-sixth are to the subnarrative of "The cosmic ocean and fertility". Again, the structure of this recurrence confirms my interpretation, that the dominant message which the king wished to convey was that his capital mirrored the heaven of Sakra on the top of the cosmic mountain.

The recurrence of reference to the narratives of "The world of the *cakravarti*" and "The world of the gods" was meant to impress both the Kandyan nobles and commoners, as well as the European ambassadors. But of course to be impressed by this recurrence one had to be familiar with the narratives to which the landscape referred. Unfortunately most of the Europeans did not know them or understand their significance. Nor did they recognize the iconic, linguistic, and behavioral synecdoches which referred to them. They therefore could not have had a similar reading of the rituals to that of the Kandyans, who for the most part did recognize them. Most of the symbolism of the god-king at the center of the world encoded both in the landscape and in ritual action was wasted on them. Unfortunately for all

From landscape to civic ritual: a kingly reading

concerned, the Europeans also became impatient or angered by the elaborate nature of the ritual and the demands for deference that were made of them. The Kandyans treated the Europeans just as *cakravartis* since time immemorial had treated vassal kings, whereas the Europeans expected to be treated as equals. Ambassador MacDowall ([1800] 1932, 457) summed up his feelings about Kandyan court ceremonial in his report to Governor North in Colombo:

> Last night was fixed for the first audience and with the usual ceremonies I reached the palace about one o'clock this morning, having commenced my march from this place at eight o'clock in the evening. It is unnecessary to trouble your Excellency with a detail of the trifling ceremonies and disgusting servility of that frivolous court . . . I did not return to the rest house till six o'clock this morning.[25]

In this chapter I have examined three civic rituals; the funeral and inauguration, the Asala Perahara, and the ambassador's audience with the king, showing that each represented a political and religious argument made in the vocabulary of ritual within a highly symbolic physical setting. For the most part this argument was made indirectly through recurrent references to the major narratives that informed Kandyan political life. These narratives, as we have seen in the last two chapters, were communicated metonymically through the use of synecdoches, many of which were profoundly geographic, for they were composed in stone, spatial arrangements, and place-related ritual actions.

8

From landscape to discourse: contestatory readings and material interests

> Ritual is used to constitute power, not just reflect power that already exists.
> (Kertzer 1988, 25)

Introduction

Much work has been done on the question of how religious buildings and general urban form encode cultural, religious, and political values (Fritz 1986; Geertz 1980; Heine-Geldern 1942; Krautheimer 1983; Mus 1937; Panofsky 1957; Tambiah 1976; Wheatley 1971; 1977). This body of work has been premised upon two assumptions: first, that a set of religious or political texts have been transformed into the medium of the built environment, and second, that this transformation has helped foster political legitimacy. For the most part, this work has successfully demonstrated the link between written religious and political texts and built form as a textual transformation which speaks of political and religious power. It has been much less successful, however, at demonstrating how these ideologies encoded in the environment have been received. The assumption, common to these writers, is that these environmental "texts" not only communicated dominant ideologies, but that the people's readings of these texts were dictated by the dominant ideology.

The notion that there is a single correct interpretation of a given text has been challenged in literary theory by reception theorists (Barthes 1977b; Iser 1978; Fish 1980; Tompkins 1980). Whereas I do not believe it is useful to follow some of the reception theorists to their more extreme conclusion that each reader of a text has the autonomy to "author" a new and unique text, these theorists have alerted us to the necessity of calling into question the hegemony of the author's original intentions. The lesson for geographers here is that if the political efficacy of textual messages encoded in the built environment is to be assessed, it should be studied not only from the point of view of those who build it, but also from the point of view of those who read it.

There are several reasons why researchers have not focused on how the built environment is actually read by those whose behavior it is assumed to affect. The most compelling reason is that much of the work done in this area, such as that by Wheatley (1971, 1977), Fritz (1986), and Mus (1937), is based upon archaeological evidence and there is virtually no evidence of reception, textual or otherwise. In the light of this absence of data on interpretation, scholars were faced with the choice of either ignoring the question of the political efficacy of these environmental texts or of assuming that people read them as they were intended to be read by those in power. There are some good reasons to believe that environmental texts were in fact usually read in accordance with the hegemonic perspective. After all, the encoding of religious and political texts in the built environment was very common in South, East and Southeast Asia, and it seems unlikely that rulers would persist in so expensive a practice if it yielded little political advantage.

But what if we do not assume that people invariably read the landscape text exactly as the rulers wished? The question then becomes one first of trying to establish what it was the rulers wished to communicate and second of how various groups did in fact read the landscape. This approach brings us back to reception theory, for if we are to judge the political efficacy of the environmental text we must try to ascertain whether the various readings affirm or contest the ruler's reading.

Although much of reception theory is individualistic to the point of being anarchic, a sociological dimension can be added to it through the incorporation of the related concepts of discourse, discursive field, and textual community. The notion of discourse (Foucault 1976) helps us understand that the construction of meaning is not unique to an individual, but is shaped by a discourse or set of discourses within a broader discursive field. The emphasis here is on the social and material conditions of reception. As discussed above in chapter 2, a discursive field consists of competing or conflicting discourses which shape and are shaped by social institutions and interacting groups, each of which may have differing material interests. Some discourses may be hegemonic while others may form the basis for serious challenges to existing practice. As modes of signification, discourses are embodied in texts broadly construed, including landscapes. They provide modes of conceptualizing; they "position" subjects in relation to others. Hence Kandyan discourse on kingship positions the king *vis-à-vis* the nobles, the *sangha*, the *rajakariya* laborers, and the rest of the population. The discursive field thus becomes a site of negotiation and struggle over meanings, privileges, and duties. Discourses enable as well as constrain; they are constitutive of, as well as constituted by, social and political relationships.

The concept of a textual community developed by Stock (1983) has a similar but more restricted scope. It refers to a group of people who come together around a shared reading of a set of texts. They form a community in that their shared reading serves as the basis for social action on the part of the group.

The Kandyan Kingdom of the early nineteenth century provides an excellent case study of the political efficacy of built form and the struggle between textual communities. In this case the meaning pivots on the relation of kingship and city building. As I have indicated previously, the terms of the struggle are contained within a single Indian–Asian discursive field made up of interrelated but potentially conflicting discourses pertaining to kingship, the Asoka, and the Sakran. Here in Kandy, as we have seen, not only was there a tradition of both charismatic and enlightened kingship, there was also a highly textualized urban environment which played a prominent role in the articulation of political power. Furthermore, and most importantly from a modern scholar's point of view, there exists a series of texts that provide some fragmentary evidence of the reception of the claims of kingship as expressed in the built environment.

What has emerged from late-eighteenth- and early-nineteenth-century Kandy is a series of texts. Some reaffirm the king's reading of the built environment, others contest that reading. Those commentaries on urban form were also directed towards the king himself and his role as a city builder. Therefore they served as an integral part of the struggle for power in the kingdom. Those commentaries on kingship and urban form, both by those that supported and those that opposed the king, were not idiosyncratic personal statements; they were drawn from a common textual tradition.

Although a majority of the members of Kandyan society were illiterate, the culture of the society was as a whole highly textualized. For as Stock (1986, 12) has pointed out, for a textual community to exist "the minimum requirement was just one literate, the *interpres*, who understood a set of texts and was able to pass his message on verbally to others." For example, political behavior depended upon a series of historical texts to authorize it. These texts formed a discourse of politics about how a king should act and how a capital should be laid out. Various political factions each clustered around a particular reading of kingly behavior or urban form and used their readings to gain political advantage over their opponents. Thus these groups acted in concert as textual communities.

Sri Vikrama's building program and the politics of interpretation

In 1803 Sri Vikrama won a great victory over an invading British army. In the ensuing years of peace he set about consolidating his power, although it appears that he was never able to fully control the Sinhalese nobles who were continually plotting among themselves and with the British against him.

From landscape to discourse: contestatory readings 157

When threatened by this simmering rebellion, he turned to a time-honored tradition of South Indian kings, an expensive building program. In so doing he played the part of a god-king, behaving like his mythic counterpart the god Indra (Sakra), whose earthly manifestation he was. After his defeat of the *asuras* (demons) Indra too rebuilt both his palace and his capital, with the help of Visvakarma, the divine architect. At the same time the king emulated those earlier monarchs of Lanka who had engaged in building programs after military victories.

Unfortunately, unlike some of the earlier kings of Lanka whose capitals of Anuradhapura and Polonnaruva were located in the agriculturally productive irrigated dry zone of Lanka, the kings of Kandy ruled over a poor kingdom.[1] Unable to pay his workmen, Sri Vikrama relied entirely on *rajakariya* (*corvée* labor). This raised a twofold problem. First, the building program was so large that the normally accepted amount of *corvée* labor was greatly exceeded. Second, there was a question of whether it was indeed appropriate to demand *rajakariya* for Sakran-type building programs. These after all glorified the king while the benefit to his subjects was only derivative. Perhaps, it was darkly pondered, *rajakariya* was best reserved for Asokan-type religious or charitable programs.

What was the point of this massive building program in a poor kingdom? I contend that it can best be understood as a political strategy on the part of the king to consolidate power by reinforcing his charisma. This he did by building an impressive landscape to serve as an allegorical portrait of his power. As there is no evidence that the king was cynical about the magical power of parallelism, we must assume that this was an equally important component of his strategy. Let us briefly review the major elements of the last king's building program and then examine how the king, the nobles, and the peasants interpreted it.

The principal project undertaken by the king was the impounding of a stream that flowed through marshy ground at the city's southern edge (see figure 4). This was a major task, as a very large dam had to be constructed at the western end of the marsh and retaining walls had to be built around the lake.[2] This project drew numerous laborers from the provinces and lasted from 1810 to 1812. The second major project was the addition of five new streets in the western portion of the city.[3]

The third project was the building of a number of additions to the palace. This project included the construction of new exterior walls, a new gateway, an octagonal tower called a *pattirippuwa*, and a symbolic moat. The gateway served as a unified entrance to both the Temple of the Relic and the palace. The *pattirippuwa* was attached to the Temple of the Tooth, and from it the king could address the populace assembled on the esplanade. The moat was dug along a line that ran north across the front of the palace/temple complex, and continued west along the front of the Visnu Devale and finally turned north once again to partially encircle the city (see figure 8).[4] There is evidence that the king also planned to move the palace from the sacred rectangle's eastern side to its center. This repositioning would have necessitated the demolition of the Natha and Pattini Devala and the deracination of the sacred bo tree; apparently the king was dissuaded from doing this.[5]

The king's interpretation

Sri Vikrama's interpretation of his building program is recorded in the *Ingrisi Hatana* ([c.1812] 1906), a poem written at his behest to reflect his point of view; it is a eulogy honoring his great victory over the English army that invaded Kandy in 1803. Elements of his interpretation can also be gleaned from poems such as the *Daḷadā Vittiya* (1974) and several *sannasas* (royal grants usually inscribed on copper) again written for him during the final years of his reign. These interpretations are intertextual in that they directly reference a series of religious models and allude to accounts of the city building of the hero-kings of Lanka as described in the *Culavamsa* (1953a; 1953b). The *Ingrisi Hatana* ([c.1812] 1906), although containing some allusions to the Asokan model of kingship, is argued preponderantly within the terms of a Sakran discourse.

Two important points are made early in the poem to legitimate Sri Vikrama's rule. The first is that the future Buddha had sent him to protect the country: the poem baldly states, "God Natha who protects Lanka sent Sri Vikrama to protect the country" (*Ingrisi Hatana* [c.1812] 1906, 7 v.49). The second point is that he is careful to observe the customs of Lankan kingship by consulting with the aristocracy: thus, "He summoned the ministers, capable of protecting the world, knowing all of the rules and regulations, and what should and should not be done" (*Ingrisi Hatana* [c.1812] 1906, v.82). This second issue was particularly sensitive as the nobles felt that Sri Vikrama was usurping their power and moving with an independence that tradition did not sanction. Intended to allay fears and disarm accusations that the king had arrogated autocratic prerogatives, the implicit message of the poems was that his building program was undertaken after consultation with those "knowing all of the rules and regulations, and what should and should not be done."

Sri Vikrama desired a capital "filled with all the wealth and requisites of cities, and which flourishes with the prosperity of the fortunate city of Indra (as if) reflected on the mirror of the earth" (*Moligoda Sannasa* 1814). However, until he completed his building program in 1812, it could be argued

From landscape to discourse: contestatory readings

that his city was an imperfect reflection of Indra's city. Inspired by the quest for parallelism so essential to Sakran kingship he set out to remedy the discrepancies by bringing the city into closer compliance with Sakra's city in heaven. This was one very powerful impetus to rebuild the palace, which had been damaged by the British occupation in 1803, to dig a moat, which was like the sea around Mount Meru, to construct gardens, which were like those of Sakra, and to impound a lake, which was like the Ocean of Milk, or "Sakra's pond" as it was alternatively conceived. The king, therefore,

> brought master builders of all types from the three areas of the island who were like the God Visvakarma in their ability. They measured the length and width of the city leveling the land and making it into a perfect square so that the expenditures and income of the kingdom would be equal. (*Ingrisi Hatana* [*c*.1812] 1906, 27, v.249)

Here we can see the king comparing the city builders to the God Visvakarma, the divine architect who rebuilt Indra's city after Indra had defeated the *asuras* in battle. Through accurate measurement he believed not only that the city could be made to correspond perfectly to the square cities of the gods, but also that this parallelism could enlist the help of the gods in the balancing of the state budget.

> They then built a group of three-storey buildings with golden roofs within the palace and surrounded it with a great wall so that it resembled Sakra's palace. Around the wall was a moat as deep as the sea.
>
> The great, noble, high, umbrella-shaped shining *pattirippuwa* was built and decorated with flags and bells which gave a pleasant sound as they blew in the wind.
>
> He built royal gates, and *pandoles* [ceremonial arches], and balconies in this beautiful, shining palace.
>
> He built twelve streets consisting of shops, having gold, gems, and other valuables and constructed two *pandoles* at the ends of each street.
>
> He planted trees as in the Nandana garden of Sakra and so the city was made to ressemble the heavenly city of Sakra. *Ingrisi Hatana* [*c*.1812] 1906, vv.250-253, 255)

Here he argues that his palace was now more like Sakra's, and that, like Sakra's, it was surrounded by the circular mountain wall and ocean that encircles Mount Meru. Also, it is pointed out, the eight-sidedness and umbrella shape of the *pattirippuwa* are both symbols of the *cakravarti*.

Furthermore, the additional streets increased the capital's conformity to a microcosmic version of the provinces of the kingdom. The text also suggests that the gardens were designed to mirror the Nandana gardens in Sakra's heavenly city.

The text has curiously little to say about the largest building project that Sri Vikrama undertook during this period: the artificial lake. This he apparently wished to incorporate into the mythic geography of the city of Kandy, as he named it the Ocean of Milk, but it was given only one verse in the *Ingrisi Hatana* ([c.1812] 1906, 27, v.254).

> The great lake was filled with red *manel* (hydra) flowers from which bees collected nectar. Golden swans swam upon its broad waters and fish played in its waves.

It is possible that this poem made little mention of the lake because it was a source of great tension among the aristocracy, the *sangha*, and the common people, as we shall see shortly.

Whereas it is clear from this description that the king conceived of his city building as an attempt to more closely model his court upon that of Sakra, he undoubtedly also wished to replicate important elements of the cities of the hero-kings of Lanka as well.[6] In the *Ingrisi Hatana* ([c.1812] 1906, 22, v.203), Sri Vikrama's entry into Kandy after the defeat of the English is compared to King Parakramabahu's triumphal return to Polonnaruva. The *Culavamsa* (1953a, 346–348; 1953b, 1–20), a text with which Sri Vikrama would have been intimately familiar, recorded that King Parakramabahu rebuilt his capital after a great military victory. Parakramabahu had also attempted to mirror Sakra's capital by building palaces, walls, moats, a Nandana garden and an artificial lake (ibid).

The one area in which Sri Vikrama's description of his rebuilding program was at variance with Parakramabahu's was that the latter gave great attention to constructing buildings for the *sangha*, whereas Sri Vikrama made no mention of any such buildings in his program. While one could perhaps argue that the amounts of construction for religious purposes by Parakramabahu was overstated by the monks who authored the *Culavamsa*, it is nevertheless striking that the *Ingrisi Hatana* should make no mention of such building. One can take this to mean that not only did Sri Vikrama not build structures for the *sangha* at this time, but that relations with the *sangha* had deteriorated to such a degree that not even a gesture, however token, was made. One of the few mentions of Buddhism in the *Ingrisi Hatana* ([c. 1812] 1906, 31 v.282, 32 v.287) occurs late in the poem, where it is stated that Sri Vikrama rules "with a constant faith in Buddhism" and in accordance with "the ten royal principles".

From landscape to discourse: contestatory readings

The *Ingrisi Hatana* stands as a remarkable document, not only because it provides insight into what Sri Vikrama thought of his building program, but also into how far down the road towards Sakran kingship he had traveled. The near-total absence of Asokan imagery and attention to the *sangha* in this document points to the grave political abyss into which the king was rapidly sinking.

The nobles' interpretation of the building program

Throughout the history of Kandy there had been power struggles between the kings and the nobles. At times the balance shifted in favor of the king while at other times, the nobles gained the upper hand. Raja Sinha II (1635–1687) held great power, but during the reigns of his son and grandson power increasingly lay in the hands of the nobility. Throughout the eighteenth century it was the nobility who were dominant while kings were at times reduced to the status of figureheads. The Nayakkars maintained power during this period of aristocratic domination by pursuing three principal strategies. First, they tried to limit the power of the nobles by playing different factions among the nobility off against one another. Second, they portrayed themselves as pious and often became lavish patrons of Buddhism. As such they strove to conform to an Asokan ideal. Third, they increasingly yielded control over the provincial bureaucracy and foreign affairs to the nobles. This abdication of authority did not, however, include control over the palace bureaucracy, which they tended to retain. The kings attempted to compensate for this loss of power by retreating into the display of royal pomp and splendid symbolism drawn from the Sakran discourse on kingship. Through this threefold strategy they were able to remain in power, for they did not seriously threaten the power of the nobles and their skillful combination of Asokan and Sakran public displays meant that they were seen as charismatic rulers by the people.[7]

One persistent source of tension between the kings and the nobles during the eighteenth century was the large number of Nayakkar relatives who had accompanied the kings' South Indian brides to Kandy. In fact, after the death of the last ethnically Sinhalese king in 1739, the Nayakkars became an increasingly separate royal community within Kandy. This community, growing in numbers as well as in political and economic importance throughout the century, came to pose a political and economic threat to the nobility.

By the early nineteenth century the Kandyan nobles often found themselves excluded from the inner circle within the palace bureaucracy and frequently in debt to the relatives of the king. The nobles nevertheless maintained greater political power, as they controlled the provincial bureaucracy. The last king, Sri Vikrama was installed in power by the first *adikar* Pilima Talavve and was, at first, a puppet of the *adikar*. However, as the young king became more confident after the defeat of the English army in 1803, he attempted to break away from the control of the first *adikar* and reclaim some of the powers that the nobles had come to take for granted as their own. The nobles in turn attempted to resist the king's ambitions by plotting among themselves and with the English. The king eventually responded to these threats by having Pilima Talavve beheaded and severely punishing a number of the leading noble families. Rather than discouraging the nobles' ambitions, this finally served to unite them in their hostile opposition. This culminated in the revolt of 1814, led by the new first *adikar*, Ahalepola, which was suppressed after Ahalepola fled to British territory.

The leading members of his faction, including his wife and children, were executed in a particularly gruesome public display in Kandy (Davy 1821, 322). The ferocity of Sri Vikrama's response to this revolt and the increasingly indiscriminate nature of his revenge on the nobles galvanized the factions against the king. Sri Vikrama, then, failed in one of the principal strategies which the Nayakkar kings had used to maintain power, which was to keep the various competing factions within the nobility from joining ranks.

Sri Vikrama's political difficulties were further exacerbated by worsening relations with the *sangha*. In the latter years of his reign, as we shall see, he even went so far as to expropriate temple lands and execute a well-known monk who he thought was implicated in the 1814 Ahalepola's plot. As the senior levels of the *sangha* were drawn from the aristocracy, in the end the *sangha* and the nobles joined forces against the king.[8] Rather than devoting his resources to an Asokan program of building *dagobas* and *viharas* as had his predecessor Kirti Sri, the king took the unprecedented step of using resources customarily allocated to the *sangha* in order to promote the building program of palaces, moats, and lakes. Having abandoned the second of the traditional strategies for maintaining legitimacy, he lost the support of the *sangha*.

Through the first decade of the nineteenth century, however, Sri Vikrama still had the support of the common people.[9] In fact he was popular with them, in part because he defended them against the depredations of some of the nobles. Also the people were apparently receptive to the legitimating rhetoric of the elaborate civic rituals he staged in the capital, and impressed with his success in the war against the English. The highly charismatic, Sakran style of rule appealed to the people, as there was nothing as yet in his behavior to suggest, to the common people at least, that he was not also a righteous Buddhist king.

The people's attitude apparently began to change, however, in 1810, because of the massive building projects he undertook in the capital. He greatly exceeded the customary demands of *rajakariya* by dragooning unusually large numbers of people to work on these projects and employing them over a much longer period of time than was traditional (Colvin R. De Silva 1953, 141). There was also the question of whether *rajakariya* should be used for massive public works that were Sakran rather than Asokan in character (Dewaraja 1972, 150; R. Pieris 1951, 272). The king's violent reaction towards what he saw as footdragging by workers, supervisors, and nobles who opposed his building projects caused great tension (Dewaraja 1972, 224). In the end the building project, which had been designed to increase the king's charisma, cost him the support of the common people.

The first *adikar* Ahalepola began his campaign to become king with an unsuccessful revolt in 1814. A month before the British invasion of Kandy in 1815, from the safety of exile in Colombo, he wrote a letter to the chiefs of Maturaṭa urging them to defect to the British side (Ehelepola [Ahalepola] 1815). The letter is interesting because in it a recognizable subtext structures the articulation of Ahalepola's ambitions. The letter, which obviously was meant to appeal to the interests of the nobles rather than those of the common people, starts by affirming his "pure loyal attachment to Sinhalese Sovereignty" and his opposition to the Nayakkar dynasty and their relatives, who as H.L. Seneviratne (1976, 59) points out, were increasingly in direct conflict with the economic interests of the nobles. He continues, "However, owing to the Vaḍuga [Nayakkar] dynasty the Sinhalese people are being destroyed in every way. When we hear of the cruelties committed by the wandering Vadugayas who have flocked to our country, we cannot contain ourselves with grief[10] . . . Daily our troubles are increasing because the rule of the King though firm on us does not touch these people who are appropriating all our possessions." The reason for all these problems he concludes, no doubt with an eye to his own future, is that the king is foreign. "All these misfortunes have come upon us because our own dynasty has ceased to exist." He then concludes by arguing that the English king would be more accommodating to Sinhalese interests and that the governor has assured him that within twenty-five years the English would return to the coast leaving Kandy to the Sinhalese. There is good reason to believe that the nobles including Ahalepola thought that the English would leave much sooner than that and that a Sinhalese dynasty would be restored.

After 1815, when Kandy had fallen to the British and the king had been exiled, Ahalepola was seen by the British as foremost among the nobles and treated with special deference. Immediately he began making his claims to kingship through a series of highly visible public actions meant to impress the nobles, but especially to garner support among the common people. When the Tooth Relic was brought back to the capital in 1815, he caused a furor among the nobles from other factions by riding at the end of the procession upon a horse. This was a public claim to kingship, for until that time it had been the exclusive prerogative of the king to ride a horse on the Kandyan side of the river and to follow the *perahara* on horseback. Another way in which Ahalepola sought to put forward his claims to kingship with the people in the capital was by commissioning a number of heroic poems about himself of the kind that were reserved for kings.

Let us now examine two of these poems for not only do they tell us about the kind of things that Ahalepola thought might advance his interest with the people, but they also offer a noble's perspective on the king's building program. The *Kirala Sandęsaya* (1958) and the *Ahalepola Varnanava* or *Vaḍuga Haṭana* (n.d.) were commissioned by Ahalepola shortly after the removal of the king in 1815. As their purpose was to advance Ahalepola's claims to the throne, they were phrased within the terms of the Kandyan discourse on kingship. However, as we have seen, the Asokan and Sakran discourses on kingship coexisted uneasily under normal circumstances and at times came into direct conflict. Since Ahalepola had been Sri Vikrama's principal opponent, one would expect that he would indicate his opposition to the king's Sakran style by emphasizing Asokan ideals. This was in fact the case.

The textual basis of Ahalepola's claims and the structure of his argument are derived from the *Mahavamsa's* (1950) accounts of the struggles of the Sinhalese hero-kings of old against Tamil usurpers. The authors of the Ahalepola poems first document in great detail the injustices against the *sangha* and the people committed by Sri Vikrama and then present Ahalepola as a hero-king who saves the people and the *sangha* by driving the wicked Tamils away and establishing a just Sinhalese Buddhist dynasty.

Although written by different authors, the two poems should be seen as part of a general political program. They do, however, differ in emphasis. The *Kirala Sandesaya* refers to the king's city building program in only very general terms, focusing attention nearly exclusively on the issue of the king as a Tamil oppressor of the people and the *sangha*. The *Ahalepola Varnanava* on the other hand, although touching upon these same themes, discusses the king's city building program in greater detail.

Let us now analyze these two poems to see how a faction among the nobility interpreted the king's city building program, and also to begin to understand the role this program played in the struggles for power in the early nineteenth century. These poems repeated two principal themes. First that Sri Vikrama was unfit to be king because he had violated the central tenets of kingship and second that Ahalepola's rebellion against him should be seen as a Sinhalese attempt to drive out a foreign dynasty. The poems support these claims by documenting a number of violations of kingship, all of which relate to the king's building program. Thus the landscape of Kandy was placed at the center of the discourse concerning legitimate kingship.

Two general types of violation were specified. The first was a violation of custom, and the second a violation of religious practice. From the nobles' point of view, the king's building program encapsulated both. The following description of the building program stands in sharp contrast to the king's description which we read earlier. First we have an account of how the building program violated the traditional religion:

> To bo trees located at different places in Senkadagala Nuvara [Kandy] were cut down and removed and the preaching hall built in the name of Arawwawala was demolished and its statues were pulled down. (*Ahalepola Varnanava* n.d., 51 v.22)

These represented extremely serious charges, for sacrilege was a heinous crime in the kingdom. The destruction or theft of temple property was one of the most serious offences against religion, short only of the murder of a monk. In 1769 monks claimed that sacrileges such as defacing *dagobas*, cutting down bo trees, or the theft of temple property were offences punishable by death (Hayley 1921, 120). The *Kirala Sandesaya* (1958, 7 vv.37–39) goes on to list some of his other offences against the religion.

> The King acted to destroy the Buddha *Sāsana* [religion]. Books of the *Dhamma* [doctrine proclaimed by the Buddha] were destroyed. Temples and temple lands were confiscated and their treasures seized. Monks were killed and others were driven out of their temples.

These kinds of charges were consistent with a traditional political discourse which accused the king of failing to uphold the tenets of Asokan kingship. They were typical of traditional Sinhalese commentaries in the histories of Lanka in portraying the Tamils as destroyers of Buddhism. In fact, there is reason to believe that some of these charges against Sri Vikrama were true. He did, for example, appropriate to his household two villages belonging to the Temple of the Tooth, a sacrilege which caused great resentment among the *sangha* and the people (C.O. 54/52. [1814] 1953). Sri Vikrama also fueled the discontent in 1814 by imprisoning six monks whom he believed to be implicated in Ahalepola's rebellion (Colvin R. De Silva 1953, 148) and he earned the *sangha*'s implacable hostility when he executed Paranatala or Moratota Kuda Unnanse, a monk noted for his learning and piety (Colvin R. De Silva 1953, 150). In fairness to Sri Vikrama, however, there is evidence that Paranatala was indeed complicit in Ahalepola's rebellion

(Colvin R. De Silva 1953, 150). Parantala's guilt notwithstanding, this was a tactical error by Sri Vikrama; in this he stands in contrast to the more astute Kirti Sri who, when faced with a similar type of rebellion of nobles and monks in 1760, executed the nobles but wisely spared the monks for fear of offending the citizenry (Dewaraja 1972, 110).

The *Ahalepola Varnanava* (n.d., 52 vv.26–28), then goes on to discuss the building of the lake in Kandy:

> All of the houses and trees in Kotagadolle [an area in the southwestern corner of the city] were removed in order to construct a lake. He then congregated people from various provinces and counties in order to build a great dam of soil five chains in height.[11]
>
> Tamil guards carrying sticks supervised this work and would not even allow the workers to stop to answer the call of nature. They worked them without stop day and night without food.
>
> The people although they worked unceasingly were beaten by the Tamil guards like the water buffaloes working in the rice fields. In this way the dam was built to a height of five chains with soil brought from the big hill in Kotagadolle.

John D'Oyly, the British agent whose job it was to monitor all activity in the Kandyan Kingdom and to undermine the power of the Kandyan king through carefully placed bribes and promises to leading nobles, recorded the feverish building activity that went on in Kandy between 1810 and 1812. His diary (D'Oyly [1825] 1917), based upon the almost daily reports of his spies, together with some later British reports, provides us with some confirmation of these claims. The following are some of the entries from his diary for the years 1811 and 1812 (D'Oyly [1825] 1917, 55, 69, 72–73).[12]

> January 25, 1811. There is no work proceeding in Kandy except making a dam of . . . Weywa [the lake] and finishing the wall and gateway around Kandy [palace].

> December 21, 1811. A great number of people are gone to Kandy from the Seven Korales to work on the dam.

> December 23, 1811. Pusweylle Disawe went to Kandy with fifteen hundred men for work on the dam, which when done will completely surround Kandy . . . [lake]. The people of the Seven Korales are very much disaffected.

> December 24, 1811. All the inhabitants of the Gabada, Wihara and Dewala Gan are bound and carried away by force to Kandy. The inhabi-

tants of some villages have made resistance. They are sent away ostensibly to make the dam and are employed at that work but people suppose it is the King's real object to have a large force in Kandy to provide against the attack which is expected from the English.

Whereas the king was entitled to demand *rajakariya* of between thirty and ninety days per year from individuals living in the *Gabadagam* (villages for his personal maintenance; Bandarage 1983, 32), it was an infringement of custom and an affront to religion for the king to demand *rajakariya* from villagers whose labor should have been reserved for *vihare* and *devale*. Sri Vikrama tried to justify this use of the labor of peasants who lived on temple lands by arguing that the work on the lake was an act of piety (Colebrooke [1832] 1956, 196). Such an explanation, however, apparently failed to convince either the *sangha* or the people.

D'Oyly's spies noted that resistance to *rajakariya* began to develop in some of the king's southern provinces (D'Oyly [1825] 1917, 74–75, 89, 104, 123, 154):

> December 28, 1811. Because a great number of people are seized and sent to Kandy to work at the tank [lake], very many persons in the Seven Korales left their villages and are living in concealment.

> December 30, 1811. The Disawe of Ihala Dolos P., after residing at Mawatagama, having gone to Kandy is now residing at the village of Ambateynne and collecting and sending people for the work of the dam of the tank . . . The Disave of the Four Korales residing at Manikkawa, is collecting people at the rate of two and three from each family, sending them forcibly to the work of the dam, and tears down and breaks the roofs of the houses of some men who absconded.

> February 10, 1812. Two thousand or three thousand men are still employed raising a dam and the work will be never finished.

> April 5, 1812. It is said that a Mohammedan, an *aratchy* and a Kankan of the Gabadawa [minor officials of the King's villages] have been impaled, for releasing people who came on *rajakariya* to work and taking money from them.

> June 30, 1812. The dam in Kandy is finished and for some time the common people have had rest from labour.

> December 29, 1812. All the people are disaffected to the King and in fear of him.

Two other nineteenth-century reports lend credence to the reports of disaffection among the common people caused by the construction of the lake. Lawrie (1896, 278) cites the following account told by Gannoruwe Tikiri Gammahe in 1819:

> I was at the time Gammahe of Gannoruwa, and the building of part of the wall of the Kandy lake belonged to my people and part to the people of Parakatawela Arachchi. The King went to look and found my part not finished while the rest was, so I was sent for and flogged and imprisoned.

The second account comes from J.B. Siebel, an advocate in Kandy during the 1850s (1954, 171).

> Thousands of persons were compelled to labour at the embankments by the order of the last King, and I remember very well that most of the old villagers who came to me, either as clients or as witnesses in cases, in the early part of my professional career about thirty-five years ago, when asked their age said, "Anney Hamuduroo, mamat pas eddha!" "Alas Sir, I also carried earth!" meaning thereby that they assisted in the formation of the lake in the beginning of the century.

The *Ahalepola Varnanava* (n.d., 52 vv.29–32, 53 vv.33–35, 54 vv.43–44, 55 v.47) then goes on to discuss the impact of the king's building program both on the layout of the city and upon the people:

> Then large numbers of people were brought to the city in order to rebuild it. Many houses and trees were removed in order to build new streets and roads. And what was accomplished by all of this? Great mountains of soil were collected throughout the city and the people were told that this was preparing the ground.
>
> A number of these soil mountains were made by destroying the well-known Bogambara Lake and Kadavatha street. At the other end of the city the Maha Maluva [esplanade in front of the lake] was dug to a depth of one and a half yards and the soil was collected into a mountain close to the great, sacred and famous Devale [Natha Devale].
>
> This great mountain of soil which rose to the height of a sacred bo tree was used as a place where dogs and foxes defecated at night. This evil mountain soon became even dirtier as people began to use it for their toilet.
>
> He then altered the Kataragama and Natha Devale and built a wall in front of the well-known *vahalkada* [gate in front of the Temple of the Tooth]. The Sandakada Pahana [moonstone] in front of the

Dalada Maligava [Temple of the Tooth] which people greatly admired was even destroyed. These were among the countless obstinate things which he did.

Plans were even made to destroy the Natha Devale. In the past the earth would have opened up and this cruel and unjust Tamil would have fallen straight to Hell because of the mischievous deeds which he did.

A huge *pattirippuwa* was constructed exceeding in height the great two-storied palace where the Lord Buddha's right Tooth Relic was placed. It was furnished with chairs, tables and beds. He even dared enjoy the company of women in this place. Because of this he has greatly increased the number of his sins and will have to pay in his next life.

He also caused great misery to the workers building the road to Geytembe and to those tilling the ground in various places around Kandy where Royal gardens were planned.

He stood like a *Yakkha* [devil] on the *Pattirippuwa* and shouted at the people that they must work harder. He couldn't see the hunger of the people and caused them much trouble. He then ordered all of the coconut trees be cut on the Maluwa where the Poya Karma [ordination place for monks] was held. He also destroyed the Vihara Geya.

When the people of the city assembled to discuss the destruction of this *vihara* he had them buried up to their shoulders in the ground and then impaled on sharp poles. Finally he had their wives taken into custody.

He destroyed and dug up the Dalada Street and then finally he destroyed all of the huge old *valavvas* [manor houses] of his ministers and made a new street by the name of Atawak street that was very long and broad.

At one level this account is simply an emotionally charged attack by an opponent of the king. Its success, as a political tract, however, lay in its subtext which in turn drew its power from the discourse of Asokan kingship. Ahalepola used his critical assessment of the building program as a vehicle to argue that Sri Vikrama had failed in almost every respect to conform to the pattern of behavior expected of an Asokan monarch. First, he is charged with failing to defend and support Buddhism, and with undermining it by destroying religious buildings, killing monks and allegedly fornicating in a building that was connected to the Temple of the Tooth. Second, he violated custom in a number of important ways. This was an extremely damaging charge, for legitimate rule had to be supported by custom.

Whereas in theory the king's power was absolute, for he was the Bhupati (the lord of the soil), in fact his rule was to be guided by *sirit* (the customs of the country) and if he did not observe these customs public opinion would turn against him (Dewaraja 1972, 150–151). He was to follow the *nitiya* (laws or customs) ordained by the ancient kings (LeMesurier and Panabokke 1880, 2);[13] these laws of the country which regulated his relations with the people were thought to be above the king (P.E. Pieris 1945a, 2). Changes in custom could take place under certain circumstances, but such changes were rare and were sanctioned only through consultation with the principal nobles and monks (D'Oyly 1929, 1). If the king simply ignored custom, he was seen as irresponsible and contemptible (Drekmeier 1962, 255).

According to the *Ahalepola Varnanava*, one of the most significant violations of *sirit*, besides the excessive demands of *rajakariya* described above, was the king's disruption of the traditional plan of the city in a number of important ways that caused hardship for the people. Whether he in fact violated custom in this regard is clearly open to debate. As I argued in chapters 5 and 6; if we consider his overall building plan for the city, these changes would have to be seen as part of an ongoing process of urban change that had been taking place ever since the founding of the city. As the nobles were well aware, the changes in the landscape were also very much in line with the Sakran building practices of kings in South India and parts of Southeast Asia. As such, one could argue that his overall plans did not violate custom. If, however, he was responsible for the destruction of bo trees and monasteries then he was most certainly in violation of custom. However, the charge that he wished to move the Malwatta Vihare[14] and the Natha Devale (and it is important to note that they were not in fact moved) might not necessarily constitute a violation of custom, for such removals had apparently taken place without repercussions in the recent past. For example, there appears to be no record of any criticism of Kirti Sri for removing the Visnu Devale from Alutnuwara to Kandy in 1747.

What is important to note is that, although the *Ahalepola Varnanava* is clearly based upon the Asokan view of kingship, there is no explicit criticism of the Sakran model. Nowhere are Sri Vikrama's claims to be a god-king directly attacked. This is especially curious when we consider that the whole point of his city building was to enhance these claims. The *Ahalepola Varnanava* was unwilling to concede Sri Vikrama that motivation. Rather, throughout the poem his building program is treated as the work of a man who is irrational, who creates great mountains of earth throughout the city to no purpose, who disrupts the street pattern with no end in mind, and who builds a great lake for a reason that the poet fails to mention.

Why did Ahalepola not attack Sakran kingship? The answer, I believe, is that he wished to become king and planned to employ elements of this model

From landscape to discourse: contestatory readings 171

himself. Although both of these poems are virtually devoid of Sakran imagery, the *Kirala Sandesaya* (1958, 3 v.12, 15 v.88) does make reference to Kandy as being like Sakra's city and Udawattakelle forest behind the palace as being like the Nandana forest of Sakra. Nevertheless, Ahalepola probably intended to become a more Asokan type of king than Sri Vikrama, for he is spoken of in these poems as the liberator of the Sinhalese from under the Tamil yoke, as was the great hero-king Dutthagamani (*Kirala Sandesaya* 1958, 9 v.48) and is referred to in both the *Kirala Sandesaya* (1958, 12 v.68) and the *Ahalepola Varnanava* (n.d., 79 v.175) as a *bodhisattva* rather than as Sakra, the king of the gods.

Both of the Ahalepola poems end by presenting him as the savior of Buddhism and the Sinhalese people. As we can see from the following passages (*Kirala Sandesaya* 1958, 8 v.47, 9 vv.48–49, 51, 12 v.68) he modeled himself explicitly on the hero-kings of Polonnaruva and Anuradhapura who freed the country from the curse of foreign Tamil dominion.

> Seeing the terrible harm that the evil Tamils were doing to the Sasana, the hero Ahalepola decided to drive them out of the country so as to help the people.
>
> Just as King Dutugamani organized an army against the Tamils, so he also organized an army and sent it to the Tamil Camp.
>
> Seizing the Tamil King who earlier had been powerful and destroyed the Sinhala country, he beat him mercilessly.
>
> Thus by removing the people's fear of the King he allowed people to live happily. Having demonstrated his heroism throughout the country, Ahalepola became the King of Kandy.
>
> Prisoners who had been sentenced to death by the last king were released and said Ahalepola is a *bodhisattva*.

The nobles' interpretation of the king's building program was very different from the king's own. Both, however, were politically motivated. But while the nobles' view claimed to speak for the people, we should be as wary of this claim as we are of the claim that the king's view reflected the view of all Kandyans. Let us, therefore, now turn to a consideration of what the people's view of this building program was. We have already caught a glimpse of it in the British commentaries and anticipate that their view of the creation of the city of the god-king would be less than favorable.

The peasants' interpretation of the building program

As we have seen in the preceding section, there are very few scraps of direct evidence of the common people's views of the king's building program.[15] Nearly all of our information is filtered through the lens of Ahalepola's highly partisan critique of the king or the reports of spies who often had a stake in leading the British to believe that there was widespread discontent with the king. Given this lack of direct evidence we must turn to the only source of information available to us: a series of ritual texts that were performed during the Kandyan period. While one cannot assume that rituals necessarily reflect people's perceptions or that all the common people shared a single view, I would argue that in a society that was as highly textualized as the Kandyan in the eighteenth and early nineteenth century, ritual based on written and oral texts often recorded and shaped perceptions.

The texts in question are a series of allegories dealing with two mythical kings, the good king of Soli and the evil king of Pandi. These allegories were a part of a larger set of thirty-five ritual texts that were originally composed between the fifteenth and sixteenth centuries and were derived from earlier South Indian texts. Obeyesekere (1984) argues that the rituals had been modified somewhat to reflect events that transpired in the Kandyan kingdom since that time. The texts were collected and their ritual performances observed by Obeyesekere (1984) during the 1950s, at a time when such ritual performances were disappearing rapidly. During the time of the Kandyan kings these same rituals were performed in the southern and western provinces, which were often less tightly controlled by the kings of Kandy than were the highland provinces (Tambiah 1976, 178), and which since the rebellion of 1811 had been suspected of disaffection (Colvin R. De Silva 1953, 138).

The ritual that I focus on here is the *pataha* (pond ritual), for its subject matter was the building program of the evil king of Pandi. Obeyesekere argues that this ritual, although ostensibly about a mythical Indian king, in fact represented the common people's view of Sakran kingship and of the related idea that the king's capital is a microcosm of the city of the gods. He further argues that such rituals were a form of grass-roots protest against excessive *rajakariya* and kings who failed to conform to the Asokan model of kingship. He then goes on to suggest that this ritual was most probably a peasant response to the city building programs of Kandyan kings such as Raja Sinha II, Kirti Sri, and Sri Vikrama. I will argue that the ritual Obeyesekere observed was an extremely detailed allegorical attack upon Sri Vikrama's building program from 1810–1812. While this version of the ritual was clearly based on earlier versions, I believe that by comparing the ritual as described by Obeyesekere to other material on the king's building program, including Ahalepola's accounts, one can see how closely this ritual conformed to Ahalepola's account of the king's building program and yet diverged from it in one absolutely critical respect.

The following is drawn from Obeyesekere's (1984, 326–333) account of a performance of the *pataha* ritual. The narration which Obeyesekere

From landscape to discourse: contestatory readings

witnessed was accompanied by a great deal of rough horse play designed to make the evil king of Pandi appear ridiculous. Obeyesekere's account of this ritual will be interspersed with my own commentary in the light of what we know about the last king's building program.

The narrator began by telling the audience that the king of Pandi, who was a powerful tyrant, had a wonderful city, which resembled the city of the gods, built by Visvakarma, the divine architect.

> No kind thought ever ripened in his mind
> His power, however, ripened from day to day
> His mind, like a fearful demon's, "ripened"
> Like warrior-faced Ravana ripened his strength.
>
> He'd acquired merit by giving alms in a previous birth
> He wore a crown studded with gold and gems
> The Cakravartin Pandi king with three eyes[16]
> Was pleased with the blessed sight of his city.
>
> He thought deep like the great ocean
> This king, lord of the earth, born of a pure dynasty
> Thought: "I am a chief of the gods and chief of kings"
> He summoned his ministers to the top storey of his palace.
>
> Great wise ones of the "court"
> Scholars possessed of sharp wisdom
> Brave generals and ministers of the "court"
> Bowed before the *danda* and worshipped the king.
>
> The king's mind was full of happiness
> Like the "infertile" banana tree that always thrives.
> "In what respect is our city different from heaven?"
> It is a thought that'll bring disaster on him.

So far the description of the king of Pandi's city sounds very much like that of Kandy before the beginning of Sri Vikrama's building program in 1810. He and the kings before him considered themselves to be *cakravartis* and like Sakra and they considered Kandy to be like Sakra's capital. Recall that Sri Vikrama had also spoken metaphorically of Visvakarma as the builder of Kandy. Sri Vikrama, like the king of Pandi, was also dissatisfied and asked himself, "In what respect is our city different from heaven?" And similarly that question brought disaster upon Sri Vikrama.

The chief minister read the king's mind and replied:

> O mighty one, lord of the seven world systems [*sakvalas*]
> O warrior powerful as Sakra himself

> Like Sakra himself possessing three eyes
> Is it your pleasure that we build a pond?

This apparently was the conclusion which Sri Vikrama arrived at as well. He decided that a large body of water representing Sakra's pond or the Ocean of Milk was needed in order to make Sri Vikrama's city a more perfect copy of Sakra's capital in heaven.

So far this account of the king's building program is different from Ahalepola's account in two respects. First, this account is explicitly allegorical, while Ahalepola's claims to be realist. Second, and much more important, the peasant's account is clearer about the king's motivations. It claims that the king (Pandi as Sri Vikrama) did indeed model himself on Sakra and he reinforced the similarity through the power of parallelism by reproducing a mythic landscape of the king of the gods. Ahalepola's refusal to acknowledge what the peasants understood can be explained by his desire to avoid a direct attack on Sakran kingship.

The king then said:

> You have a warrant from Īśvara
> You handsome men learned in mathematics
> Intelligent as the teachers of the gods themselves
> Choose a good moment through your astrology.

The chief minister then told the king that it was impossible to find an auspicious moment on the particular day when the king wished construction to begin.

> The great Pandi king blessed and powerful
> Heard what the group of counselors had to say
> Like a bull he uttered idiotic words:
> "There is no astrology except merit and sin."

Obeyesekere (1984, 337) argues that this last line is probably a veiled attack on King Kirti Sri who, as a pious Buddhist monarch, publicly scorned astrology. If Obeysekere's interpretation is correct and the king of Pandi represents Kirti Sri here, then it is unclear why the villagers claim in a previous verse that the king asked his advisors to choose a good moment through astrology. An alternative explanation of these two verses is that they are allegorical references to Sri Vikrama rather than to Kirti Sri. According to Dollapihilla (1959, 95), Sri Vikrama rejected the services of all of the best-known astrologers in the kingdom because their names had been submitted by the nobles whom he thought might block his building plans and chose instead an unknown astrologer whom he thought would do his bidding. It is

From landscape to discourse: contestatory readings 175

entirely possible that when Sri Vikrama was asked to justify the choice of such an inexperienced astrologer, he might have craftily fallen back on canonical Buddhism's opposition to astrology by saying: "There is no astrology except merit and sin."

But this ploy would have failed to impress the villagers, who knew little of canonical Buddhism and practiced astrology as a part of their village Buddhist religion. Thus, I would suggest, the villagers were probably criticizing him for using an inexperienced and biased astrologer. In fact all the kings of Kandy, including Kirti Sri, would have believed in astrology, regardless of the fact that it was not sanctioned by canonical Buddhism. Astrology was terribly important in all building projects for if construction was not undertaken at an astrologically auspicious time it was feared that the whole building project would fail (Shukla n.d., 36). Just as a king sought to create a parallel between his behavior and that of the gods and between the layout of his capital with that of the heavenly cities, so also astrology established a temporal parallelism by bringing the kingdom and the heavens into harmony (see Heine-Geldern 1942, 15).

According to the poem, the king then commanded the people to commence work on the pond. But the ministers protested that it was an enormous task and would take time:

> O powerful Pandi king who knows what's right
> Five hundred sorrows are involved in cutting a pond
> Under the shadows of your command we suffer
> O righteous king, one cannot dig a pond in a day.

Brushing their protests aside, the king had ordered them to dig a pond "huge in both length and breadth" within seven days. Messengers were then sent out to summon the workers. In the next part of the ritual the workers' suffering, as they labor from morning till evening, is described.

> Within a radius of fifty-five *yodun* in the king's city
> They come to dig the Pandi king's pond
> The assembled crowd dig out stumps and roots
> They speak to each other about their heads.

> He [the king] summoned Brahmans, watchers, and supervisors
> To break the laziness in the camp
> Young lads were tied up together
> And beaten to make them work.

> Like Sakra his glory spread around
> Whirling his gem-studded Sakra sword o'er his head

> Like Ravana entering the field of battle
> Came the great king of Pandi to the pond one day.
>
> He grabs hold of idlers and beats out their brains
> He cuts their bodies and slaughters the lads
> He brandishes the powerful sword in his hand
> Sparks fly out wherever it strikes.
>
> A foolish king in spite of his broad forehead
> To please him we carry large baskets on our heads
> We suffer a thousand sorrows and misfortunes
> Our heads are bald from carrying these baskets.
>
> We dig up stones, trees, and heap the earth
> But, these efforts are worthless, like husking a coconut without the kernel.
>
> People gather to work like a sheaf of reeds
> Their mouths were so parched, that they even forgot their suffering
> Like bulls they bit their lips and bore it all
> Who can escape the sins of past births?

The king then says

> These are idle workmen, they should be impaled on an *ula* [sharpened stake]. No inquiry is necessary.

The resemblance between these passages in this peasant ritual and those in the Ahalepola accounts of the building of the Kandy lake is striking. In both cases there is a strong implication that *rajakariya* had been violated by a king. The king is portrayed as the antithesis of the Asokan monarch, for he oppressed his people by forcing them to work on projects that appeared to have neither public utility nor religious merit. The building of the lake is seen as a misguided ploy by an evil and vain king bent on self-glorification. Although his people toiled endlessly to build his lake the king oppressed them even further by punishing them for not working fast enough. Here again we can see the parallel with Sri Vikrama's punishment of workers, a parallel which extends even to the detail of impaling slothful workers.

Again there is a parallel between the workmen digging endlessly for the king of Pandi and those digging endlessly for Sri Vikrama. The narrator of the *pahata* ritual says: "We dig up stones, trees, and heap the earth. But, these efforts are worthless, like husking a coconut without the kernel." The peasants thought such things were useless, not only because they had been begun without properly consulting astrologers and were therefore bound to fail (Obeyesekere 1984, 330), but also because they had now come to see

Sakran kingship itself as flawed. Probably because of the king's misdeeds, they were disabused of the traditional view that a god-king could also be a righteous Asokan monarch. They now had taken up one traditionally possible, but historically rare position, that it was ridiculous to think that a king, no matter how powerful, could ever become like a god.

The *Ahalepola Varnanava* (n.d., 52 v.29) also claims that the digging in Kandy was useless, but the criticism lacks the bite of the peasant's critique for it fails to single out either the folly of Sakran kingship or improper astrology as the reason why. The poem merely claims that the king was irrational.

The ministers informed the king that it was impossible to complete the pond unless more workers were summoned. The king then suggested that laborers from the eighteen regions be brought to the capital. He wrote letters to the eighteen kings within his sphere of influence ordering them to appear before him:

> We do not doubt that you'd be pleased to pay us a visit
> It would be good if you meet us without dallying on the way
> The moment you read this letter come to work on our pond
> If you don't our armies will answer you with war.

The kings from seventeen of the regions come and work on the king's pond.

> Even the kings who lived in the shade of goodness
> Didn't have a thing to eat the livelong day
> They draw loads of earth and heap them on both sides
> They suffer terribly like rounded up cattle.

I would argue that the allegorical kings of the eighteen regions represent the *disavas* of the outer provinces of the Kandyan Kingdom. Just as it was contrary to custom for a king to demand labor from vassal kings, so it was, as we have already argued, contrary to custom for the king of Kandy to demand this type of *rajakariya* from the outer provinces.

The good king of Soli refused to come and so the king of Pandi took an army to Soli to defeat him. Soli, with the help of Sakra, caused a great flood which destroyed the king of Pandi's army. When the king of Pandi returned to his own city he cursed the country of Soli to be without water for seven years and seven months and the country was subsequently devastated by drought, famine and pestilence. Finally, after much suffering, Sakra interceded with the goddess Pattini, who had the power to relieve suffering from disease and drought. She in turn intervened and ended the drought.

Just as the good king of Soli, who was portrayed as an ideal Asokan monarch, refuses to come and work for the evil king, so Ahalepola who portrayed himself as both a hero-king and an Asokan monarch refused to come to Kandy when summoned by Sri Vikrama in 1814. Sri Vikrama responded by sending an army to the provinces of Sabaragamuva and the Three and Four Korales where Ahalepola's rebellion was based. After a series of defeats by troops loyal to the king, Ahalepola's ill-prepared army fled into English territory. Sri Vikrama responded to Ahalepola's treason by punishing the people of these provinces just as the king of Pandi punished Soli.

As early as 1812 there was unrest in these provinces due to droughts, famines and pestilence. D'Oyly's ([1825] 1917, 129) spies reported that the people of these provinces "ascribe their present calamities of sickness and famine to the injustices and wrongs committed by the King." Drought, famine and sickness in Lanka were traditionally attributed to unjust rule (LeMesurier and Panabokke 1880, 2; B.L. Smith 1978a, 82).[17] In fact, the belief that an unjust king causes environmental calamity was widespread throughout South Asia. Coomaraswamy (1931, 41) quotes the *Manimekhalai*, a third century A.D. South Indian Buddhist text, on this issue:

> If the king swerve ever so little from righteousness, the planets themselves will desert their orbits; if the planets change their course, rainfall will diminish; with a shortage of rainfall, all life on earth will cease; the king will often cease to be regarded as king, because he would seem not to regard all life as his own.

To summarize then, in this chapter we have explored the struggle over the meaning of both urban form and sacral kingship by focusing on the building program undertaken by Sri Vikrama between 1810 and 1812. No single hegemonic view of either the nature of urban form or of kingship emerged. The king, drawing upon a Sakran discourse, viewed the building program as an opportunity to create a more charismatic rule by recreating the landscape of his capital in the image of the city of Sakra in heaven.

Ahalepola, on the other hand, interpreted the city-building program largely within an Asokan frame of reference and focused upon the injustices which the king committed in the course of the work. His reading, however, contained no direct critique of the Sakran model. Instead he portrayed the king as an irrational tyrant. He aspired to the kingship himself and had he succeeded he would undoubtedly have adopted many of the Sakran elements of self-glorification. Ahalepola's reading, therefore, just as the king's before him, was guided by what he perceived to be his own interests.

The peasants of the western provinces gave a third interpretation, which was more radically Asokan than that of Ahalepola. Although their critique resembled his in its focus upon the building of the lake and the record of injustice and hardship inflicted upon the workers, it went further, to attack

From landscape to discourse: contestatory readings 179

the very claims of Sakran kingship. In their eyes the king's city building project was unjust, not only because it oppressed the people, but also because they had been radicalized to the point of viewing it as ridiculous as well, because the very notion of kings emulating the king of the gods and re-creating the city of the gods was absurd. This critique of the very idea of a cosmic landscape was radical within the discursive field of South Asian kingship, and for this reason Ahalepola could not have accepted it.

All three of these interpretations of city building were politically inspired. Each reflected the interests of the group within society that held it. While each was confined within a larger discursive field which pertained to kingship, each was shaped in opposition to the discourses of the opposing interests. In this case the king's reading of the landscape did not prevail. One could argue that the building program acted as a catalyst, which brought into play competing textual models of kingship which were employed by the nobles and the peasants to undermine the legitimacy of the king. The king's model was derived from a Sakran reading of the *Mahavamsa* and other political texts such as the *Arthasastra*. The nobles' model was based on a largely Asokan reading of these texts with a tacit acceptance of some Sakran claims. The peasants' model, on the other hand, had become relentlessly Asokan. One could also see in the peasants' interpretation the indirect influence of older Indian texts such as the *Brahmavaivarta Purana* and the *Manimekalai* (Madhaviah 1923). In fact, the former goes so far as to suggest that even the city of Sakra (here called Indra) in heaven was an illusion (*Brahmavaivarta Purana*, quoted in O'Flaherty 1984, 270):

> The architect of the gods, named Visvakarman ["All-Maker"] was employed by Indra to build a spectacular city. When Indra's pride and impatience and insatiability drove him to make constant demands for architectural improvements, Visvakarman sought help from the gods. They sent to Indra a young boy, who first complimented Indra on his city and then remarked that of the Indra's before him none had ever had such a wonderful city. When Indra expressed his astonishment and disbelief, the boy – who was Vishnu in disguise – dwarfed Indra's achievement with a cosmic description of millions of Indra's like a parade of ants, and millions of palaces, all of them vanished long ago.

One can see here a textual model that supported an argument against the royal pride that oppresses the people in order to create cities of the gods. The moral of this text is that if such cities are illusory and transient, then mere mortals who chase after such dreams are as dangerous as they are foolish.

The *Manimekalai* takes a rather different tack, satirizing the king's city built in the image of the city of the gods by describing it as the highly polluting cremation ground, the archetypal place of death (*Manimekalai*, quoted in O'Flaherty 1984, 270–271):

> The cremation ground, with its pyres, [has four gates] . . . The great Mayan [Sanskrit: Maya] created this Cosmos Ground . . ., [which] shows, each in its proper place: Mount Meru standing at the center of the sphere, the seven types of mountain ranges rising around it, the encircling oceans, the four islands, and the other features . . . Here and there people burn corpses; others just abandon them . . . The flesh-eating hoot-owl screeches, and the Man's Head Bird, who seizes and devours heads of corpses, sounds his cry . . . Out in the open, people who dine on corpses serve their guests from pots reeking with human fat.

Here in this South Indian Buddhist text we see an argument that the cosmic city is not merely a foolish idea, as the tale of Indra's city suggests, but a vicious idea as well.[18]

Perhaps the major point that both the nobles' and the peasants' interpretations of the king's city-building program make is that it has produced suffering and death for the common people. For both of these groups, what the building program produced was more like a cremation ground than a cosmic and sacred city.

No reading is innocent; each of the readings we have examined had a political agenda. In a highly textualized society like the Kandyan one, both the urban landscape itself and the way people respond to it are shaped by texts. The fact that the form of protest was highly intertextual, employing allegorical rituals that had been used in earlier centuries, is one piece of evidence that the whole society including illiterate peasants was highly textualized. There are, however, as we have shown, multiple and contestatory texts that comprise a discursive field, and that becomes the site of a power struggle. To struggle for and against political legitimation in the Kandyan Kingdom was in large part a matter of bringing certain texts and particular readings to the forefront of political discourse. In this sense one would have to agree with Jacob Neusner (1975, 195) that "the point and purpose of tradition is not to pass on historical facts but both to create and to interpret contemporary reality, to intervene in history."

9

Conclusion

This book has been devoted to an exploration of the relationship between a landscape and the competing discourses within the discursive field of which it is a constitutive part. While it is perhaps no surprise that a landscape is shaped by discourses, it may be less well understood how the landscape as a signifying system embodying cultural practices can "act back" on the competition between discourses, at times thrusting certain ones to the fore and forcing others into the background.

The particular landscape in which I examined this dialectic, the royal capital of Kandy, was one in which two textually based discourses served as the basis of a volatile politics of interpretation. The latent tension which had long existed between these discourses had been carefully managed and syncretized over the centuries by the monkhood and the court, for each discourse had served an important purpose within the socio-political realm. One, the Asokan, provided a set of guidelines for Buddhist kings in their responsibility for protecting the religion and the people while the other, the Sakran, provided a model of the pomp and ceremony appropriate to divine kingship. Both in their different ways served as models of charismatic rule. These discourses were not merely ways of thinking or talking about kingship, they were given material expression in the landscape and in civic ritual.

In this study I have focused on the manner in which a set of narratives that compose the Sakran discourse were actualized in the landscape by the last king. Such a focus upon the relationship between a discourse, a landscape, and civic rituals presupposes that landscapes and rituals can fruitfully be conceptualized as texts that can be read both by those who experience them and by scholars who study them. These narratives were encoded in the landscape and in ritual in the form of linguistic and iconographic tropes such as synecdoches and recurrent motifs.

Important elements of the landscape such as the palace, walls, the audience hall, and the Temple of the Tooth, contained multiple synecdoches referring to the same narrative as well as multivalent synecdoches referring to several different narratives simultaneously. This recurrence, across different elements of the landscape and within each element, was one of the most important tropes through which the landscape communicated. It impressed upon the Kandyans again and again that they were in the presence of a god-king whose capital was like a mirror of the heavens.

But landscapes never have a single meaning; there always exists the possibility of different readings. Neither the production nor reading of landscapes is ever "innocent." Both are political in the broadest sense of the term, for they are inextricably bound to the material interests of various classes and positions of power within a society. The landscape of Kandy was produced to further the perceived interests of the Kandyan kings. It was consciously designed to foster a certain hegemonic reading that spoke of the power, benevolence and legitimacy of the kings in their capital.

This "kingly" reading customarily syncretized the Asokan and Sakran discourses of kingship. As such, it was dependent upon a landscape that embodied both discourses. The last king's building program, however, produced a Sakran landscape that caused segments of the population to react from within an increasingly entrenched Asokan discourse. Consequently, it also allowed the king's opponents among the nobility to mobilize the support of the peasantry against him. Because of the clear visual evidence in the material environment of the king's neglect of his Asokan duties and his enhancement of his image as a divine god-king, the "balanced" reading that was traditionally accepted as proper by the populace became harder to support. While a shift towards Sakranism within the realm of language and ritual may have cost little in material terms, the same cannot be said for a corresponding shift within the rhetoric of landscape.

Sri Vikrama's Sakran-inspired building program, was so labor-intensive that it mobilized opposition to the king among the peasants over the issue of what constituted the proper behavior of a monarch. Had he in his quest to become a Sakran god-king, betrayed the tenets of Asokan kingship? Had he gone against custom? Was the building of the Ocean of Milk really a religious project? The changes that the king made to the landscape of Kandy lay at the heart of this controversy and revealed the contradictions within the larger discursive field of kingship. They prompted the nobles and the peasants to reconsider and shift their thinking about abstract conceptions of kingship.

The peasants in the provinces from which most of the labor for these Sakran building projects was drawn turned against the king because of the illegitimate demands he made upon them. Their ritual critiques of his actions, although allegorical, were nevertheless treasonous. They assaulted the building program, the narratives that were encoded in the landscape of the capital, and by extension the whole discourse of Sakran kingship. Because they were trapped within the same discursive field as the king, their opposition to him was necessarily limited to the only textually legitimate critique available: the Asokan discourse on kingship.

Conclusion

The noble Ahalepola was also entrapped in the same discursive field, but his critique took a somewhat different tack, for his interests were different from those of the peasants. Like that of the peasants, his critique was Asokan in inspiration; however, he avoided the peasants' direct attack upon the Sakran discourse because, aspiring to become king himself, he saw the potential benefit to himself of Sakranism. He therefore, craftily attacked the king's failure to conform to the Asokan discourse rather than his decision to embrace the Sakran.

Ahalepola's attack on the king, like that of the peasants, was largely focused upon the king's building program, but unlike the peasants, his use of the landscape was purely strategic. He exploited the unpopularity of this program in order to mobilize support among the peasants to depose a king whose rule he and the other nobles found increasingly onerous. Had Sri Vikrama been a docile puppet of the nobles as they hoped he would be, they might have allowed him his building program and more actively helped suppress peasant unrest in the disaffected provinces. But because the king and his Nayakkar relatives attempted to reduce the power of the nobles, they seized upon this imbalance between the two discourses of kingship and used it to justify the king's removal.

Ultimately the contradictions which had lain latent for so long within the discursive field of kingship were made manifest. The monks, the nobles, and the peasants, whose cooperation had allowed the syncretism of the discourses, began, for varying reasons, to question the prevailing order, for they saw in the tension between the discourses, a space for contestation. The irony of all this is that the king had hoped that his city-building project would solidify his power by reinforcing both his charisma and magical power.

Landscape as one of the most pervasive and highly visible cultural productions in any society acts as an important signifying system. In the case of Kandy in the early nineteenth century a struggle over political power focused on the meaning of the landscape of the capital precisely because that landscape encapsulated the intersection of competing discourses and competing material interests.

Finally, let me conclude with some remarks about the broader implications of this book for the study of landscape. While I am sensitive to the many problems of transferring concepts used in the analysis of one place and time to another, I would hope to have something to say to those wishing to work in other parts of the world. The way to resolve this dilemma, I believe, is by admitting that while the world most certainly is not early-nineteenth-century Kandy writ large, neither is Kandy out of this world, although at times to a late-twentieth-century reader it may have appeared so. The very fact that in interpreting the landscape of Kandy I have found useful concepts such as textual community, employed by Stock (1983) to understand religious practices in twelfth-century France; discourse, developed by Foucault to understand medieval and modern France; and the notion of tropes such as synecdoche, metonymy, and recurrent narrative structure used by literary theorists to understand Western literature, suggests that there may be broader implications of this work. Such implications, of course, do not stem from the particular character of the Kandyan Kingdom, but from the more general character of the concepts. Landscapes anywhere can be viewed as texts which are constitutive of discursive fields, and thus can be interpreted socio-semiotically in terms of their narrative structure, their synecdoches, and recurrence. This applies as much to late-twentieth-century America as it does to early-nineteenth-century Kandy. The way that these concepts are articulated with reference to different times and places will, of course, vary greatly. Nevertheless, the thrust of the interpretive method will be the same – to uncover the underlying multivocal codes which make landscapes cultural creations, to show the politics of design and interpretation and to situate landscape at the heart of the study of social process.

Appendix

Table 1. *Location of synecdoches for the narrative "The world of the cakravarti"*

The narrative "The world of the *cakravarti*" is composed of three subnarratives:
(A) Control over the whole world through reproduction of centrality and the cardinal directions.
(B) Control over the kingdom through microcosmic reproduction.
(C) Reproduction of the cities of the Sinhalese hero-kings.

Location	Synecdoche	Medium	Sub narrative
Western rectangle	Rectangular shape	Concrete	C
Western rectangle	Divide into quarters	Concrete	A
Western rectangle	Divide into halves	Concrete	B
Western rectangle	4 gates	Concrete	A
Western rectangle	4 ferries	Concrete	A
Western rectangle	21 blocks	Concrete	B
Bogambara lake	Lake	Concrete	C
Artificial lake	Lake	Concrete	C
Island	Island park	Concrete	C
Lake wall	4 triangles	Concrete	A
Lake wall	Circle below triangles	Concrete	A
Lake wall	7 triangles wave	Concrete	A
Eastern rectangle	Rectangle	Concrete	C
Center of rectangle	Bell	Concrete	C
Center of rectangle	Bowl	Concrete	C
Center of rectangle	Assembly place	Concrete	C
Palace	Eastern location	Concrete	C
Palace wave wall	4 triangles	Concrete	A
Palace wave wall	Circle below triangles	Concrete	A
Palace wave wall	2 triangles beside wave	Concrete	A
Palace wave wall	7 triangles/wave	Concrete	A
Palace wave wall	Outer palace wall	Concrete	C
Palace wall	Wall	Concrete	C
Palace wall	Embossed pillars	Concrete	C

Appendix

Location	Synecdoche	Medium	Sub-narrative
Palace building	Symbol of 4 quarters	Concrete	A
Palace building	Lotus base	Concrete	A
Palace building	Row of lotuses	Concrete	A
Palace building	Embossed pillars	Concrete	C
Palace door	Sun and moon	Concrete	C
Palace bridge	5 cones	Concrete	A, C
Palace moat	Moat	Concrete	C
Palace gate	4 trefoil openings	Concrete	A, C
Palace gate	5 cones	Concrete	A, C
Palace/temple	Joined complex	Concrete	C
Temple	Relic in temple	Concrete	C
Temple wave wall	4 triangles	Concrete	C
Temple wave wall	Circle below triangles	Concrete	A
Temple wave wall	2 triangles beside wave	Concrete	A
Temple wave wall	7 triangles/wave	Concrete	A
Temple moat	Moat	Concrete	C
Temple wall	Lotus	Concrete	A
Temple wall	Pillars	Concrete	C
Cloud wall	Cloud pattern	Concrete	C
Cloud wall	Trefoil niches	Concrete	C
Cloud wall	4 trefoils	Concrete	A, C
Cloud wall	Circle below trefoil	Concrete	A, C
Cloud wall	7 trefoil/cloud	Concrete	A, C
Pattirippuwa	Octagon	Concrete	A
Shrine	Painting of cosmos	Concrete	A
Base of shrine	Lotus	Concrete	A
Shrine wall/ceiling	Suns	Concrete	C
Shrine wall/ceiling	Moons	Concrete	C
Shrine wall/ceiling	Painting of kings	Concrete	C
Shrine wall/ceiling	Name of kings	Language	C
Shrine	Relic on 2nd floor	Concrete	C
Shrine	7 *dagobas* for relic	Concrete	A
Shrine	8-sided altar	Concrete	A
Audience hall	Center of palace/temple	Concrete	A, C
Audience hall	Octagonal pillars	Concrete	A, C
Audience hall	7 pillars in hall	Concrete	A
Visnu wave wall	4 triangles	Concrete	A
Visnu wave wall	Circle below triangles	Concrete	A
Visnu wave wall	2 triangles beside wave	Concrete	A
Visnu wave wall	7 triangles/wave	Concrete	A
Visnu moat	Moat	Concrete	C
Visnu cloud wall	4 trefoils	Concrete	A
Visnu cloud wall	Circle below trefoil	Concrete	A

Appendix 187

Location	Synecdoche	Medium	Sub-narrative
Visnu cloud wall	2 beside drift	Concrete	A
Visnu cloud wall	7 trefoil/cloud	Concrete	A
Natha wall	Lotus base	Concrete	A
Pattini wall	Lotus base	Concrete	A
Canals	Canals	Concrete	C
Provinces	*Disa*	Language	A
Provinces	4 major	Language	A
Provinces	8 minor	Language	A

Table 2. *Location of synecdoches for the narrative "The world of the gods"*

The narrative "The world of the gods" is composed of three subnarratives:
(A) The cities of the gods, especially Sakra's city.
(B) The Ocean of Milk, fertility and creation.
(C) The cosmic axis, especially the cosmic mountain and the cosmic tree.

Location	Synecdoche	Medium	Sub-narrative
Western rectangle	Rectangle	Concrete	A
Kataragama Devale	Kataragama	Language	A
Kataragama Devale	Western rectangle	Concrete	A
Kataragama Devale	Meru gate	Concrete	A, C
Bogambara Lake	Anotatta	Language	B
Bogambara Lake	Lake	Concrete	B
Artificial lake	Ocean of Milk	Language	B
Artificial lake	Lake	Concrete	A, B
Artificial lake	Myth of white tortoise	Language	B, C
Lake wall	Wave pattern	Concrete	B, C
Lake wall	Wave wall	Language	B, C
Lake wall	Triangle (fire)	Concrete	B, C
Lake wall	Triangle (leaf)	Concrete	B, C
Lake wall	4 triangles	Concrete	B
Lake wall	Circle below triangles	Concrete	B
Lake wall	2 triangles beside wave	Concrete	B
Lake wall	7 triangles/wall	Concrete	B

Appendix

Location	Synecdoche	Medium	Sub-narrative
Moat joins lake	Confluence	Concrete	B
Lake and E. rectangle	Lake borders rectangle	Concrete	B, C
Canal	Canal	Concrete	A, B, C
River	River	Concrete	A, B, C
E. rectangle	Rectangle	Concrete	A, C
Palace	Eastern location	Concrete	A, C
Palace	Sakra's palace	Language	A
Palace	Mount Mandara	Language	C
Palace moat	Moat	Concrete	A, B, C
Palace wave wall	Wave pattern	Concrete	A, B, C
Palace wave wall	Triangle (fire)	Concrete	B, C
Palace wave wall	Triangle (leaf)	Concrete	B, C
Palace wave wall	Wave wall	Language	B
Palace wave wall	4 triangles	Concrete	B
Palace wave wall	Circle below triangles	Concrete	B
Palace wave wall	2 triangles beside wave	Concrete	B
Palace wave wall	7 triangles/wave	Concrete	B
Palace wall	Lotus	Concrete	B, C
Palace wall	Embossed pillars	Concrete	C, A
Palace building	Lotus base	Concrete	B
Palace building	Trefoil niches	Concrete	A, C
Palace building	Symbol of 4 quarters	Concrete	C
Palace building	Row of lotuses	Concrete	B
Palace building	Embossed pillars	Concrete	A, C
Palace door	Sun and moon	Concrete	C
Palace bridge	Carved elephants	Concrete	A, B
Palace bridge	5 cones	Concrete	C
Palace gate	Meru gate	Language	A, C
Palace gate	4 trefoil openings	Concrete	A, C
Palace gate	5 cones	Concrete	A, C
Palace	Elevated	Concrete	A, C
Palace/temple	Joined complex	Concrete	A
Palace/temple	Both called Maligawa	Language	A
Temple moat	Moat (as river)	Concrete	A, B, C
Temple wave wall	Wave pattern	Concrete	A, B, C
Temple wave wall	Wave wall	Language	B
Temple wave wall	Triangle niches	Concrete	A, B, C
Temple wave wall	4 triangles	Concrete	A, B, C
Temple wave wall	Circle below triangles	Concrete	A, B, C
Temple wave wall	2 triangles beside waves	Concrete	A, B, C
Temple wave wall	7 triangles/wave	Concrete	A, B, C
Temple moat	Moat (as Ocean)	Concrete	A, B, C
Temple wall	Lotus	Concrete	B

Appendix

Location	Synecdoche	Medium	Sub-narrative
Temple wall	Pillars	Concrete	A, C
Cloud wall	Cloud drift pattern	Concrete	A, B, C
Cloud wall	Celestial rampart	Language	A, B, C
Cloud wall	Trefoil niches	Concrete	A, C
Cloud wall	4 niches	Concrete	A, B, C
Cloud wall	Circle below trefoil	Concrete	A, B, C
Cloud wall	2 trefoil beside drifts	Concrete	A, B, C
Cloud wall	7 trefoil/drift	Concrete	A, B, C
Temple	Trefoil niches	Concrete	A, C
Temple	Relic in temple	Concrete	A
Temple	Sakra's palace on earth	Language	A
Temple	Elevated	Concrete	A, C
Temple	Located in east	Concrete	A, C
Temple door	*Makara torana*	Concrete	B, C
Pattirippuwa	Octagon	Concrete	A, C
Shrine	Center of temple	Concrete	C
Shrine	Painting of Cosmos	Concrete	C
Base of shrine	Lotus	Concrete	B, C
Shrine wall/ceiling	Suns	Concrete	C
Shrine wall/ceiling	Moons	Concrete	C
Shrine wall/ceiling	Paintings of Tavatimsa	Concrete	A
Shrine wall/ceiling	Name of Tavatimsa	Language	A
Shrine wall/ceiling	Painting of Sakra	Concrete	A
Shrine wall/ceiling	Name of Sakra	Language	A
Shrine wall/ceiling	Painting of Brahma	Concrete	A
Shrine wall/ceiling	Name of Brahma	Language	A
Shrine wall/ceiling	Painting of gods' assembly	Concrete	A
Shrine wall/ceiling	Name "Assembly of gods"	Language	A
Shrine wall/ceiling	Painting Laksmi	Concrete	A
Shrine wall/ceiling	Name of Laksmi	Language	A
Shrine door	*Makara torana*	Concrete	B, C
Shrine	Relic on 2nd floor	Concrete	A
Shrine	7 *dagobas* for relic	Concrete	A, C
Shrine	8-sided altar	Concrete	C
Shrine	Silver table on altar	Concrete	B
Shrine	Octagonal cupola on pillars	Concrete	C
Shrine	3 crystal *dagobas*	Concrete	A, C
Shrine	Gold lotus-relic on wire	Concrete	A, B, C
Audience hall	Center of palace/temple	Concrete	A, C
Audience hall	Octagonal pillars	Concrete	A, C
Audience hall	7 pillars in hall	Concrete	A, B, C
Audience hall	Elevated	Concrete	A, C
Visnu wave wall	Wave swell pattern	Concrete	A, B, C

Location	Synecdoche	Medium	Sub-narrative
Visnu wave wall	Wave wall	Language	B
Visnu wave wall	Triangular niches	Concrete	A, B, C
Visnu wave wall	4 triangles	Concrete	A, B, C
Visnu wave wall	Circle below triangles	Concrete	A, B, C
Visnu wave wall	2 triangles beside wave	Concrete	A, B, C
Visnu wave wall	7 triangles/wave	Concrete	A, B, C
Visnu moat	Moat	Concrete	A, B, C
Visnu cloud wall	Cloud drift pattern	Concrete	A, B, C
Visnu cloud wall	Celestial rampart	Language	A, B, C
Visnu cloud wall	Trefoil niches	Concrete	A, C
Visnu cloud wall	4 trefoils	Concrete	A, C
Visnu Devale	Elevated	Concrete	A, C
Visnu Devale	Located in north	Concrete	A, C
Visnu Devale	Meru gate	Concrete	A, C
Road to Visnu Devale	Vaikuntha	Language	A, C
Devata Bandara Devale	Next to Visnu Devale	Concrete	A
Natha Devale	Located in south	Concrete	A, C
Natha Devale	Natha-Siva/Maitreya	Concrete	A, C
Natha Devale	Natha-Siva/Maitreya	Language	A, C
Natha Devale	Elevated	Concrete	A, C
Natha Devale	Meru gate	Concrete	A, C
Natha wall	Lotus base	Concrete	B, C
Natha wall	Lotus	Language	B, C
Pattini Devale	Located in west	Concrete	A, C
Pattini Devale	Elevated	Concrete	A, C
Pattini Devale	Pattini-Parvati/Bosat	Concrete	A, C
Pattini Devale	Pattini-Parvati/Bosat	Language	A, C
Pattini wall	Lotus base	Concrete	A, C
Center of rectangle	Bo tree	Concrete	C
Center of rectangle	*Dagoba*	Concrete	A, C
Center of rectangle	Bowl relic	Concrete	A
Center of rectangle	Bell	Concrete	A
Center of rectangle	Assembly place	Concrete	A

Table 3. *Location of synecdoches during civic rituals for the narrative "The world of the* Cakravarti"

The narrative "The world of the *cakravarti*" is composed of three subnarratives:
(A) Control over the whole world through reproduction of centrality and the cardinal directions.
(B) Control over the kingdom through microcosmic reproduction.
(C) Reproduction of the cities of the Sinhalese hero-kings.

Location	Ritual	Synecdoche	Medium	Sub-narrative
City	All	4 festivals	Behavior	A
Western rectangle	All	1st *adikar* has half	Behavior	B
Western rectangle	All	2nd *adikar* has half	Behavior	B
Palace/city	All	White elephant	Concrete	C
Palace/city	All	White horse	Concrete	C
Palace	All	White cattle	Concrete	C
Palace	All	King as Sakra	Language	C
Audience hall	All	King as Sakra	Language	C
Provinces	All	4 Major *disava*	Concrete	B
Provinces	All	4 Major *disava*	Language	B
Provinces	All	8 Minor *disava*	Concrete	B
Provinces	All	8 Minor *disava*	Language	B
Cremation ground	Cremation	7-storey pyre	Concrete	C
Cremation ground	Cremation	7-foot canopy	Concrete	C
River	Cremation	Ashes in river	Behavior	C
Cemetery	Interment	Interment in *dagoba*	Behavior	C
Center of rectangle	Consecration	Queen/*chank*/water	Behavior	C
Center of rectangle	consecration	Brahmin/*chank*/water	Behavior	C
Center of rectangle	Consecration	Pearl umbrella	Behavior	C
Center of rectangle	Consecration	Slippers	Behavior	C
Center of rectangle	Consecration	Chowrie	Behavior	C
Center of rectangle	Consecration	Head split in 7	Language	C
Center of rectangle	Consecration	Pavilion in center	Concrete	A, C
Center of rectangle	Consecration	Ascension of pavilion	Behavior	A, C
Center of rectangle	Consecration	Throne in pavilion	Concrete	A, C
Center of rectangle	Consecration	Pavilion of Mandapa	Concrete	A, C
Center of rectangle	Consecration	Throne of Mandapa	Concrete	A, C
Visnu Devale	Consecration	Blessing of god	Behavior	C
Coronation stone	Consecration	Raised square stone	Concrete	C
Coronation stone	Consecration	Stone on 4 pillars	Concrete	C
Coronation stone	Consecration	Face northwest	Behavior	C
Coronation stone	Consecration	Brow fillet	Behavior	C
Coronation stone	Consecration	Sword	Behavior	C
Coronation stone	Consecration	Name	Language	C
City streets	Consecration	Circumambulate	Behavior	A, B, C
City	Perahara	Perahara	Behavior	C
Eastern rectangle	Perahara	Perahara	Behavior	A
4 Devala	Perahara	Kapa	Concrete	A
City	Perahara	Kumbal Perahara	Behavior	A, B, C
City	Perahara	4 *nilame* of Devala	Behavior	B
Octagon	Perahara	King stands there	Behavior	A
Octagon	Perahara	King's 8-sided hat	Concrete	A
Front of palace	Perahara	Throne/sun/moon	Concrete	A, C
City	Perahara	Representative of provinces	Behavior	B, C
City	Perahara	21 days	Behavior	B
Center of rectangle	Embassy	Bo tree	Concrete	A
Palace	Embassy	Great gate	Language	A, C
Throne room	Embassy	Partition/sun/moon	Concrete	C
Throne	Embassy	Lions and suns	Concrete	C

Appendix

Table 4. *Location of synecdoches during civic rituals for the narrative "The world of the gods"*

The narrative "The world of the gods" is composed of three subnarratives:
(A) The cities of the gods, especially Sakra's city.
(B) The Ocean of Milk, fertility and creation.
(C) The cosmic axis, especially the cosmic mountain and the cosmic tree.

Location	Ritual	Synecdoche	Medium	Sub-narrative
Palace	All	King as Sakra	Language	A
Palace	All	Functions like Sakra's	Behavior	A
Palace	All	White cattle	Concrete	A, B
Temple	All	Functions like Sakra's	Behavior	A
Palace/temple	All	King produces rain	Behavior	A, B
Palace/temple	All	*Kapruka*	Concrete	A, B, C
Palace/temple	All	*Kapruka*	Language	A, B, C
Temple	All	Relic produces rain	Concrete	A, B
Temple	All	Nilame produces rain	Behavior	A, B
Temple	All	Nilame produces rain	Language	A, B
Palace/city	All	White elephant	Concrete	A, B
Palace/city	All	White horse	Concrete	A, B
Cremation ground	Cremation	7-storey pyre	Concrete	A, C
Cremation ground	Cremation	7-foot canopy	Concrete	A, C
River	Cremation	Ashes in river	Behavior	A, B, C
Visnu Devale	Consecration	Blessing of god	Behavior	A
Coronation stone	Consecration	Raised square stone	Concrete	A, C
Coronation stone	Consecration	Stone on 4 pillars	Concrete	A, C
Coronation stone	Consecration	Face northwest	Behavior	A
Coronation stone	Consecration	Brow fillet	Behavior	A
Coronation stone	Consecration	Sword	Behavior	A
Coronation stone	Consecration	Name	Language	A
Center of rectangle	Consecration	Pavilion in center	Concrete	A, C
Center of rectangle	Consecration	Ascension of pavilion	Behavior	A, C
Center of rectangle	Consecration	Throne in pavilion	Concrete	A, C
Center of rectangle	Consecration	Pavilion of Mandapa	Concrete	A, B, C
Center of rectangle	Consecration	Throne of Mandapa	Concrete	A, B, C
City streets	Consecration	Circumambulate	Behavior	A, C
City streets	Perahara	July/August moon	Behavior	A, B
Visnu Devale	Perahara	*Kapa*	Concrete	A, B, C
Natha Devale	Perahara	*Kapa*	Concrete	A, B, C
Pattini Devale	Perahara	*Kapa*	Concrete	A, B, C
Kataragama Devale	Perahara	*Kapa*	Concrete	A, B, C
4 *devala*	Perahara	Eastern branch for *kapa*	Concrete	A
4 *devala*	Perahara	White cloth on *kapa*	Concrete	A, B
4 devala	Perahara	Milk on *kapa*	Concrete	B
4 *devala*	Perahara	*Kapa* 3 around Devala	Behavior	A, C
4 *devala*	Perahara	Gods 3 around Devala	Behavior	A, C
City	Perahara	Kumbal Perahara	Behavior	A, B, C
City	Perahara	Pattini circumambulation	Behavior	A, C
City	Perahara	Natha circumambulation	Behavior	A, C
City	Perahara	Visnu circumambulation	Behavior	A, C
City	Perahara	Kataragama circumambulation	Behavior	A, C
City	Perahara	Relic circumambulation	Behavior	A, B, C
City	Perahara	King circumambulation	Behavior	A, C
Octagon	Perahara	King stands there	Behavior	A, C

Appendix

Location	Ritual	Synecdoche	Medium	Sub-narrative
Octagon	Perahara	King's 8-sided hat	Concrete	A, C
City	Perahara	Howdah like Sakra's	Concrete	A, C
City	Perahara	King on white horse	Behavior	A, B, C
City	Perahara	Chariot/8 horses	Behavior	A, B, C
Eastern rectangle	Perahara	Circumambulate 3	Behavior	A, C
City	Perahara	Flowers strewn	Behavior	B
City	Perahara	Elephants	Concrete	A, B
River	Perahara	Water cutting	Behavior	A, B
Temple	Perahara	Tooth emerges	Behavior	A, B, C
Route to city	Embassy	Difficult road	Behavior	A, C
Route to city	Embassy	Climb mountain	Behavior	A, C
Route to city	Embassy	Climb mountain	Language	A, C
Route to city	Embassy	Delay movement	Behavior	A, C
Route to city	Embassy	Letter in white	Concrete	A
Route to city	Embassy	Letter on head	Behavior	A
Route to city	Embassy	5 carry letter	Behavior	A
Route to city	Embassy	33 attendants	Behavior	A
Route to city	Embassy	Music for letter	Behavior	A
Route to city	Embassy	Presents in white	Concrete	A
Route to city	Embassy	32 cases presents	Concrete	A
Houses on route	Embassy	Square	Concrete	A
Houses on route	Embassy	Letter at Center	Concrete	C
Houses on route	Embassy	4 doors at cardinal	Concrete	C
Houses on route	Embassy	Improve near Kandy	Concrete	A, C
Geytembe	Embassy	Enter Kandy	Behavior	A
Geytembe	Embassy	Bo tree	Concrete	A, C
Kandy	Embassy	King–shoes/rides	Behavior	A
Boundary	Embassy	7 markers	Concrete	A, B, C
Eastern rectangle	Embassy	Met by *adikar*	Behavior	A, C
Center of rectangle	Embassy	Bo tree	Concrete	C
Palace	Embassy	King is great gate	Language	A
Palace	Embassy	7 levels to king	Behavior	A, B, C
Audience hall	Embassy	Raised	Concrete	A, C
Audience hall	Embassy	7 curtains	Concrete	A, B, C
Audience hall	Embassy	White drapes	Concrete	A, B
Audience hall	Embassy	Attendants in white	Concrete	A, B
Audience hall	Embassy	Golden weapons	Concrete	A
Audience hall	Embassy	Burn charcoal	Behavior	A
Audience hall	Embassy	King's speech	Behavior	A
Throne room	Embassy	Partition/sun/moon	Concrete	A, C
Throne	Embassy	Elevated	Concrete	A, C
Throne	Embassy	Suns	Concrete	A, C
Throne	Embassy	Female deity	Concrete	A

Notes

1. INTRODUCTION

1. Perhaps the closest most cultural geographers come to relating landscape to cultural process is in the study of the relationship between landscape and the diffusion of culture. The questions of what those landscapes mean to those who built them or those who later lived in them, however, are rarely addressed.
2. For a discussion of hermeneutics see Giddens (1976; 1979), Ricoeur (1974; 1981), Gadamer (1986). For a sympathetic critique of Gadamer see Eagleton (1983) and Wright (1984).
3. Whereas the approaches of Barthes and De Certeau are often quite structural, Geertz's approach is more hermeneutic. Much of Geertz's work lies within the field of ethnohistory. Other major figures in this movement include: Abrams (1982), Darnton (1984), Davis (1983), Ginzburg (1982), Ladurie (1979; 1987), LeGoff (1980), and Muir (1981).
4. Cosgrove and Daniels' recent edited volume entitled *The Iconography of Landscape* (1988) offers a wealth of stimulating, theoretically informed essays on landscape interpretation.
5. The most useful discussion of intertextuality for social scientists I have come across is found in Stock (1983). In literary theory the term usually refers to the interaction of autonomous texts. For a critique of this type of reified, non-sociological approach see Duncan and Duncan (forthcoming), in which we discuss the notion of intertextuality and literary theories in relation to landscape interpretation.
6. Examples of works in art history and iconology which are relevant to landscape interpretation include: Baxandall (1972; 1985), Berger (1972), E.H. Gombrich (1961), Gombrich, Hochberg, and Black (1972), Goodman (1976), Hemeren (1969), Mitchell (1980; 1986), Panofsky (1957), and Shapiro (1973).
7. Obeyesekere (1984, 344–345) devotes two pages of his book to this question and suggests that a study of Kandy be done. There have, however, been several studies of the Temple of the Tooth and its rituals, the most important ceremonial building in Kandy (Hocart 1931; H.L. Seneviratne 1978a; 1985).
8. Curiously, although the underpinnings of customary law were written down, customary law itself was not (A. Gunasekara 1978, 122). This should not be taken to imply, however, that because it was part of the oral tradition, it was not textualized.

2. LANDSCAPE AS A SIGNIFYING SYSTEM

1. For example, see Barthes (1979a; 1982; 1986a, b; 1987), De Certeau (1985), Krautheimer (1983), Millon and Nochlin (1978), Pratt (1986). Daniels (1987; 1988), Cosgrove and Daniels (1988), Cosgrove (1982; 1985; 1989), Duncan and Duncan

(1988), Ley (1987; 1989), Rowntree (1988), Anderson (1987; 1988), Domosh (1987), and Mills (1988).
2. For a critique of this position see Duncan and Ley (forthcoming).
3. For fine examples of the historical reconstruction of the consciousness of peasants see Davis (1983), Ginzburg (1982; 1985), and Ladurie (1979; 1987).
4. For example, see Clarence Glacken's (1967) comprehensive study of European attitudes toward the natural landscape, Tuan's (1974) examination of environmental perception and values, or Lowenthal's (1985) exploration of attitudes towards landscapes of the past. Also see Sauer's (1975; 1980) volumes on European attitudes to North America and David Lowenthal and Hugh Prince's (1965) perceptive study of English attitudes towards landscape.
5. See Meinig (1983), and Sauer (1969a).
6. See the edited collection by Seamon and Mugerauer (1985).
7. For an excellent discussion of the relation between theory and description and the question of theory-neutrality versus theory-ladenness see Sayer (1984; 1985).
8. There is an extensive literature which challenges the notion of ethnographic realism. Some of this is hermeneutic in that it acknowledges the researcher's own discursivity and the problem of the hermeneutic circle. Examples of hermeneutic approaches are those of Geertz (1973a; 1983a), Gadamer (1986), Giddens (1976; 1979; 1984), or Ricoeur (1981). Some, who are also anti-foundationalist and anti-essentialist, tend to take a more radically relativist stance in claiming that because we cannot have absolutely certain knowledge, we cannot make any claims to authority. They question whether there is any positive relation between our theories and reality "out there." Implicit in this stance is an unwillingness to confront critically the question of validity, values, or political implications. Examples of such relativist positions include Rorty (1979), Lyotard (1984), and Goodman (1976). Criticisms of the politically conservative nature of radical anti-foundationalism are found in Jameson (1981) and Eagleton (1983). Interesting alternatives to both ethnographic realism and extreme forms of relativism are proposed in the critical theories such as those of Norris (1985), Lentricchia (1983), Jameson (1981), and Eagleton (1983). Perhaps the most useful alternatives are found in scientific realist positions as they are expounded by Outhwaite (1987) and Sayer (1984; 1985). Despite the confusing use of the term "realism" here, scientific realism contrasts sharply with ethnographic or "naive realism" in that it entails epistemological fallibilism and a keen sensitivity to the hermeneutic between the conceptual frameworks of the observer and the observed. See Giddens (1984, 228).
9. For an expanded definition of text see Clifford and Marcus (1986), Geertz (1980), Darnton (1984), Barthes (1979a, b), Ricoeur (1974), and Brown (1987).
10. Although more Althusserian than my own approach, I regard Harootunian's (1988) *Things Seen and Unseen: Discourse and Ideology in Tokugawa Nativism* as an interesting and valuable empirical study employing the concept of competing discourses. For a survey of theories of discourse highlighting the more structural conceptions see Diane Macdonell (1986). An argument which emphasizes the production of subjectivities is found in Chris Weedon (1987). For a critique of the use of discourse analysis in the study of ideology see Thompson (1984).
11. See Macdonell (1986).
12. See Mitchell (1980; 1986), E.H. Gombrich (1972), Panofsky (1957; 1972; 1982), and Barthes (1977a).

13. For discussions of allegory see Frye (1971), Fletcher (1964) and De Man (1979). Also, an interesting discussion of allegory can be found in J. Clifford's (1986) essay on allegory in ethnographic writing.
14. On metonymy and its relation to other tropes, see Hayden White (1978). Also see Kenneth Burke (1945) especially his appendix, "Four master tropes," pp. 503–517, and Roman Jakobson (1960, 350–377).
15. The use of repetition in literature is analysed in Suleiman (1980a; 1980b). For a discussion of the socio-psychological implication of repetition in ritual see Leach (1966, 404) and Rappoport (1979, 175–176).
16. On the use of tradition in political discourse also see Neusner (1975), Shils (1981), Hobsbawm and Ranger (1983), Baker (1985), Heesterman (1985) and Agnew (1989).

3. THE DISCURSIVE FIELD OF KANDYAN KINGSHIP

1. The intermingling of Buddhist and Hindu beliefs was continuous from the founding of Buddhism. During certain periods, such as the ninth to early eleventh centuries, the penetration of Hindu beliefs was particularly strong (F.E. Reynolds 1974, 70).
2. For a discussion of the Nayakkar dynasty in South India see Dirks (1987).
3. See *Mahavamsa* (1950), *Culavamsa* (1953a; 1953b).
4. When the European powers conquered the coastal kingdoms of Lanka, the Kandyan royal family remained the only source of *ksatriyas* on the island, and when King Narendra Sinha died without legitimate heir in 1739, the Sinhalese dynasty ended. The absence of *ksatriyas* pretenders to the throne was not in and of itself an insuperable problem for the Sinhalese, as at times non-*ksatriyas* had successfully claimed the throne through marriage to a *ksatriya* princess. For example, Vimala Dharma Sūriya I, who was not a *ksatriya*, seized the throne in 1592 and afterward took a *ksatriya* queen to legitimate his power. The *radaḷa* noble Ahalepola also made an unsuccessful bid for the crown after 1815.
5. Dewaraja (1972, 42–43) notes that the Nayakkars who came to Kandy were *sudras* and not *ksatriyas* as the Sinhalese believed.
6. More detailed discussions of the economic and administrative organization of the Kandyan Kingdom are found in R. Pieris (1956), K.M. De Silva (1981), and Bandarage (1983). The following summary draws upon these three sources.
7. Towards the end of his reign, the last king added a third *adikar* in order to attempt to further divide power among different factions of the nobility.
8. Perhaps the best studies of the symbolic diffusion of political power out of a capital have been conducted by Agulhon (1982; 1985).
9. The term Sakran comes from Sakra, the king of the gods, whom the kings of Kandy emulated. For further discussions of Sakran and Asokan models of kingship see Obeyesekere (1984).
10. Some kings of Lanka such as Kassapa I in Sīgiri modeled themselves upon the god Kuvera (Paranavitana 1950).
11. Although I refer to the Sakran model as Hinduized, there was in fact no single Hindu model of kingship. Throughout South Asian history conceptions of such aspects of kingship as the source of kingly authority, *rāja dharma* (the duty of kings), sacrality, authoritative relations with other power structures, the king as *cakravarti* (world ruler), the king as self-aggrandizing monarch, and the king as self-sacrificing,

benign protector of the moral order of society vary widely. The historiography of kingship in South Asia reveals it as a complex and controversial topic. Clearly there were contrasting and conflicting ideals among which a balance was sought. Some of these ideals corresponded more closely to the Asokan model and others to the Sakran. In the case of Kandyan kingship the more Hinduized model contrasted with the Buddhist Asokan model by emphasizing the self-aggrandizing, sacral model. For a discussion of South Asian kingship see Obeyesekere (1984), Dirks (1987), Drekmeier (1962), Heesterman (1985), Richards (1978), and Smith (1978a).

12. Sakra is the name of the tribe from which the Buddha came. In this way the Buddha and the king of the gods were associated through descent.

13. There is some reason to believe that the conversion to Buddhism by the Nayakkar kings was purely a political move for public consumption and that privately they remained Hindu followers of the god Siva (see R.F. Gombrich 1971, 35). Derrett (1956) argues that in spite of the Kandyan kings' adherence to Buddhism, there were hardly any features of Kandyan kingship that distinguished it from Indian kingship.

14. This did not protect him from an assassination attempt led by a faction among the nobility and the chief monk of the Malwatte Vihare, one of the two major monasteries in Kandy, who wished to install a more pliable monarch, a prince smuggled in from Thailand. The plot was revealed to the king by another faction among the nobility in conjunction with the leadership of the Asgiri Vihare, the rival monastery in Kandy.

4. CONCRETIZING THE SAKRAN DISCOURSE: FROM LANDSCAPE OF THE GODS TO LANDSCAPE OF THE HERO-KINGS

1. Mount Meru is also often referred to as *Mahāmeru*, *Sumeru*, or *Sineru* in South Asia.

2. A *yoduna* is generally estimated to be approximately sixteen miles, although some consider it to be twelve miles. Mount Meru is sometimes considered to be 168,000 *yoduns*. Trikuta is 30,000 *yoduns*.

3. There are variations on this theme. One late-eighteenth-century document fails to speak of the seven annular seas, simply placing "Mahameru in the middle of seven mountains in the milky sea" (see *Saṅgarāja Vata* 1955, 112, v.296).

4. The details of this system will be explored in greater detail below. The Buddhist view of the universe is a variation on the Hindu view. According to the latter, the world consists of a central, circular continent known as Jambudvipa. At the center of this continent lies Mount Meru around which the sun, the moon, and the stars revolve. The heaven of the gods lies upon Meru's top. This heaven is surrounded by the heavens of the eight *Lokapālas* or guardians of the world. Jambudvipa is surrounded by seven annular oceans and seven annular continents. The last of the oceans is surrounded by a huge mountain wall. (See Heine-Geldern 1942, 17). In fact Buddhist kings in Lanka appear to have borrowed freely from both of these models of the universe, treating them as if they were virtually synonymous.

5. The symbol of the cosmic tree and the lotus will be dealt with in detail in chapters 5 and 6.

6. As usual in South Asian mythology, there is disagreement upon the location of Lake Anotatta. For example, it is sometimes considered to be one of the seven great lakes of the Himalayas (see *Mahavamsa* 1950, 3), while at other times it is equated

with the pond of Sakra, which would place it on top of Mount Meru rather than Himalaya (Obeyesekere 1984, 334). Sakra's palace on the top of Meru did in fact have a lake, although it is questionable that it was Anotatta (Godage 1945, 57). Mabbett (1983, 66, 69) also associates Meru with Lake Anotatta, as does Rowland (1953a, 70), who writes that a shaft magically arises out of the lake on Meru every morning lifting up a throne for the sun at noon, and then sinking back into the lake again in the afternoon.

7. The *Anotatta Waruna* departs from the usual symbolism of the elephant at the eastern gate (see for example, T.B. Karunaratne's (1978, 113–114) discussion "The Astamangala figure on an *attani* pillar of Sena I from Kivulekada, Sri Lanka." Perhaps the author of the *Kavi* thought that a lion should occupy the exalted eastern position because of the lion's prominence in Sinhalese mythology.

8. This account of the Ahas Ganga flowing out of Lake Anotatta appears to be based upon a *Puranic* account of the waters flowing off Meru. According to the *Puranas*, after the heavenly Ganges falls upon the summit of Meru it divides into four branches, flowing towards the four cardinal points. The four branches pass through four rocks carved in the shape of animal heads: to the south a bull, to the west a horse, to the east an elephant, and to the north a lion. Before the heavenly stream divides in four it encircles Meru through seven channels for a space of 84,000 *yoganas*. After this each falls off Meru into a lake and hence into the ocean. (See Ali 1973, 61–62).

9. See Mahabharata (1973), *Visnu Purana* (1952).

10. Culavamsa (1953b, 49) notes that the *danavas* are *asuras*.

11. According to the *Mahabharata* the poison was swallowed by Siva, which accounts for the discoloration of his throat (see Stutley and Stutley 1984, 265).

12. The *Visnu Purana* (1952) attributes the seizure of the *amrita* to the demon Rahu who causes the eclipse of the moon. This account omits any reference to the *danavas*.

13. Mahabharata, volume I, 15–17, 23 in O'Flaherty (1980); Zimmer 1974, 16–18; Stutley and Stutley 1984, 265.

14. *Rg Veda* (I.23, 19–20) quoted in Stutley and Stutley 1984, 11.

15. *Rg Veda* (VII.57, 6; IX.74, 4; X.139, 6). See Stutley and Stutley 1984, 11.

16. Remember that at the time of the churning the cow of fertility emerged, as did the white elephant who is seen as a theriomorphic form of the rain-producing cloud. I will return later in more detail to the theme of the elephant as a symbol of fertility.

17. See the myth of the emergence of the moon from the ocean and of Rahu's attempt to swallow the *amrita* in it.

18. Technically, *amrita* is a celestial elixir while *soma*, by ritualistic definition, is a sacrificial libation offered to the gods and then drunk by the officiating priests. Although this distinction is not always made, the former is usually described in mythical terms while the latter is thought to be derived from a plant. During the Gupta period the term *soma* was applied to twenty-four different types of plants. It was used medicinally in order to prevent death and the decay of the body. The juice of the *soma* plant was ritually extracted by pricking the bulb with a golden needle and trapping the milky sap in a golden vessel (see Stutley and Stutley 1984, 11, 283). Here we can see that although *soma* is "natural" in that it comes from a plant, it has the properties of *amrita*.

19. *Rg Veda* (III.48, 2) quoted in Stutley and Stutley 1984, 282.

20. Whereas this model applies in areas of Asia influenced by India, it does not as Eliade suggests apply to the ancient Near East. J.Z. Smith (1987, 16), citing R.J. Clifford (1972), argues that Eliade misinterpreted the Near Eastern material when he

claimed that the temple was assimilated to the cosmic mountain.
21. Gogerly (1884, 195) cites *Samyutta Nikaya* (1917) to the effect that the sun and the moon circle Meru half-way up its sides.
22. There are a variety of different accounts of the shape of Mount Meru in the *Puranas*. Some say that it is an inverted cone, others that it is quadrangular, octagonal or twisted like a braided hair (Ali 1973, 48). We shall see in chapters 6 and 7 how these various shapes of Mount Meru are reproduced in Kandyan architecture.
23. According to the *Asura Bhawana Kavi* (1954, 89), Mount Meru rests upon three peaks and the *asuras* live in the valleys between these peaks.
24. This city is also known as Masakkasana (Godage 1945, 57).
25. According to the Puranic version of the myth of Meru (Dimmitt and Van Buitenen 1978, 28), not only the city of Sakra and his thirty-two gods, but also the cities of Brahma, Siva, and Visnu are located on the square top of Meru.
26. Tambiah (1976, 102–103) notes that more complex systems have a central point surrounded by the nine directions, hence the prevalence of five- and eight-unit spatial and political systems throughout Indian Asia. These systems are frequently encountered in the Kandyan landscape.
27. There are some similarities between this mode of thought and that which is described by Foucault (1970) as a sixteenth-century paradigm of resemblances. For an account of magical belief and its decline in Europe, see Thomas (1978). Examples of the use of tropes such as metaphor, metonymy, and synecdoche to characterize different modes of consciousness can be found in Frye (1982), White (1978), Vico (1968), K. Burke (1945), and Benveniste (1971). Also, it could be argued (as per White 1978, 26) that Marx's analysis of commodities in *Capital*, volume 1 (1967, 71–83) uses the theory of tropes to understand the "language of commodities." For a review of magical and mythic conceptions of space see Sack (1980, chapter 6).
28. For a more general discussion of ancient Indian cities see Puri (1966), and Chaudhury (1969).
29. See also *A Guide to Anuradhapura* (1981).
30. The symbolism of consecration will be discussed in detail in chapter 7.
31. See Eliade (1959), especially chapter 1, entitled "Archetypes and Repetition."
32. For more detail on the layout of Sigiri see R.H. De Silva (1971), and Bandaranayake (1984).
33. Mount Kailasa is thought to be one of the mountains in the cosmic Himalayas, and one of the abodes of the gods Siva, Kuvera, and occasionally of Sakra (see B.L. Smith 1978a, 92; Zimmer 1974, 198; Ali 1873, 55–56; Obeyesekere 1984, 97, 100.) Sakra is thought to abide there, as elements of Siva are appropriated to Sakra in some Lankan myths.
34. For a detailed description of Polonnaruva see *Ancient City of Polonnaruva* (1967), *A Guide to Polonnaruva* (1982), Prematilleke (1982a; 1982b).
35. We shall see that the last king of Kandy, Sri Vikrama, sought to emulate Parakramabahu by constructing the great artificial lake which formed the southern border of his capital in the early nineteenth century.
36. As Obeyesekere (1984, 342) points out, in Buddhist thought the *makara* is a mythical dragon.
37. This problem of the tension between doing good works and building to achieve the cosmic metaphor is very interesting. See chapter 8 for an examination of the difficulties which the last king of Kandy faced when he undertook just such a large project in the early nineteenth century.

5. THE KANDYAN LANDSCAPE, 1312–1815

1. Paranavitana (1943, 310) points out that the Sinhalese believed that the gods dwelt in old trees and that the *na* or ironwood tree (*mesua ferrea*) was particularly favored by the gods. The *na*, along with the bo tree, being inhabited by gods was prohibited from being cut down. Natha is thought by the Sinhalese to be Maitreya, the future Buddha who will attain enlightenment under a *na* tree (R.F. Gombrich 1971, 162).
2. Codrington (1943, 28) argues that Viravikrama possibly had the *devale* rebuilt.
3. One must, as Obeyesekere (1984, 345) reminds us, beware of accepting Knox's words as the absolute truth for although he was detained in the Kandyan Kingdom for twenty years and was relatively free to roam about, he spent little time in Kandy itself.
4. For a definition and discussion of allegorical portraiture see Hemeren (1969).
5. He is also thought of at times as the minister of the god Kataragama (Obeyesekere 1963, 144).
6. It is unclear from the text where this reservoir was located. Perhaps it was near Gampola.
7. The role that the river played in court ritual in the eighteenth century will be discussed in detail in chapter 7.
8. It should be kept in mind that this account was written to honor Ahalepola, ex-first *adikar*, pretender to the throne, and enemy of the late king. It therefore sought to portray the king in an unfavorable light.
9. There is some dispute as to where exactly the Bora Veva was located. L.J.B. Turner (1918, 76) places this pond at the northern end of the city whereas Dolapihilla (1959, 276) places it in the southwestern portion of the city next to Lake Bogambara. The confusion arises because the pond was drained in 1820 during the construction of the road to Kurunegala (see *Ceylon National Archive* (1820); Colvin R. de Silva (1933, 211)). I assume that Karunaratne and Turner are correct about the location of the pond and that Dolapihilla is misinformed.

6. FROM DISCOURSE TO LANDSCAPE: A KINGLY READING

1. Eck (1982) has used a similar approach in her interpretation of the city of Banaras as a text which acts as a synecdoche for the whole of India. Blier (1987) has used the concepts of narrative, metaphor, and synecdoche in her interpretation of the housing of the Balammalika of Togo and Benin.
2. Actually Sinhalese monasteries in the ninth century conformed to this ideal plan better than cities did. They were square with two streets in the shape of a cross, four main gates and a rigorous orientation.
3. Hocart (1970, 250) writes that the traditional Indian capital stands for the whole world. Its parts represent regions of the world.
4. For a general discussion of natural symbols see Douglas (1970).
5. Raghavan on *Manu* 9, 321, quoted in O'Flaherty (1980, 214).
6. *Matsya Purana*, 175, 23–63 quoted in O'Flaherty (1980, 226).
7. Kertzer (1988, 11) argues that multivocality and ambiguity in ritual are useful as they allow political solidarity to be constructed even when there is no consensus. See also Munn (1973, 580), V. Turner (1967, 50), and G. Lewis (1980, 9).
8. *Matsya Purana*, 166.1–4; 167.58–59 in O'Flaherty (1980, 237).
9. The use of images and architecture as modes of instruction, what Pelikan (1974, 94)

termed "books for the illiterate" has a long history in the West. Discussions of this point with reference to Byzantium can be found in Pelikan (1974, 91–98) and Kitzinger (1954); with reference to France and Italy see Duby (1981, 77, 78, 134, 135, 211, 265), Panofsky (1957, 44), and Baxandall (1972); with reference to Africa see Blier (1987, 36), and to Asia see Wheatley (1983, 424). For a discussion of the role of place in moral teaching see Basso (1987).

10. See Rowland (1953a, 15) and Davy (1821, 151) for a discussion of solar and lunar symbols on *dagobas*.

11. For a discussion of Meru gates see Rowland (1953a, 16).

12. The display described here took place in 1893 (Cumming 1893, 206–208).

13. Coomaraswamy (1972, 9, 47–49) points out that the Buddha was often substituted for Brahma in myth.

7. FROM LANDSCAPE TO CIVIC RITUAL: A KINGLY READING

1. In many respects my analysis in this chapter follows in the tradition of historians and anthropologists who have studied political rituals. Perhaps the classic work on the topic is Kantorowitz's *The King's Two Bodies* (1957). Of late there have been many interesting studies on this topic by researchers working at the interface of anthropology and history, see Kertzer (1988), Dirks (1987), Willentz (1985), Cannadine and Price (1987), Muir (1981), and Trexler (1980). A number of scholars have drawn attention to the importance of the role of place and landscape in the enactment of civic rituals, see Muir and Weissman (1989), Kertzer (1988, 9), Kuper (1972, 411–425), Trexler (1973, 126–127), Matthews (1971), Elias (1983), and Cancik (1985–1986).

2. This is a description of the cremation of Mahestane, heir to the throne of Kandy in 1612.

3. It is interesting to note that, in Thailand, Meru not only refers to the cosmic mountain, but to a royal funeral pyre as well (Griswold and Nagara 1975, 88). In nineteenth-century Bali the funeral tower was thought of both as Meru and as the heavens (Geertz 1980, 119).

4. For a detailed discussion of the *rājāsuya* see Heesterman (1957).

5. The irony of this was that only two of the four South Indian Nayakkar kings of Kandy in the eighteenth century could claim some connection to royal Indian lineage. Furthermore, the Nayakkars were of *sudra*, not *ksatriya*, descent as the Sinhalese believed, and therefore technically ineligible to be kings (Dewaraja 1972, 42–43). Needless to say, however, as far as the Sinhalese were concerned the Nayakkars were of pure *ksatriya* descent.

6. Before the Visnu Devale was built in Kandy in 1747 it is possible that the kings came to this same spot to receive the blessing of Dedimunda (Devata Bandara).

7. For an examination of the links between processions and social control in Europe and North Africa see Kertzer (1988, 23), Graham and Johnson (1979), Bergeron (1971), Strong (1973), and Geertz (1983b, 162).

8. It is interesting to note that V. Turner (1961; 1967; 1969) found that in Central Africa trees with white sap were also used in rituals to symbolize fertility and semen.

9. The most detailed descriptions of the Asala Perahara are found in Aluvihare (1952) and H.L. Seneviratne (1978a) and I draw heavily upon their descriptions in my own discussion of the festival.

10. This howdah was built in the time of Kirti Sri (*Sangaraja Vata* 1955, 104, v. 239).
11. Dutch embassies were often delayed in the late 1730s due to the illness of the king (Arasaratnam 1974, 13) and it is possible that this was the cause of Schnee's delay.
12. Boyd ([1782] 1973, 178–179) wished to bring fifty soldiers with him to Kandy in 1782 in order to impress the king. The Kandyans, on the other hand thought five or six should be adequate. They compromised with twenty-five, but Boyd worried about the impression that such a small number would make for, as he said, the soldiers "were by far the best part of my appearance."
13. The Dutch during the eighteenth century sent presents worth 10,000 to 15,000 guilders per year. These included rare birds and animals which they procured from their trading posts in India, Southeast Asia and the Middle East, and European goods of a more mundane nature such as needles and pins, mirrors, children's toys, and white shoulder-length wigs (Arasaratnam 1974, 8; Jonville 1948, 3; P.E. Pieris 1909, 193).
14. It is unclear whether the resthouses between Colombo and Kandy had doors leading to the four quarters. Jonville and Percival failed to note it if they did. Boyd ([1782] 1973, 162) described a resthouse made of small squares but with the central one both larger than the rest and elevated above the others. Again, it is unclear whether this elevation was common to the other resthouses, but went unnoted by the other ambassadors.
15. The Kandyans insisted that Boyd ([1782] 1973, 175–176) enter Kandy from this point even though it would take him thirty-seven difficult miles out of his way in order to do so.
16. In 1546 the Portuguese Ambassador De Souza was delayed at the river for five days until an auspicious time was suggested (O.M. de Silva 1967, 39).
17. In addition to the Kandyan troops who were irregulars serving only a small portion of each year, the king had his own personal guard of about 300 men who guarded the palace, plus non-Kandyan mercenaries who were Malays and Malabars (P.E. Pieris 1945a, 2).
18. European embassies often disputed the exact nature of the obeisance that they should pay the king. The Kandyans for their part treated the king with the respect due a god. All who came before the king had to make obeisance by three prostrations and receive all his orders and communicate with him on their knees, with head covered and without weapons (P.E. Pieris 1945a, 1, 3; D'Oyly 1929, 2).
19. This throne was presented to King Vimala Dharma Suriya II (1687–1707) by the Dutch Governor of Ceylon, Thomas Van Rhee, probably in the year 1693. It appears in the Dutch list of gifts for the years 1690–1700 as "one throne with accessories." It was probably manufactured in Colombo by Sinhalese craftsmen under Dutch supervision or in one of the Dutch settlements in India (Pearson 1929, 381–382). King Rajadhi (1780–1798) had it raised on a platform (Pearson 1933–1934, 383).
20. There is some dispute as to whether this four-cornered hat was a crown or not. It was certainly not a typical European crown in style, even though Andrews and Jonville refer to it as a crown. It is unclear whether the king was wearing his four-cornered hat when Boyd ([1782] 1973, 214) described him as wearing "a large crown," or whether it was such a hat that was sold at auction in London as part of the king's regalia in the year 1820 (W. Smith 1820).
21. High chiefs under the rank of *disava* or *adikar*, unless of royal descent, were forbidden to have gold embroidery on their hats. Only the king could wear a frill at the

edge of his hat and only members of the royal family could wear a spray of gems from the center of their hats (Nevill 1887, 4–5).

22. This is perhaps a measure of the influence which the first *adikar* Pilima Talavve exerted over the young king in 1800, for Andrews (J.P. Lewis 1917, 13) noted in 1796 that both *adikars* sat *outside* the king's alcove, one to the left and the other to the right. Hocart (1924–1928c, 208) cites Codrington (1921, 151), who said that chiefs were divided into *dakuṇu amsaya* and *varn amsaya* (right and left) according to their position in the hall of audience. The inscriptions on the pillars of the council hall in Polonnaruva show that these officials had their positions fixed on the right and left of the throne as early as the thirteenth century (Rhys Davids 1873, 246). If, as Hocart (1924–1928c, 208) believes is the case, the throne in Polonnaruva was at the southern end of the audience hall facing north, then the heir to the throne and the top nobles who sat on the king's right hand side sat on the auspicious eastern side. The throne in Kandy was at the southern end of the hall facing north and it is very likely that the first *adikar* Pilima Talavve sat to the right on the eastern side of the throne.

23. Apparently during the eighteenth century audiences with the king had become increasingly ritualized. Whereas in 1671 Raja Sinha II forbade his nobles direct contact with Europeans (Vimalananda 1973, lix) and spoke for hours directly to Ambassador Van Bystervelt (1890, 360), such interaction was not possible by the time of Ambassador Schnee's embassy in 1731–1732. Virtually all business of state was conducted between the ambassador and the nobles after the ambassador's audience with the king. Boyd ([1782] 1973, 218) in 1782 told the nobles during his audience with the king that he wished to talk to the king about trade, but the *adikars* refused to pass his message to the king, telling Boyd that they would discuss this with him after the audience. So powerful were the nobles at the beginning of the nineteenth century that Governor North complained "All communication with the king or the court by any other means than through the first *adigar* was impossible. I had tried to make known [to the king] my pacific wishes through the chief priest and the Dessave of Leuke but in vain" (North, n.d.).

24. The only ambassador during the eighteenth century who was given accommodation within the city of Kandy was Pybus in 1762. After some footdragging on the part of the Kandyans he was granted this request because the court was anxious to persuade the British to aid them against the Dutch. Pybus was, however, confined to his house in Kandy and was allowed to have no unsupervised communication with any of the people in the city. In the sixteenth and early seventeenth centuries, however, ambassadors were regularly lodged in a resthouse within the city (O.M. De Silva 1967, 2; P.E. Pieris 1913, 321).

25. Jan Schreuder ([1762] 1946, 11), the Dutch Governor of Ceylon in 1762 was equally disgusted with court ceremonial. "We cannot even stir, much less derive suitable profits from our conquest, [of the coastal portion of the Island] if we did not continually, indeed to our loathing, flatter and caress the Court . . . [We] almost continually have to play the crouching little dog . . ."

8. FROM LANDSCAPE TO DISCOURSE: CONTESTATORY READINGS AND MATERIAL INTERESTS

1. The poverty of Kandy was compounded by the Europeans, who cut off much of the kingdom's lucrative trade with the outside.

2. Upon his arrival in Kandy with the English army in 1815 Lieutenant De Bussche (1815, 42) observed that the Kandy lake was enclosed on three sides by a stone wall, the fourth side being formed by the Kotagadolle Mountain.
3. Actually the *Ingrisi Hatana* claims that the king added twelve new streets. However, the Turner map of Kandy in 1815 (figure 8) only shows five new streets. It is unclear whether other small lanes were added that did not appear on the map, or if twelve was chosen as a more impressive number.
4. It is likely that Sri Vikrama was following some of the old canals dug around the city by Raja Sinha II in the seventeenth century.
5. See *Ahalepola Varnanava* (n.d.). Also see Dolapihilla (1959). The moving of a *devale* was not unheard of; in fact, as mentioned earlier, the Visnu Devale in Kandy was moved from Alut Nuvara in 1747 during the reign of Kirti Sri.
6. The irresolvable difficulty that all of the Nayakkar kings of Kandy faced was that the Tamils were the traditional enemies of the hero-kings of Lanka. Thus it must have been with a mixture of irony and fear that Sri Vikrama heard himself described in the *Ingrisi Hatana* ([c.1812] 1906, 5 v.34) as killing "the English as Dutthagamini [perhaps the greatest of the Sinhalese hero-kings] killed the Tamils."
7. On the use of ceremony to prop up unstable regimes in other parts of the world see Kuhrt (1987), Cameron (1987), and McMullen (1987).
8. Much more comprehensive accounts of the revolt that led to the fall of the Kandyan Kingdom are provided by P.E. Pieris (1945b), Colvin R. De Silva (1953), R. Pieris (1956), K.M. De Silva (1973), and Malalgoda (1976).
9. Governor North confided to General MacDowall in 1803 that the "king is more powerful than at any period since he mounted the throne, and his adherents appear to be strongly attached to his cause" (C.O. 54/10 1803d 1973).
10. The name Vadugas was derogatory and was used to stress the foreignness of these kings (Wijetunga 1958, 125).
11. A chain is sixty-six feet in length, which would make the dam 330 feet high. I have seen the dam at the end of the lake and it is probably no more than twenty feet in height. The figure of 330 feet is a typical example of hyperbole for dramatic effect that was employed in such types of court poetry.
12. The dots in the text represent words which the editor of D'Oyly's diaries was unable to decipher.
13. In the Kandyan Kingdom this meant not only following the laws of the kings of Lanka but also the Laws of Manu. Throughout Indian Asia it was thought that Manu had established laws and it was the king's duty to study and interpret them, not to be an innovative lawmaker himself (Griswold and Prasert Na Nagara 1975, 35–38). The Kandyans believed that their kings, as members of the Solar Dynasty, were descended from Mahasammata, the first king elected at the beginning of the *kalpa*. Manu, the law giver was also of this line (A. Gunasekara 1978, 132–133).
14. Sri Vikrama decided to remove the Malwatte Vihare outside of the city in order to expand the area of his planned lake. The monks of the *vihare* strongly opposed this plan, however, and presented him with a petition which, although it did not condemn the proposed action, placed the entire responsibility for the move upon the king. Sri Vikrama then reluctantly reversed his decision (Dewaraja 1972, 134).
15. For good examples of the small but growing literature on the historical reconstruction of peasants' attitudes see P. Burke (1978, 65–87), Ginzburg (1982; 1985), Sabean (1984), and Ladurie (1979; 1987).

16. Obeyesekere (1984, 334) notes that this refers to the third eye which Siva had in the middle of his forehead. Although the king saw himself as like Sakra in Lanka, attributes of Siva were often transferred to Sakra.

17. It is interesting to note that in the summer of 1983 there was a drought in Kandy and I heard people claim that the drought was caused by the misrule of the president of the country.

18. For a more detailed discussion of the cosmos as a cremation ground in the *Manimekalai* see Richman (1988, especially chapter 5).

References

Abrams, P. 1982. *Historical Sociology*. Ithaca: Cornell University Press
Agnew, J.A. 1989. The devaluation of place in social science. In *The Power of Place: Bringing Together Geographical and Sociological Imaginations*, ed. J.A. Agnew and J.S. Duncan, pp. 9–29. London: Unwin Hyman
A Guide to Anuradhapura. 1981. Central Cultural Fund. Colombo: Ministry of Cultural Affairs
A Guide to Polonnaruva. 1982. Central Cultural Fund. Colombo: Ministry of Cultural Affairs
Agulhon, M. 1982. *The Republic in the Village*. Cambridge: Cambridge University Press
  1985. Politics, images, and symbols in post-revolutionary France. In *Rites of Power: Symbolism, Ritual and Politics Since the Middle Ages*, ed. S. Willentz, pp. 177–205. Philadelphia: University of Pennsylvania Press
Ahalepola Varnanava/Vaduga Hatana. No date (originally early nineteenth century). Ed. B. Gunasekara. Colombo
Ali, S.M. 1973. *The Geography of the Puranas*. New Delhi: Peoples Publishing House
Althusser, L. 1971. *Lenin and Philosophy*. New York: Monthly Review Press
Aluvihare, R. 1952. *The Kandy Perahera*. Colombo: M.D. Gunasena
Ananthalwar, M.A. and A. Rao. 1921. *Indian Architecture. Volume I. Architectonics or Silpa Sastra*. Madras: A.Y.T. Iyer and Sons
Ancient City of Polonnaruva. 1967. Colombo: Archaeological Department of Ceylon
Andaya, B.W. 1978. Statecraft in the reign of Lu Tai of Sukhodaya (c.1347–1374). In *Religion and Legitimation of Power in Thailand, Laos, and Burma*, ed. B.L. Smith, pp. 2–19. Pennsylvania: Anima
Anderson, K. 1987. "Chinatown" as a public nuisance: the power of place in the making of a racial category. *Annals, Association of American Geographers*, 77: 580–598
  1988. Cultural hegemony and the race definition process in Chinatown, Vancouver, 1880–1980. *Environment and Planning D: Society and Space*, 6: 127–149
Anotatta Waruna. 1954 (originally eighteenth century). In *Sinhala Verse (Kavi)*, collected by H. Nevill, ed. P.E.P. Deranyagala, vol. I, p. 289. Colombo: Ceylon National Museums Manuscript Series, vol. IV
Arasaratnam, S. 1963. Vimala Dharma Suriya II (1687–1707) and his relations with the Dutch. *Ceylon Journal of History and Social Science*, 6: 59–70.
  1964. *Ceylon*. Englewood Cliffs: Prentice-Hall.
  1974. Introduction to J.S. Van Gollenesse, *Memoir of Julius Stein Van Gollenesse (Governor of Ceylon, 1734–1751). For His Successor Gerrit Joan Vreeland, 28 February 1751*, trans. and ed. S. Arasaratnam. Colombo: Department of National Archives

List of references

Ariyapala, M.B. 1956. *Society in Medieval Ceylon*. Colombo: K.V.G. De Silva
Aryan, K.C. 1981. *Basis of Decorative Element in Indian Art*. New Delhi: Rekha Prakashan
Asgiriye Talpata, 1969. Ed. M. Rohanadeera. Colombo: Privately published
Asura Bhawana Kavi. 1954 (originally sixteenth century). In *Sinhala Verse (Kavi)*, collected by H. Nevill, ed. P.E.P. Deranyagala, vol. II, p. 89. Colombo: Ceylon National Museums Manuscript Series, vol. IV
Baker, K.M. 1985. Memory and practice: politics and the representation of the past in eighteenth-century France. *Representations*, 11: 134–164
Baldeus, P. 1752. *Ceylon*. London: W.H. Allen
Bandarage, A. 1983. *Colonialism in Sri Lanka: The Political Economy of the Kandyan Highlands, 1833–1886*. Berlin: Mouton
Bandaranayake, S. 1984. *Sigiriya Project: First Archaeological Excavation and Research Report (January–September 1982)*. Unesco–Sri Lanka Project of the Cultural Triangle, Central Cultural Fund. Colombo: Ministry of Cultural Affairs
Barthes, R. 1977a. Rhetoric of the image. In *Image, Music, Text*, trans. S. Heath. New York: Hill and Wang
  1977b. The death of the author. In *Image, Music, Text*, trans. S. Heath, pp. 142–148. New York: Hill and Wang
  1979a. *The Eiffel Tower and Other Mythologies*. Trans. R. Howard. New York: Hill and Wang
  1979b. From work to text. In *Textual Strategies: Perspectives in Post-Structural Criticism*, ed. J.V. Harari, pp. 73–81. Ithaca: Cornell University Press
  1982. *Empire of Signs*. trans. R. Howard. New York: Hill and Wang
  1986a. *Mythologies*, trans. A. Lavers. New York: Hill and Wang
  1986b. The Blue Guide. In *Mythologies*, trans. A. Lavers, pp. 74–77. New York: Hill and Wang
  1987. La lumière du sud-ouest. In *Incidents*. Paris: Editions du Seuil
Basso, K. 1987. "Stalking with stories": names, places, and moral narratives among the western Apache. In *On Nature: Nature, Landscape, and Natural History*, ed. D. Halpern. San Francisco: North Point Press
Baxandall, M. 1972. *Painting and Experience in Fifteenth Century Florence*. Oxford: Oxford University Press
  1985. *Patterns of Intention: On the Historical Explanation of Pictures*. New Haven: Yale University Press
Bechert, H. 1978. The beginnings of Buddhist historiography: Mahavamsa and political thinking. In *Religion and Legitimation of Power in Sri Lanka*, ed. B.L. Smith, pp. 1–12. Chambersburg, Pa.: Anima
Bell, H.C.P. 1904. *Report on the Kegalla District*. Reprint of Archaeological Survey of Ceylon, 19, 1892. Colombo: Government Printer
  (ed. and trans.) 1915–1916. Letter from the Kandyan Court: 1726. *The Ceylon Antiquary and Literary Register*, I: 118–123
Bell, H.C.P. and A. Mendis Gunasekara Mudaliyar. 1915–1916. Kelani Vihara and its inscription. *The Ceylon Antiquary and Literary Register*, I: 145–161
Belsey, C. 1980. *Critical Practice*. London: Methuen
Benveniste, E. 1971. Remarks on the function of language in Freudian theory. In *Problems of General Linguistics*. Coral Gables, Fla.: University of Miami Press
Berger, J. 1972. *Ways of Seeing*. Harmondsworth: Penguin Books

Bergeron, D.M. 1971. *English Civil Pageantry*. London: Edward Arnold
Bertolacci, A. 1817. *A View of the Agricultural, Commercial and Financial Interests of Ceylon*. London: Black, Parbury, and Allen
Blier, S.P. 1987. *The Anatomy of Architecture: Ontology and Metaphor in Batammaliba Architectural Expression*. Cambridge: Cambridge University Press
Bloch, M. 1974. Symbols, song, dance and features of articulation: is religion an extreme form of traditional authority? *European Journal of Sociology*, 15: 55–81
Boyd, H. [1782] 1973. A journal of an embassy from the government of Madras to the king of Candy, in Ceylon in the year 1782. In *Miscellaneous Letters of Hugh Boyd*, ed. H. Boyd, pp. 107–264. Louisville, Ky.: Lost Cause Press
Brown, R. 1987. *Society as Text: Essays on Rhetoric, Reason, and Reality*. Chicago: University of Chicago Press
Burke, K. 1945. *A Grammar of Motives*. New York: Prentice Hall
  1969. *A Rhetoric of Motives*. Berkeley: University of California Press
  1970. *The Rhetoric of Religion: Studies in Logology*. Berkeley: University of California Press
Burke, P. 1978. *Popular Culture in Early Modern Europe*. New York: Harper and Row
Butler, C. 1984. *Interpretation, Deconstruction and Ideology*. New York: Oxford University Press
Buultjens, A.E. (trans.). [1765] 1899. Governor Van Eck's expedition against the king of Kandy, 1765. *Journal of the Ceylon Branch of the Royal Asiatic Society*, 16: 36–78
Cameron, A. 1987. The construction of court ritual: the Byzantine *Book of Ceremonies*. In *Rituals of Royalty: Power and Ceremonials in Traditional Societies*, ed. D. Cannadine and S. Price, pp. 106–136. Cambridge: Cambridge University Press
Campbell, J. 1974. *The Mythic Image*. Princeton: Princeton University Press
Cancik, H. 1985–1986. Rome as sacred landscape: Varro and the end of republican religion in Rome. *Visible Religion*, 4–5: 249–265.
Cannadine, D. and Price, S. (eds.) 1987. *Rituals of Royalty: Power and Ceremonials in Traditional Societies*. Cambridge: Cambridge University Press
Casie Chitty, S. 1834. *The Ceylon Gazetteer*. Ceylon: Cotta Church Mission Press
Ceylon National Archive. 1820. March 21 Board of Commissioners
Chaudhury, B.N. 1969. *Buddhist Centres in Ancient India*. Calcutta: Sanskrit College
Clifford, J. 1986. On ethnographic allegory. In *Writing Culture: The Poetics and Politics of Ethnography*, pp. 98–121. Berkeley: University of California Press
Clifford, J. and G.E. Marcus (eds.). 1986. *Writing Culture: The Poetics and Politics of Ethnography*. Berkeley: University of California Press
Clifford, R.J. 1972. *The Cosmic Mountain in Canaan and the Old Testament*. Cambridge, Mass.: Harvard University Press
Clifford, R.T. 1978. The Dhammadipa tradition of Sri Lanka: three models within the Sinhalese chronicles. In *Religion and Legitimation of Power in Sri Lanka*, ed. B.L. Smith, pp. 36–47. Chambersberg, PA.: Anima
C.O. (=Colonial Office) 54/10. [1803a] 1973. Letter to Lord Hobart from F. North, February 25, 1803. Reproduced in T. Vimalananda, *The British Intrigue in the Kandyan Kingdom of Ceylon*. Colombo: M.D. Gunasena
  [1803b] 1973. Letter to F. North from H. MacDowall, February 24, 1803.

Reproduced in T. Vimalananda, *The British Intrigue in the Kandyan Kingdom of Ceylon*. Colombo: M.D. Gunasena

[1803c] 1973. Translation of a Chingalese report of the Appoohamies lately sent to Candy with a letter, February 15, 1803. Reproduced in T. Vimalananda, *The British Intrigue in the Kandyan Kingdom of Ceylon*. Colombo: M.D. Gunasena

[1803d] 1973. Letter from F. North to H. MacDowall, March 18, 1803. Reproduced in T. Vimalananda, *The British Intrigue in the Kandyan Kingdom of Ceylon*. Colombo: M.D. Gunasena

C.O. 54/44. [1812] 1984. Copy number 16 written to the British by Ehelapola, September 6, 1812. Reproduced in T. Vimalananda, *Sri Wickrama, Brownrigg and Ehelepola*. Colombo: Gunasena

C.O. 54/52. [1814] 1953. Letter from D'Oyly to Brownrigg, August 16, 1814. Cited in C.R. De Silva, *Ceylon Under British Occupation: 1795–1833. Volume I: Its Political and Administrative Development*, pp. 144–150. Colombo: The Colombo Apothecaries' Company

Codrington, H.W. 1909. The Kandyan navandanno. *Journal of the Ceylon Branch of the Royal Asiatic Society*, 21: 221–253

(trans.). 1916–1917. The date of Kirttisri's accession. *Ceylon Antiquary and Literary Register*, 2: 156–157

1921. Right hand and left hand. *Journal of the Ceylon Branch of the Royal Asiatic Society*, 28: 151–152

(trans.). 1943. The Kandy Natha Devale Inscriptions. In *Epigraphia Zeylanica*, vol. IV (1934–41): 27–34, ed. S. Paranavitana. Oxford: Oxford University Press

Coedes, G. 1947. *Pour mieux comprendre Angkor*. Paris: Adrien Maisonneuve

Colebrooke, W.M.G. [1832] 1956. Report of Lieutenant-Colonel Colebrooke upon the compulsory services to which the natives of Ceylon are subject. Reproduced in G.C. Mendis (ed.), *The Colebrooke-Cameron Papers: Documents on British Colonial Policy in Ceylon, 1796–1833*, vol. I, pp. 189–211. Oxford: Oxford University Press

Coomaraswamy, A.K. 1931. *Yaksas Part 2*. Washington D.C.: Smithsonian Institution

1956. *Medieval Sinhalese Art*. 2nd edn. New York: Pantheon

1972. *Elements of Buddhist Iconography*. New Delhi: Munshiram Manoharlal

Cosgrove, D.E. 1978. Place, landscape and the dialectics of cultural geography. *Canadian Geographer*, 22: 269–282

1982. The myth and stones of Venice: an historical geography of a symbolic landscape. *Journal of Historical Geography*, 8: 145–169

1983. Towards a radical cultural geography: problems of theory. *Antipode*, 15: 1–11

1985. *Social Formation and Symbolic Landscape*. Totowa, N.J.: Barnes and Noble

1989. Power and place in the Venetian territories. In *The Power of Place: Bringing Together Geographical and Sociological Imaginations*, ed. J. Agnew and J.S. Duncan. London: Unwin Hyman

Cosgrove, D.E. and S. Daniels. 1988. *The Iconography of Landscape: Essays on the Symbolic Representation, Design, and Use of Past Environments*. Cambridge: Cambridge University Press

Culavamsa Part 1. 1953a. Trans. and ed. W. Geiger. Colombo: Ceylon Government Information Department

Culavamsa Part 2. 1953b. Trans. and ed. W. Geiger. Colombo: Ceylon Government Information Department

Cumming, C.F.G. 1893. *Two Happy Years in Ceylon*. London: Chatto and Windus
Dalada Vittiya. [c.1812] 1974. Ed. Puchibandara Sanasgala. No publisher
D'Alwis, J. 1858–1859. Notes on the mythological legends of the Sinhalese. *Journal of the Ceylon Branch of the Royal Asiatic Society*, 3: 10–42
Dambuve Nayaka Unnanse. [1857] 1956. Evidence in Malwatta Vihara Land Case, cited in R. Pieris, *Sinhalese Social Organization: The Kandyan Period*. Colombo: Ceylon University Press Board, p. 3.
Daniels, S. 1985. Arguments for a humanistic geography. In *The Future of Geography*, ed. R.J. Johnston, pp. 143–158. London: Methuen
  1987. The implications of industry: Turner and Leeds. *Turner Studies*, 9: 10–17.
  1988. The political iconography of woodland in later Georgian England. In *The Iconography of Landscape: Essays on the Symbolic Representation, Design, and Use of Past Environments*, ed. D.E. Cosgrove and S. Daniels, pp. 43–82. Cambridge: Cambridge University Press
Darian, S.G. 1978. *The Ganges in Myth and History*. Honolulu: University of Hawaii Press
Darnton, R. 1984. A bourgeois puts his world in order: the city as text. In *The Great Cat Massacre and Other Episodes in French Cultural History*, pp. 106–143. New York: Basic Books
Davis, N.Z. 1983. *The Return of Martin Guerre*. Cambridge, Mass.: Harvard University Press
Davy, J. 1821. *An Account of the Interior of Ceylon*. London: Longman, Hurst, Rees, Orme, and Brown
De Bussche, L. 1815. *Letters on Ceylon, 1815*. Typescript, Ceylon Room, University of Peradeniya library
De Casparis, J.G. 1961. New evidence on cultural relations between Java and Ceylon in ancient times. *Artibus Asiae*, 24: 241–248
De Certeau, M. 1984. *The Practice of Everyday Life*. Berkeley: University of California Press
  1985. Practices of space. In *On Signs*, ed. M. Blonsky, pp. 122–145. Baltimore: The Johns Hopkins University Press
De Man, P. 1979. *Allegories of Reading*. New Haven: Yale University Press
Derrett, J.D.M. 1956. The origins of the laws of the Kandyans. *University of Ceylon Review*, 14: 105–150
De Queyroz, F. [1687] 1930. *The Temporal and Spiritual Conquest of Ceylon*, trans. S. G. Perera. 2 volumes. Colombo: A.C. Richards, Acting Government Printer
De Silva, C.M.A. 1963–1965. The Satara Varan Devas or the Four Guardian Gods in Buddhism with a special study of their bronze statuettes in the Colombo National Museum. *Spolia Zeylanica*, 30: 165–172
De Silva, Colvin R. 1933. Colebrooke's secret reports on forced labor. *Ceylon Literary Register*. Third Series. Vol. III
  1953. *Ceylon Under British Occupation: 1795–1833. Volume I: its Political and Administrative Development*. Colombo: The Colombo Apothecaries' Company
De Silva, C.R. 1972. *The Portuguese in Ceylon, 1617–1638*. Colombo: Cave
De Silva, K.M. 1973. The Kandyan Kingdom and the British: the last phase, 1796–1818. In *University of Ceylon History of Ceylon*, III, ed. K.M. De Silva, pp. 12–33. Colombo: Colombo Apothecaries' Company
  1981. *A History of Sri Lanka*. Berkeley: University of California Press

List of references

De Silva, L. 1978. The symbolism of the Indrakila in the Parittamandapa. In *Senerat Paranavitana Commemoration Volume*, ed. K. Indrapala, L. Prematilleke, and J.E. Van Lohuizen de Leeuw, pp. 234–250. Leiden: E.J. Brill
  1980. *Buddhism: Beliefs and Practices in Sri Lanka*. Colombo: Wesley Press
De Silva, O.M. 1967. *Vikrama Bahu of Kandy: The Portuguese and the Franciscans (1542–1551)*. Colombo: M. D. Gunasena
De Silva, R.H. 1971. *Sigiriya*. Colombo: Department of Archaeology
Devorohane 1954. In *Sinhala Verse (Kavi)*, collected H. Nevill, P.E.P. Deranyagala, vol. II, p. 190. Colombo: Ceylon National Museums Manuscript Series, vol. V
Dewaraja, L.S. 1972. *The Kandyan Kingdom of Ceylon 1707–1760*. Colombo: Lake House
Dharmadasa, K.N.O. 1976. The Sinhala–Buddhist identity and the Nayakkar dynasty in the politics of the Kandyan kingdom, 1739–1815. *The Ceylon Journal of Historical and Social Studies*, new series, 6: 1–23
Dimmitt, C. and Van Buitenen, J.A.B. 1978. *Classical Hindu Mythology: A Reader in the Sanskrit Puranas*. Philadelphia: Temple University Press
Dirks, N.B. 1987. *The Hollow Crown: Ethnohistory of an Indian Kingdom*. Cambridge: Cambridge University Press
Dolapihilla, P. 1959. *In the Days of Sri Wickramarajasingha, Last King of Kandy*. Maharagama: Saman Press
Domosh, M. 1987. Imagining New York's first skyscrapers: 1875–1910. *Journal of Historical Geography*, 13: 233–248
Douglas, M. 1970. *Natural Symbols*. London: Barrie and Rockliff
D'Oyly, J. [1825] 1917. *Diary of Mr. John D'Oyly*, ed. H.W. Codrington. Colombo: Colombo Apothecaries
  1929. A sketch of the constitution of the Kandyan kingdom. *Ceylon Historical Journal*, 24. Colombo: Tisara Prakasakayo
Drekmeier, C. 1962. *Kingship and Community in Early India*. Palo Alto, Calif.: Stanford University Press
Duby, G. 1981. *The Age of Cathedrals: Art and Society 980–1420*. Trans. E. Levieux and B. Thompson. Chicago: University of Chicago Press
Duncan, J.S. 1980. The superorganic in American cultural geography. *Annals, Association of American Geographers*, 70: 181–198
Duncan, J.S. and N.G. Duncan. 1984. A cultural analysis of urban residential landscapes in North America: the case of the anglophile elite. In *The City in Cultural Context*, ed. J.A. Agnew, J. Mercer, and D.E. Sopher, pp. 255–276. London: Allen and Unwin
  1988. [Re] Reading the landscape. *Environment and Planning D: Society and Space*, 6: 117–126
Forthcoming. *The Text in the World: Toward a Critical Theory of Landscape Interpretation*. Baltimore: The Johns Hopkins University Press
Duncan, J.S. and D. Ley. Forthcoming. Cultural geography. In *Rethinking Human Geography: Society, Space and the Social Sciences*, ed. G. Smith, R. Martin, and D. Gregory. London: Macmillan
Eagleton, T. 1983. *Literary Theory: An Introduction*. Minneapolis: University of Minnesota Press
Eck, D. 1982. *Banaras: City of Light*. Princeton: Princeton University Press
  1987. The city as sacred center. In *The City as Sacred Center: Essays on Six Asian Contexts*, ed. B. Smith and H.B. Reynolds, pp. 1–11. Leiden: E.J. Brill

Eco, U. 1986. *Semiotics and the Philosophy of Language*. Bloomington, Ind.: Indiana University Press
  1987. Travels in hyperreality. In *Travels in Hyperreality*, pp. 1–58. Bungay, Suffolk: Picador
Ehelepola [Ahalepola]. 1815. *Letter from Ehelepola to the Maturata Chiefs*. Transcript, Ceylon Room. University of Peradeniya library
Eliade, M. 1959. *Cosmos and History: The Myth of Eternal Return*. New York: Pantheon
  1973. *Patterns in Comparative Religion*. Westford, Mass.: New American Library
Elias, N. 1983. *The Court Society*, trans. E. Jephcott. New York: Pantheon
Epigraphia Zeylanica 1912. *Jetavanarama Slab Inscription (No. 1) of Mahinda IV (circa 1026–1042 A.D.)*. Vol. I (1904–1912), pp. 213–229. Oxford: Oxford University Press
  1943a. *The Ampitiya Rock Inscription*, trans. H.W. Codrington, ed. S. Paranavitana, vol. IV (1934–1941), pp. 271–273. Oxford: Oxford University Press
  1943b. *The Sagama Rock Inscription of Bhuvanaikabahu V*, trans. and ed. S. Paranavitana, vol. IV (1934–1941), pp. 296–311. Oxford: Oxford University Press
  1943c. *The Gadaladeniya Inscription of Senasammata Vikrama Bahu*, trans. H.W. Codrington, ed. S. Paranavitana, vol. IV (1934–1941), pp. 8–15. Oxford: Oxford University Press
  1943d. *The Kandy Natha Devale Inscriptions*, trans. H.W. Codrington, ed. S. Paranavitana, vol. IV (1934–1941), pp. 27–34. Oxford: Oxford University Press
Evers, H.D. 1972. *Monks, Priests and Peasants: A Study of Buddhism and Social Structure in Central Ceylon*. Leiden: E.J. Brill
Fernando, C.M. 1896. The inauguration of the king in ancient Ceylon. *Journal of the Ceylon Branch of the Royal Asiatic Society*, 14: 125–130
Filliozat, J. 1954. Le Symbolism du monument de Phnom Bakheng. *Bulletin de l'Ecole Française d'Extreme-Orient*, 44: 527–554
Fish, S. 1980. *Is There a Text in This Class?* Cambridge, Mass.: Harvard University Press
Fletcher, A. 1964. *Allegory: the Theory of a Symbolic Mode*. Ithaca: Cornell University Press
Foucault, M. 1967. *Madness and Civilization: A History of Insanity in the Age of Reason*, trans. R. Howard. London: Tavistock
  1970. *The Order of Things*. New York: Random House
  1975. Film and popular memory: an interview with Michel Foucault. Trans. M. Jordin. *Radical Philosophy*, 11: 24–29
  1976. *The Archaeology of Knowledge and the Discourse on Language*. New York: Harper and Row
Fritz, J.M. 1986. Vijayanagara: authority and meaning of a South Indian imperial capital. *American Anthropologist*, 88: 44–55
Frye, N. 1971. *Anatomy of Criticism*. Princeton: Princeton University Press
  1982. *The Great Code: The Bible and Literature*. San Diego, Calif.: Harcourt, Brace, Jovanovich
Gadamer, H.-G. 1986. *Truth and Method*. New York: Crossroad
Geertz, C. 1973a. *The Interpretation of Cultures*. New York: Basic Books
  1973b. Thick description: toward an interpretive theory of culture. In *The Interpretation of Cultures*, pp. 3–32. New York: Basic Books

1973c. Deep play: notes on the Balinese cockfight. In *The Interpretation of Cultures*, pp. 412–454. New York: Basic Books
1980. *Negara: The Theatre State in Nineteenth Century Bali*. Princeton: Princeton University Press
1983a. Blurred genres: the refiguration of social thought. In *Local Knowledge: Further Essays in Interpretive Anthropology*, pp. 19–35. New York: Basic Books
1983b. Centers, kings, and charisma: reflections on the symbolics of power. In *Local Knowledge: Further Essays in Interpretive Anthropology*, pp. 121–146. New York: Basic Books
Geiger, W. 1960. *Culture of Ceylon in Medieval Times*, ed. H. Bechert. Weisbaden: O. Harrassowitz
Giddens, A. 1976. Hermeneutics, ethnomethodology, and problems of interpretive analysis. In *The Uses of Controversy in Sociology*, ed. L. Coser and O.N. Larsen, pp. 315–328. New York: Free Press
1979. *Central Problems in Social Theory: Action, Structure and Contradiction in Social Analysis*. Berkeley: University of California Press
1984. Hermeneutics and social theory. In *Hermeneutics: Questions and Prospects*, ed. G. Shapiro and A. Sica, pp. 215–230. Amherst, Mass.: University of Massachusetts Press
Ginzburg, C. 1982. *The Cheese and the Worms: The Cosmos of a Sixteenth Century Miller*. Harmondsworth: Penguin Books
1985. *The Night Battles: Witchcraft and Agrarian Cults in the Sixteenth and Seventeenth Centuries*. Harmondsworth: Penguin Books
Glacken, C.J. 1967. *Traces on the Rhodian Shore: Nature and Culture in Western Thought From Ancient Times to the Beginning of the Eighteenth Century*. Berkeley: University of California Press
Godage, C. 1945. The place of Indra in early Buddhism. *University of Ceylon Review*, 2–3: 41–72
Godakumbura, C.E. No date. *Guardstones*. Colombo: Ceylon Government Archaeological Department
Gogerly, D.J. 1884. Buddhism. *The Orientalist*, 1: 193–205
Gokhale, B.G. 1966. Early Buddhist kingship. *Journal of Asian Studies*, 26: 15–22
Gombrich, E.H. 1961. *Art and Illusion*. Princeton: Princeton University Press
1972. *Symbolic Images: Studies in the Art of the Renaissance II*. Chicago: University of Chicago Press
Gombrich, E.H., J. Hochberg, and M. Black. 1972. *Art, Perception and Reality*. Baltimore: The Johns Hopkins University Press
Gombrich, R.F. 1971. *Precept and Practice: Traditional Buddhism in the Rural Highlands of Ceylon*. London: Oxford University Press
Goodman, N. 1976. *Languages of Art*. Indianapolis, Ind., Hackett
Graham, V.E. and W.M. Johnson. 1979. *The Royal Tour of France by Charles IX and Catherine de'Medici: Festivals and Entries, 1564–1566*. Toronto: University of Toronto Press
Greenwald, A. 1978. The relic of the spear: historiography and the saga of Dutthagamani. In *Religion and Legitimation of Power in Sri Lanka*, ed. B.L. Smith, pp. 13–25. Chambersburg, Penn.: Anima
Griswold, A.B. and Prasert Na Nagara, 1975. On kingship and society at Sukhodaya. In *Change and Persistence in Thai Society: Essays in Honor of Lauriston Sharp*,

ed. G.W. Skinner and A.T. Kirsch, pp. 29–92. Ithaca: Cornell University Press

Gunasekara, A. 1978. Rajakariya or the duty to the king in the kingdom of Sri Lanka. In *The Concept of Duty in South Asia*, ed. W.D. O'Flaherty and J.D.M. Derrett. New Delhi: Vikas

Gunasekara, B. 1895. *A Contribution to the History of Ceylon: Translated from Pujavaliya*. Colombo: H.C. Cottle

Gunatilaka, R.A. 1975. Ancient stupa architecture: the significance of cardinal points and the Catummahapatha concept. *Ceylon Journal of History and Social Science*, 5: 38–48

Gunawardana, R.A.L.H. 1971. Irrigation and hydraulic society in early medieval Ceylon. *Past and Present*, 53: 3–27

Harootunian, H.D. 1988. *Things Seen and Unseen: Discourse and Ideology in Tokugawa Nativism*. Chicago: University of Chicago Press

Hayley, F.A. 1921. *A Treatise on the Laws and Customs of the Sinhalese Including Portions Still Surviving Under the Name Kandyan Law*. Colombo: H.W. Cave

Heesterman, J.C. 1957. *The Ancient Indian Royal Consecration: The Rajasuya Described According to the Yajus Texts and Annotated*. The Hague: Mouton

  1978. The conundrum of the king's authority. In *Kingship and Authority in South Asia*, ed. J.F. Richards. South Asian Studies Publication, no. 3, pp. 1–27. Madison, Wis.: University of Wisconsin Press

  1985. *The Inner Conflict of Tradition: Essays in Indian Ritual, Kingship, and Society*. Chicago: University of Chicago Press

Heine-Geldern, R. 1930. Weltbild und Bauform in Sudostasien. *Wiener Beitrage zur Kunst- und Kulturgeschichte Asiens*, 4: 28–78

  1942. Conceptions of state and kingship in Southeast Asia. *Far Eastern Quarterly*, 2: 15–30

Hemeren, G. 1969. *Representation and Meaning in The Visual Arts: A Study in the Methodology of Iconography and Iconology*. Lund: Berlingska Boktryckeriet

Heydt, J.W. [1744] 1952. *Heydt's Ceylon*, trans. R. Raven-Hart. Colombo: Ceylon Government Information Department

Hobsbawm, E.J. and T. Ranger (eds.). 1983. *The Invention of Tradition*. Cambridge: Cambridge University Press

Hocart, A.M. 1924–1928a. The four quarters. *Ceylon Journal of Science*, section G, 1: 105–111

  1924–1928b. Notes on previous articles: the four quarters. *Ceylon Journal of Science*, section G, 1: 177–178

  1924–1928c. Duplication of office in the Indian state. *Ceylon Journal of Science*, section G, 1: 205–210

  1924–1928d. Archaeological summary: town planning. *Ceylon Journal of Science*, section G, 1: 150–156

  1924–1928e. The throne in Indian art. *Ceylon Journal of Science*, section G, 1: 117–123

  1924–1928f. The coronation ceremony. *Ceylon Journal of Science*, section G, 1:27–42

  1928a. Archeological summary: town planning. *Ceylon Journal of Science*, section G, 2: 86–87

  1928b. Archeological summary: moated sites. *Ceylon Journal of Science*, section G, 2: 87–88

1931. *The Temple of the Tooth in Kandy*. London: Luzac
1970. *Kings and Councillors: An Essay in the Comparative Anatomy of Human Society*. Chicago: University of Chicago Press
Hodder, I. 1986. *Reading the Past: Current Approaches in Archaeology*. Cambridge: Cambridge University Press
Hopkins, E.W. 1915. *Epic Mythology*. Strasburg: Verlag Von Karl J. Traubner
Inden, R. 1978. Ritual, authority, and cyclic time in Hindu kingship. In *Kingship and Authority in South Asia*, ed. J.F. Richards, South Asian Studies Publication no. 3, pp. 28–73. Madison, Wis.: University of Wisconsin Press
Ingrisi Hatana. [c.1812] 1906. Colombo: Privately published
Iser, W. 1978. *The Act of Reading*. Baltimore: The Johns Hopkins University Press
Jackson, J.B. 1984. *Discovering the Vernacular Landscape*. New Haven: Yale University Press
Jakobson, R. 1960. Linguistics and poetics. In *Style in Language*, ed. T. Sebeok, pp. 350–377. Cambridge, Mass.: M.I.T. Press
Jameson, F. 1981. *The Political Unconscious: Narrative as a Socially Symbolic Act*. Ithaca: Cornell University Press
Jatakas. 1962. Vol. 1. London: Pali Text Society
Jay, M. 1986. In the empire of the gaze: Foucault and the denigration of vision in twentieth century French thought. In *Foucault: A Critical Reader*, ed. D.C. Hoy, pp. 175–204. New York: Basil Blackwell
Jayatilaka, S. 1881. Sinhalese omens. *Journal of the Ceylon Branch of the Royal Asiatic Society*, 7: 147–151
Jonville, Mons. 1948. Narrative of the journey to Kandy made on the occasion of the embassy of Major General MacDowall in 1800. *Journal of the Ceylon Branch of the Royal Asiatic Society*, 38: 1–21
Kantorowitz, E.H. 1957. *The King's Two Bodies: A Study of Medieval Political Theology*. Princeton: Princeton University Press
Karunaratna, N. No date. *From Governor's Pavilion to President's Pavilion*. Colombo: Government Printer
Karunaratne, T.B. 1978. The astamangala figure on an attani pillar of Sena I from Kivulekada, Sri Lanka. In *Senerat Paranavitana Commemoration Volume*, ed. L. Prematilleke, K. Indrapala, and J.E. Van Lohuizen De Leeuw, pp. 107–115. Leiden: E.J. Brill
Karunatilake, A.D.P. 1958. *Senkadagala Pura Itihasaya*. Colombo.
Kautiliya Arthasastra 1972. Ed. R.P. Kangle, 3 vols. Bombay: Orient Longmans
Kavmini Kondola. 1905 (originally mid eighteenth century). Ed Samarajeewa Pallegama Lekam. Colombo.
Keppitipola, T.B. 1918. Map of Kandy town about the year 1815 A.D. *The Ceylon Antiquary*, 4: 75
Kertzer, D. 1988. *Ritual, Politics and Power*. New Haven: Yale University Press
Kirala Sandesaya [c.1816] 1958. Ed. C. Godakumbure. Colombo: Privately published
Kitzinger, E. 1954. The cult of images in the age before iconoclasm. *Dumbarton Oaks Papers*, 7: 85–150
Knox, R. 1681. *An Historical Relation of the Island of Ceylon in the East Indies*. London: Richard Chiswell
Kokila Sandesa. 1918–1919. Ed. and trans. W.F. Gunawardhana. *Ceylon Antiquary and Literary Register*, 4: 157–165

Krautheimer, R. 1983. *Three Christian Capitals: Topography and Politics.* Berkeley: University of California Press

Kuhrt, A. 1987. Usurpation, conquest and ceremonial: from Babylon to Persia. In *Rituals of Royalty: Power and Ceremonial in Traditional Societies,* ed. D. Cannadine and S. Price, pp. 20–55. Cambridge: Cambridge University Press

Kuper, H. 1971. The language of sites in the politics of space. *American Anthropologist,* 74: 411–425

LaCapra, D. 1983. Rethinking intellectual history and reading texts. In *Rethinking Intellectual History: Texts, Contexts, and Language,* pp. 23–71. Ithaca: Cornell University Press

Ladurie, E.L. 1979. *Montaillou: The Promised Land of Error.* New York: Vintage 1987. *Jasmin's Witch.* New York: George Braziller

Law, B.C. 1954–1955. The life of king Parakkamabahu I. *The Ceylon Historical Journal,* 4: 23–32

Lawrie, A.C. 1896. *A Gazetteer of the Central Provinces of Ceylon (Excluding Walapane).* Vol. I. Colombo: G.J.A. Skeen, Government Printer

1898. *A Gazetteer of the Central Provinces of Ceylon (Excluding Walapane).* Vol. II. Colombo: G.J.A. Skeen, Government Printer

No date. *Kandyan Law and History: Material Collected for two Projected Works.* Five folio volumes, no page numbers. Foreign and Commonwealth Office Library

Leach, E. 1966. Ritualization in man in relation to conceptual and social development. *Philosophical Transactions of the Royal Society,* series B, 251: 403–408

LeGoff, J. 1980. *Time, Work, and Culture in the Middle Ages.* Chicago: University of Chicago Press

LeMesurier, C.J.R. and T.B. Panabokke (trans.). 1880. *Niti-Nighanduva or The Vocabulary of Law: As it Existed in the Last Days of the Kandyan Kingdom.* Colombo: Government Printer

Lentricchia, F. 1983. *Criticism and Social Change.* Chicago: University of Chicago Press

Lewis, G. 1980. *Day of Shining Red: An Essay on Understanding Ritual.* Cambridge: Cambridge University Press

Lewis, J.P. 1912. Kandyan architecture. In *The Book of Ceylon,* ed. H. Cave, pp. 324–377. London: Cassell and Company

1917. Andrews' Embassies to Kandy in 1795 and 1796. *Journal of the Ceylon Branch of the Royal Asiatic Society,* 26, no. 70: 49–100, 115–155, 172–229; no. 71: 6–36

Lewis, P. 1979. Axioms for reading the landscape: some guides to the American scene. In *The Interpretation of Ordinary Landscapes,* ed. D.W. Meinig, pp. 11–32. New York: Oxford University Press

Ley, D.F. 1987. Styles of the times: liberal and neo-conservative landscapes in inner Vancouver 1968–1986. *Journal of Historical Geography,* 13: 40–56

1989. Modernism, postmodernism and the struggle for place. In *The Power of Place: Bringing Together Geographical and Sociological Imaginations,* ed. J. A. Agnew and J.S. Duncan. London: Unwin Hyman

Lowenthal, D. 1985. *The Past is a Foreign Country.* Cambridge: Cambridge University Press

Lowenthal, D. and H.C. Prince, 1965. English landscape tastes. *Geographical Review,* 55: 186–222

List of references

Lyotard, J.-F. 1984. *The Postmodern Condition: A Report on Knowledge*, trans. G. Bennington and B. Massumi. Minneapolis, Minn.: University of Minnesota Press
Mabbett, I.W. 1983. The symbolism of Mount Meru. *History of Religions*, 23: 64–83
Macdonell, D. 1986. *Theories of Discourse: An Introduction*. Oxford: Basil Blackwell
MacDowall, H. [1800] 1932. Letter of Hay MacDowall to Frederic North, Gannoruwa, 10th April, 1800. *Ceylon Literary Register*, third series, 2: 457
Madhavia, A. 1923. *Manimekalai*. Madras: India Publishing House
Maga Salakuna. 1947. (Originally early seventeenth century). Trans. and ed. E. Peiris. *Journal of the Ceylon Branch of the Royal Asiatic Society*, 37: 205–220
Mahabharata. 1973. Vol. I. Trans. and ed. J.A.B. Van Buitenen. Chicago: University of Chicago Press
Mahavamsa: or the Great Chronicle of Ceylon. 1950. Trans. and ed. W. Geiger. Colombo: Ceylon Government Information Department
Maimataya. No date. Ed. H.P. Perera Appuhamay. Colombo: Privately published
Maitri Upanisad. 1975. In *The Thirteen Principal Upanisads*, ed. R.E. Hume, 2nd edn. New York: Oxford University Press
Malalgoda, K. 1976. *Buddhism in Sinhalese Society 1750–1900: A Study of Religious Revival and Change*. Berkeley: University of California Press
Manu Dharmasastra or the Laws of Manu. 1887. Ed. J. Jolly, trans. A.C. Burnell and E.W. Hopkins. London: Trubnells Oriental Series
Marasinghe, M.M.J. 1974. *The Gods in Early Buddhism*. Kelaniya: University of Sri Lanka, Vidyalankara Campus
Marcus, G. and D. Cushman, 1982. Ethnographies as texts. *Annual Review of Anthropology*, 2: 25–69
Marcus, G. and M. Fischer, 1986. *Anthropology as Cultural Critique: An Experimental Moment in the Human Sciences*. Chicago: University of Chicago Press
Marx, K. 1967. *Capital : A Critique of Political Economy Volume I: The Process of Capitalist Production*. New York: International Publishers
Matthews, T.F. 1971. *The Early Churches of Constantinople: Architecture and Liturgy*. University Park, Pa.: Pennsylvania State University Press
McMullen, D. 1987. Bureaucrats and cosmology: the ritual code of T'ang China. In *Rituals of Royalty: Power and Ceremonial in Traditional Societies*, ed. D. Cannadine and S. Price, pp. 181–236. Cambridge: Cambridge University Press
Meinig, D.W. 1979a. The beholding eye: ten versions of the same scene. In *The Interpretation of Ordinary Landscapes*, pp. 33–50. New York: Oxford University Press
  1979b. *The Interpretation of Ordinary Landscapes*. New York: Oxford University Press
  1979c. Symbolic landscapes: models of American community. In *The Interpretation of Ordinary Landscapes*, pp. 164–194. New York: Oxford University Press
  1983. Geography as an art. *Transactions, Institute of British Geographers*, new series, 8: 314–328
Mendis, G.C. 1945. *The Early History of Ceylon*. Calcutta: Y.M.C.A. Publishing House
Millava, Disava of Vellassa. 1817. Account of the Kandy Perahara. *Ceylon Government Gazette*, August 19, 1817. Colombo
Millon, H.A. and L. Nochlin (eds). 1978. *Art and Architecture in the Service of Politics*. Cambridge, Mass.: M.I.T. Press

Mills, C.A. 1988. Life on the upslope: the post-modern landscape of gentrification. *Environment and Planning D: Society and Space*, 6: 169–189
Mitchell, W.J.T. (ed.) 1980. *The Language of Images*. Chicago: University of Chicago Press
  1986. *Iconology: Image, Text, Ideology*. Chicago: University of Chicago Press
Moligoda Sannasa. [1814] 1904. Reproduced in H.C.P. Bell, *Report on the Kegalla District*. Reprint of Archaeological Survey of Ceylon 19, 1892, 1904. Colombo: Government Printer
Moratota Vata. 1798. Ed. C. De Silva. Colombo
Mudiyanse, N. 1959. *The Art and Architecture of the Gampola Period (1341–1415)*. Colombo: M.D. Gunasena
Muir, E. 1981. *Civic Ritual in Renaissance Venice*. Princeton: Princeton University Press
Muir, E. and R.F.E. Weissman. 1989. Social and symbolic places in renaissance Venice and Florence. In *The Power of Place: Bringing Together Geographical and Sociological Imaginations*, ed. J.A. Agnew and J.S. Duncan. London: Unwin Hyman
Munn, N. 1973. Symbolism in ritual context: aspects of symbolic action. In *Handbook of Social and Cultural Anthropology*, ed. J.J. Honigmann, pp. 579–612. Chicago: Rand McNally
Mus, P. 1937. Angkor in the time of Jayavarman VII. *Indian Arts and Letters*, 11: 65–75
Nanayakkara, V. 1977. *Return to Kandy*. Colombo: Arasan Press
Neusner, J. 1975. The study of religion as the study of tradition. *History of Religions*, 14: 191–206
Nevill, H. 1887. The Kandyan hat. *The Taprobanian*, 2: 4–5
Norris, C. 1985. *Contest of Faculties: Philosophy and Theory after Deconstruction*. London: Methuen
North on his dealings with the King and the Adigar. [No date] 1973. Reproduced in T. Vimalananda, *The British Intrigue in the Kandyan Kingdom of Ceylon*, 1973. Colombo: M.D. Gunnasena
Obeyesekere, G. 1963. The great tradition and the little in the perspective of Sinhalese Buddhism. *Journal of Asian Studies*, 22: 139–153
  1984. *The Cult of the Goddess Pattini*. Chicago: University of Chicago Press
O'Flaherty, W.D. 1980. *Women, Androgenies and Other Mythical Beasts*. Chicago: University of Chicago Press
  1984. *Dreams, Illusion and Other Realities*. Chicago: University of Chicago Press
Outhwaite, W. 1987. *New Philosophies of Social Science: Realism, Hermeneutics and Critical Theory*. London: Macmillan
Panawatta, S. 1978. Treasures of Kandy's Lake. *The Sunday Observer*, October 29, p. 17
  1983. The showpiece of Kandyan architecture. *Weekend*, July 25, p. 23
Panditha, V. 1954–1955. Buddhism during the Polonnaruwa period. *Ceylon Historical Journal*, 4: 113–129
Panofsky, E. 1957. *Gothic Architecture and Scholasticism: An Inquiry into the Analogy of the Arts, Philosophy, and Religion in the Middle Ages*. New York: Meridian

1972. *Studies in Iconography: Humanistic Themes in the Art of the Renaissance.* New York: Harper and Row
1982. *Meaning in the Visual Arts.* Chicago: University of Chicago Press
Paranavitana, S. 1928. Mahayanism in Ceylon. *Ceylon Journal of Science* 2: 35–71
  1932. Religious intercourse between Ceylon and Siam in the 13th–15th centuries. *Journal of the Ceylon Branch of the Royal Asiatic Society*, 32: 190–213
  (trans.). 1943. The Sagama Rock Inscription of Bhuvanaikabahu V. *Epigraphia Zeylanica*, ed. S. Paranavitana, vol. IV (1934–1941), pp. 296–311. Oxford: Oxford University Press
  1950. Sigiri: abode of a god king. *Journal of the Ceylon Branch of the Royal Asiatic Society*, new series, 1: 129–161
  1954. *Report of the Archaeological Survey of Ceylon, 1953.* Part 4: Education, Science and Art (G), appendix. Colombo: Government Printer
  1956. Political and social conditions of medieval Ceylon. In *Sir Paul Pieris Felicitation Volume.* Colombo: Colombo Apothecaries
  1972. *Glimpses of Ceylon's Past.* Colombo: Lake House
Parangi Hatana. No date. Ed. T.S. Hemakumar. Manuscript, Ceylon Room, University of Peradeniya library
Parker, H. 1909. *Ancient Ceylon.* London: Luzac
Pearson, J. 1929. The throne of the kings of Kandy. *Journal of the Ceylon Branch of the Royal Asiatic Society*, 31: 380–383
  1933–1934. The throne of the kings of Kandy. *Ceylon Literary Register*, third series, 3: 382–384
Pelikan, J. 1974. *The Spirit of Eastern Christendom (600–1700). The Christian Tradition: A History of the Development of Doctrine.* Volume II. Chicago: University of Chicago Press
Percival, R. 1803. *An Account of the Island of Ceylon.* London: C.R. Baldwin
Perera, E.A. 1916. *Sinhalese Banners and Standards.* Memoirs of the Colombo Museum, series A, number 2. Colombo: Government Printer
Pieris, P.E. 1909. The Dutch embassy to Kandy in 1731–32: diary of Wijesuriwardhana Maha Mudiyanse, otherwise called Lewis de Saran Maha Mudaliyar. *Journal of the Ceylon Branch of the Royal Asiatic Society*, 21: 187–220
  1913. *Ceylon: The Portuguese Period.* Vol. I. Colombo: Colombo Apothecarie
  1914. *Ceylon: The Portuguese Period.* Vol. II. Colombo: Colombo Apothecarie
  1945a. Some political conventions and social customs of the Sinhalese. *University of Ceylon Review*, 3: 1–10
  1945b. *Tri Simhala: The Last Phase 1796–1815.* Colombo: Colombo Apothecaries
  and J. Crosby. 1945. A report on Buddhism in Siam, 1689. *Journal of the Ceylon Branch of the Royal Asiatic Society*, 36: 100–111
Pieris, R. 1951. Society and ideology in Ceylon during a time of troubles, 1795–1850, Part 2, *University of Ceylon Review*, 9: 266–279
  1956. *Sinhalese Social Organization: The Kandyan Period.* Colombo: Ceylon University Press Board
Pratt, M.L. 1986. Scratches on the face of the country; or what Mr. Barrow saw in the land of the bushmen. In *"Race," Writing, and Difference*, ed. H.L. Gates, pp. 138–163. Chicago: University of Chicago Press
Prematilleke, P.L. 1982a. *Alahana Parivena Polonnaruva: Second Archaeological*

Excavation Report (October 1981–March 1982). Unesco–Sri Lanka Project of the Cultural Triangle, Central Cultural Fund. Colombo: Ministry of Cultural Affairs

1982b. *Alahana Parivena Polonnaruva: Third Archaeological Excavation Report* (April–September 1982). Unesco–Sri Lanka Project of the Cultural Triangle, Central Cultural Fund. Colombo: Ministry of Cultural Affairs

1983. *First Archaeological Excavation Report (December 1981–May 1982)*. Unesco–Sri Lanka Project of the Cultural Triangle, Kandy Project. Colombo: Central Cultural Fund

1986. Recent Archaeological Research on a Sri Lankan City Complex. Paper delivered at 15th Annual Conference on South Asian Studies. Madison, Wis., November 6–9

Przyluski, J. 1933. Pradakshina et prasavya en Indochine. *Festschrift fur M. Winternitz zum 70ten Geburtstag.*

Puri, B.N. 1966. *Cities of Ancient India*. Meerut: Meenakshi Prakashan

Pybus, J. [1762] 1958. *The Pybus Embassy to Kandy, 1762*. Ed. P.E.P. Deraniyagala. The National Museums of Ceylon Historical Series, vol. 1. Colombo: Government Press

Quaritch-Wales, H.G. 1931. *Siamese State Ceremonies: Their History and Function*. London: Bernard Quaritch Ltd

Rajaratna Karaya. No date (originally eighteenth century). Ed. W. Saddananda. Colombo: Privately published

Rajasinha Hatana. 1966. Ed. E.H.M. Somarathne. Colombo

Rajavaliya: or a Historical Narrative of Sinhalese Kings. 1900 (originally late seventeenth century). Trans. B. Gunnasekara, Mudaliyar. Colombo: Skeen

Rappoport, R. 1979. *Ecology, Meaning, and Religion*. Richmond, Calif.: North Atlantic Books

Raven-Hart, R. 1956. The great road. *Journal of the Ceylon Branch of the Royal Asiatic Society*, new series, 4: 143–212

Reynolds, F.E. 1974. Dhammadipa: a study of Indianization and Buddhism in Sri Lanka. *Ohio Journal of Religious Studies*, 2: 63–78

Reynolds, H.B. 1987. Madurai: Koyil Nakar. In *The City as Sacred Center: Essays on Six Asian Contexts*, ed. B. Smith and H.B. Reynolds, pp. 12–44. Leiden: E.J. Brill

Rhys Davids, T.W. 1873. Inscriptions at the audience hall of Parakrama Bahu. *Indian Antiquary*, 2: 246

1880. *Buddhist Birth Stories*. London: Pali Text Society

Richards, J.F. 1978. Introduction. In *Kingship and Authority in South Asia*, ed. J.F. Richards, South Asian Studies Publication no. 3, pp. iii–xi. Madison, Wis.: University of Wisconsin Press

Richman, P. 1988. *Women, Branch Stories, and Religious Rhetoric in a Tamil Buddhist Text*. Foreign and Comparative Studies, South Asia Series 12. Syracuse: Maxwell School of Citizenship and Public Affairs, Syracuse University

Ricoeur, P. 1974. The model of the text: meaningful action considered as a text. *Social Research*, 38: 529–62

1981. *Hermeneutics and the Human Sciences: Essays on Language, Action and Interpretation*. Cambridge: Cambridge University Press

Rorty, R. 1979. *Philosophy and the Mirror of Nature*. Princeton: Princeton University Press

Rowland, B. 1953a. The four beasts: directional symbolism in Ceylon. *Arts Quarterly*, 18: 11–19
    1953b. *The Art and Architecture of India: Buddhist, Hindu, Jain*. London: Harmondsworth
Rowntree, L.B. 1988. Orthodoxy and new directions: cultural/humanistic geography. *Progress in Human Geography*, 12: 575–586
Sabean, D.W. 1984. *Power in the Blood: Popular Culture and Village Discourse in Early Modern Germany*. Cambridge: Cambridge University Press
Sack, R.D. 1980. *Conceptions of Space in Social Thought: A Geographical Perspective*. Minneapolis: University of Minnesota Press
Said, E. 1983. *The World, the Text, and the Critic*. Cambridge, Mass.: Harvard University Press
Saintyves, P. 1923. Le Tour de la ville et la chute de Jericho. *Essais de Folklore Biblique*. Paris
Samyutta Nikaya. 1917. Part 1, trans. Mrs. Rhys Davids and Suriyagala Sumangala Thera. New York: Oxford University Press
Sangaraja Vata. 1955 (originally late eighteenth century). Ed. C. De Silva. Colombo: Privately published
Satara Devala Devi Puwata. 1954 (originally eighteenth century). In *Sinhala Verse (Kavi)*, vol. II, pp. 158–159, collected by H. Nevill, ed. P.E.P. Deranyagala. Colombo: Ceylon National Museum Manuscript Series, vol. V
Sauer, C.O. 1969. The morphology of landscape. In *Land and Life: A Selection From the Writings of Carl Ortwin Sauer*, ed. J. Leighly, pp. 315–350. Berkeley: University of California Press
    1975. *Sixteenth Century North America: The Land and its People as Seen by Europeans*. Berkeley: University of California Press
    1980. *Seventeenth Century North America: Spanish and French Accounts*. Berkeley: Turtle Island Foundation
Sayer, A. 1984. *Method in Social Science: A Realist Approach*. London: Hutchinson
    1985. Realism and Geography. In *The Future of Geography*, ed. R.J. Johnston, pp. 159–173. London: Methuen
Schreuder, J. [1762] 1946. *Memoir of Jan Schreuder, Governor of Ceylon Delivered to his Successor Lubbert Jan Baron Van Eck on March 17, 1762*, trans. F. Reimers. Colombo: Ceylon Government Press
Seamon, D. and R. Mugerauer (eds.). 1985. *Dwelling, Place and Environment: Towards a Phenomenology of Person and World*. Dordrecht: Martinus Nijhoff
Seneviratne, A. 1983. *Kandy*. Colombo: Ministry of Cultural Affairs
Seneviratne, H.L. 1976. The alien king: Nayakkars on the throne of Kandy. *The Ceylon Journal of Historical and Social Studies*, new series, 6: 55–61
    1978a. *Rituals of the Kandyan State*. Cambridge: Cambridge University Press
    1978b. Religion and legitimation of power in the Kandyan Kingdom. In *Religion and Legitimation of Power in Sri Lanka*, ed. B.L. Smith, pp. 177–187. Chambersburg, Pa.: Anima
    1984. Continuity of civil religion in Sri Lanka. *Religion*, 14: 1–14
    1985. An exploration of the meaning of space in the Temple of the Tooth in Kandy. *Purusartha*, 8: 177–195
Seneviratne, J.M. 1916–1917. Sinhalese royal obsequies. *The Ceylon Antiquary and Literary Register*, 2: 120–123

1918. Royalty in ancient Ceylon during the period of the "great dynasty" (5th century B.C.–4th century A.D.). *Journal of the Ceylon Branch of the Royal Asiatic Society*, 26: 109–156

1921–1922. Coronation of Sinhalese kings: origins of customs, the figwood chair and the right whorled chank. *The Ceylon Antiquary and Literary Register*, 7: 220–225

Shapiro, M. 1973. *Words and Pictures: On the Literal and the Symbolic in the Illustration of a Text.* The Hague: Mouton

Shils, E. 1981. *Tradition.* Chicago: University of Chicago Press

Siva Purana 1970. Ed. J.L. Shastri. 4 vols. Delhi: Motilal Banarsidas.

Shorto, H.L. 1963. The 32 Myos in the Medieval Mon Kingdom. *Bulletin School of Oriental and African Studies*, 26: 572–591

Shukla, D.N. (ed. and trans.). No date. *Vastu Sastra, Vol. 1: Hindu Science of Architecture.* Lucknow: Vastu-Vanmaya-Prakasana-Sala

Siebel, J.B. 1954. A dip into the story of Kandy (a series of lectures delivered in Kandy between 1889–90). *Journal of the Dutch Burger Union of Ceylon*, 44: 164–175

1955. A dip into the story of Kandy (a series of lectures delivered in Kandy between 1889–90). *Journal of the Dutch Burger Union of Ceylon*, 45: 11–22

Sinhala Upasakajanalankaraya. No date (originally early nineteenth century). Ed. D.P.R. Samaranayake. Colombo: Privately published

Sirr, H.C. 1850. *Ceylon and the Cingalese.* Vol. II. London: W. Sholberl

Smith, B.L. 1978a. Kingship, the Sangha, and the process of legitimation in Anuradhapura, Ceylon: an interpretive essay. In *Religion and Legitimation of Power in Sri Lanka*, ed. B.L. Smith, pp. 73–95. Chambersburg, Pa.: Anima

1978b. The ideal social order as portrayed in the chronicles of Ceylon. In *Religion and Legitimation of Power in Sri Lanka*, ed. B.L. Smith, pp. 48–72. Chambersburg, Pa.: Anima

1987. The pursuit of equilibrium: Polonnaruva as a ceremonial center. In *The City as Sacred Center: Essays on Six Asian Contexts*, ed. B. Smith and H.B. Reynolds, pp. 60–87. Leiden: E.J. Brill

Smith, J.Z. 1987. *To Take Place: Towards a Theory of Ritual.* Chicago: University of Chicago Press

Smith, W. 1820. *Catalogue of the Regalia of the King of Kandy Sold by Auction in London on June 13, 1820.* London: King Street, Seven Dials. Manuscript in Museum Library, Colombo

Stein, B. 1984. Mahanavami: medieval and modern kingly ritual in South India. In *All the King's Mana: Perspectives on Kingship in Medieval South India*, pp. 302–326. Madras: New Era Publications

Stock, B. 1983. *The Implications of Literacy: Written Language and Models of Interpretation in the Eleventh and Thirteenth Centuries.* Princeton: Princeton University Press

1984. Medieval literacy, linguistic theory, and social organization. *New Literary History*, 16: 13–29

1986. Texts, readers, and enacted narratives. *Visible Language*, 20: 194–301

1988. Selections from the symposium on "literacy, reading, and power," Whitney Humanities Center, November 14, 1987. *Yale Journal of Criticism*, 2: 193–232

1989. Tradition and modernity: models from the past. In *Listening for the Text.* Baltimore: The Johns Hopkins University Press

Strong, R. 1973. *Splendor at Court: Renaissance Spectacle and the Theatre of Power.* Boston: Houghton Mifflin

Stutley, M. and J. Stutley. 1984. *Harper's Dictionary of Hinduism.* New York: Harper and Row

Suleiman, S.R. 1980a. Redundancy and the "readable" text. *Poetics Today,* 1: 119–142

1980b. Introduction: varieties of audience-oriented criticism. In *The Reader in the Text: Essays on Audience and Interpretation,* ed. S.R. Suleiman and I. Crossman, pp. 3–45. Princeton: Princeton University Press

Suleiman, S.R. and I. Crossman. 1980. *The Reader in the Text: Essays on Audience and Interpretation.* Princeton: Princeton University Press

Sulu Pujavaliya. 1913 (originally mid eighteenth century). Ed. J.D.B. Perera. Colombo: Privately published

Suriya Santiya. 1954. (Originally eighteenth century). In *Sinhala Verse (Kavi),* collected by H. Nevill, ed. P.E.P. Deranyagala, vol. II, p. 20. Colombo: Ceylon National Museums Manuscript Series, vol. IV

Tambiah, S.J. 1973. Classification of animals in Thailand. In *Rules and Meanings: The Anthropology of Everyday Knowledge,* ed. M. Douglas, pp. 127–164. Harmondsworth: Penguin Books

1976. *World Conqueror and World Renouncer.* Cambridge: Cambridge University Press

1985. A reformulation of Geertz's conception of the theatre state. In *Culture, Thought and Social Action: An Anthropological Perspective,* pp. 316–338. Cambridge, Mass.: Harvard University Press

Tennent, J.E. 1859. *Ceylon: An Account of the Island.* Vol. II. London: Longman, Green, Longman, and Roberts

Thomas, K. 1978. *Religion and the Decline of Magic: Studies in Popular Belief in Sixteenth and Seventeenth Century England.* New York: Penguin Books

Thompson, J.B. 1984. *Studies in the Theory of Ideology.* Berkeley: University of California

Thupavamsa. 1947. Ed. D.E. Hettiarachchi. Colombo: Ceylon Stationers

Tompkins, J. 1980. *Reader Response Criticism: From Formalism to Poststructuralism.* Baltimore: The Johns Hopkins University Press

Trexler, R.C. 1973. Ritual behavior in renaissance Florence: the setting. *Medievalia et Humanistica,* 4: 125–144

1980. *Public Life in Renaissance Florence.* New York: Academic Press

Tuan, Y.F. 1974. *Topophilia: A Study of Environmental Perception, Attitudes, and Values.* Englewood Cliffs: Prentice-Hall

Tucci, G. 1971. *The Theory and Practice of the Mandala.* New York: Samuel Weiser

Turner, L.J.B. 1918. The town of Kandy about the year 1815 A.D. *The Ceylon Antiquary,* 4: 76–82

Turner, V. 1961. *Ndembu Divination: Its Symbolism and Techniques.* Rhodes–Livingston Papers no. 31. Manchester: Manchester University Press

1967. *The Forest of Symbols.* Ithaca: Cornell University Press

1969. *The Ritual Process: Structure and Antistructure.* Ithaca: Cornell University Press

1974. *ND, Fields and Metaphors: Symbolic Action in Human Society.* Ithaca: Cornell University Press

Valentijn, F. [1722] 1978. *Francois Valentijn's Description of Ceylon*. Trans. and ed. S. Arasaratnam. London: The Hakluyt Society

Van Bystervelt, H. 1890. Henricus Van Bystervelt's embassy to Kandy (1671). *Journal of the Ceylon Branch of the Royal Asiatic Society*, 11: 355–376

Van Gollenesse, J.S. [1751] 1974. *Memoir of Julius Stein Van Gollenesse (Governor of Ceylon, 1743–1751) For His Successor Gerrit Joan Vreeland, 28 February 1751*, trans. and ed. S. Arasaratnam. Colombo: Department of National Archives

Van Lohuizen De Leeuw, J.E. 1978. An aspect of Sinhalese influence in Thailand. In *Senerat Paranavitana Commemoration Volume*, ed. L. Prematilleke, K. Indrapala, and J.E. Van Lohuizen De Leeuw, pp. 137–141. Leiden: E.J. Brill

Vedic Hymns 1891. Trans. F.M. Muller. Sacred Books of the East, vol. 32. Oxford: Oxford University Press

1897. Trans. H. Oldenberg. Sacred Books of the East, vol. 46. Oxford: Oxford University Press

Vico, G. 1968. *The New Science*. Trans. T. Berin and M. Fisch. Ithaca: Cornell University Press

Vimalananda, T. 1963. *Udarata Maha Karalla*. Colombo: M.D. Gunasena

1973. *The British Intrigue in the Kandyan Kingdom of Ceylon*. Colombo: M.D. Gunasena

Visnu Purana. 1952. Ed. R.C. Gupta. Gorakhpur: Asian Publishing House

1978. Trans. C. Dimmitt and J.A.B. Van Buitenen. In *Classical Hindu Mythology: A Reader in the Sanskrit Puranas*, pp. 94–98. Philadelphia: Temple University Press

Volwahsen, A. 1969. *Living Architecture: Indian*. London: MacDonald

Wagner, P.L. 1972. *Environments and Peoples*. Englewood Cliffs: Prentice-Hall

Wagner, P.L. and M.M. Mikesell. 1962. General introduction: the themes of cultural geography. In *Readings in Cultural Geography*, pp. 1–24. Chicago: University of Chicago Press

Weedon, C. 1987. *Feminist Practice and Poststructuralist Theory*. Oxford: Basil Blackwell

Wheatley, P. 1971. *The Pivot of the Four Quarters: A Preliminary Enquiry into the Origins and the Character of the Ancient Chinese City*. Chicago: Aldine

1977. The suspended pelt: reflections on a discarded model of spatial structure. In *Geographic Humanism, Analysis and Social Action*, ed. D. Deskins et al., pp. 47–108. Ann Arbors, Mich.: Michigan Geographical Publication no. 17

1983. Nagara and commandery: origins of the Southeast Asian urban traditions. Chicago: University of Chicago, Department of Geography, Research Papers no. 207–208

White, H. 1978. *Tropics of Discourse: Essays in Cultural Criticism*. Baltimore: The Johns Hopkins University Press

1982. Method and ideology in intellectual history: the case of Henry Adams. In *Modern European Intellectual History: Reappraisals and Perspectives*, ed. D. LaCapra and S. Caplan, pp. 280–310. Ithaca: Cornell University Press

Wickremaratne, A. 1987. Shifting metaphors of sacrality: the mythic dimensions of Anuradhapura. In *The City as Sacred Center: Essays on Six Asian Contexts*, ed. B. Smith and H.B. Reynolds, pp. 45–59. Leiden: E.J. Brill

Wiener, M.J. 1981. *English Culture and the Decline of the Industrial Spirit*. Cambridge: Cambridge University Press

Wijetunga, W.M.K. 1958. The background of the Nayakkars of Kandy. *University of Ceylon Review*, 16: 125–130

Willentz, S. (ed.) 1985. *Rites of Power: Symbolism, Ritual and Politics Since the Middle Ages*. Philadelphia: University of Pennsylvania Press

Williams, G. 1816. *Plan of Kandy in the Island of Ceylon, showing the position of the redoubts*. Manuscript, Ceylon Room, University of Peradeniya library.

Williams, R. 1973. *The Country and the City*. London: Chatto and Windus

1982. *The Sociology of Culture*. New York: Schocken Books

Winslow, D. 1984. A political geography of deities: space and the pantheon in Sinhalese Buddhism. *Journal of Asian Studies*, 43: 273–291

Wright, I. 1984. History, hermeneutics, deconstruction. In *Criticism and Critical Theory*, ed. J. Hawthorn, pp. 83–98. London: Edward Arnold

Zelinsky, W. 1973. *The Cultural Geography of the United States*. Englewood Cliffs: Prentice-Hall

Zimmer, H. 1974. *Myths and Symbols in Indian Art and Civilization*. Princeton: Princeton University, Bolligen Series 4

Index

adikar, 92, 100, 114, 119, 132–133, 140, 145–147, 149–150, 162–163
Ahalepola, 162–172, 174, 177–178, 183
allegory, 6, 19–20, 47, 51, 88–89, 91–118, 147, 150–151, 157, 172, 174, 177, 180, 196, 200n.4
Anuradhapura, 6, 25–30, 51–54, 115, 120, 124–126, 128, 157, 171
astrology, 174–177

Bandarage, S., 34
Barthes, R., 3–4, 16–17, 154
bodhisattva, 38, 40, 45, 54, 113, 115, 120, 122–123, 125, 133, 137, 171
bo tree, 52, 70, 109, 115, 122, 124, 132, 144, 146, 150, 158, 165
Boyd, H., 145–146, 148
British conquest, 33, 78, 80
Buddha, 25, 39–41, 45, 48, 52, 113, 115, 125, 128, 137, 147

cakravarti, 39–40, 48–49, 92–95, 98, 106, 111, 120, 122, 124, 133, 147, 153, 159, 173
canal, 84
caste, 34–35
charisma, 41–42
city of the gods, 20–21, 23–24, 39–40, 42–48, 52–58, 69, 88, 91–95, 108–117, 127, 129, 132–134, 137–139, 142, 144, 147–148, 151, 158–160, 172–174, 187–190, 192–193
cities of the hero-kings, 48–58, 60, 94–95, 124, 127, 138–139, 151, 160, 185–187, 191–192
Clifford, J., 195–196
Codrington, H.W., 123–124
Coedes, G., 125

consecration ceremony, 45, 54, 70, 119–127
Coomaraswamy, A., 68, 70, 102, 105, 109, 115, 125, 129, 132–133, 137, 178
Cosgrove, D., 4, 7, 194
cosmic axis, *see* Mount Meru
cosmic waters, *see* Ocean of Milk
cosmology, 43–48, 106, 112, 116, 120, 146
court ritual, 33, 41, 87, 98, 119–153, 203
Culavamsa, 25, 40, 51, 107–108, 125, 158, 160
culture, 4, 11, 13, 15–18
cultural geography, 3–4, 11–13
customary law, 5, 37–38

dagoba, 111, 113, 115, 120, 133, 165
Daniels, S., 4, 7
Davy, J., 42, 47–48, 80, 92–94, 115, 120, 122, 125, 128, 132, 134, 136, 162
De Queyroz, F., 61–64
De Silva, C.R., 64, 66–67
De Silva, K.M., 27–28, 38, 72, 76
devalagam, 35, 129
Dewaraja, L., 33, 35, 69–70, 82, 87, 93, 119, 122, 139, 149, 151, 163, 166, 170
discourse, 4, 7, 12, 16–17, 22, 155, 183
discursive field, 4–5, 16–17, 155, 180–181
of kingship, 5–6, 24–41, 87–88, 155
Asokan kingship, 5, 35, 38–41, 78, 88, 155, 158, 161, 164–165, 169–172, 176–181
Sakran kingship, 5, 38–48, 78, 88, 155, 158–159, 161, 164–165, 170–172, 177–181

226

Index

D'Oyly, J., 33, 76, 80, 82, 84, 92, 137, 144, 147, 166–167, 170, 178
Dutch, conflict with, 32, 69–71

Eagleton, T., 11, 194–195
eastern rectangle, 94–97, 107–118, 125, 129, 132, 134, 145–146

fertility, 39, 44–49, 54, 68, 102, 106, 113, 119, 125, 128–130, 136
foreign embassies, 139–153
Foucault, M., 4, 14, 16–17, 22, 155, 183
Fritz, J.M., 154–155

Gampola, 29, 100, 200
Geertz, C., 3–4, 16, 18, 50, 71, 128, 154
Geiger, W., 128
Giddens, A., 17
god-king, 5, 38–39, 49, 54, 57, 59, 88, 108, 124, 133, 145, 148, 150, 157, 170, 177
Gombrich, R.F., 105, 115–116
goyigama, 34, 122

Heesterman, J.C., 124
hegemony, 16
Heine-Geldern, R., 50–51, 71, 125, 154, 175
hermeneutics, 3, 13, 17
hero-kings, 23–24, 27, 29, 41, 48–58
Heydt, J.W., 99, 137, 146
Hocart, A.M., 50, 52, 55, 67, 87, 92, 106, 122, 124–125, 128, 137, 151

ideology, 12, 16, 19, 58
Inden, R., 124–125, 128, 148
interpretation, 11–18
  politics of, 16, 179–184
intertextuality, 4–6, 22–24, 49, 58, 87, 113, 118, 154, 158, 172, 180–181

Jaffna, kingdom of, 30–31
Jameson, F., 20, 195
Jonville, M., 140, 142, 145–146, 148–150

Kandy
  social structure, 34–37
  economy, 34–35, 58
  territorial organization, 36–37, 92–93, 117, 133
  growth of the city, 59–84
  foundation myth, 90–91, 100–101
  city as allegorical landscape, 91–118
Kataragama, 63, 72–74, 94–95, 116, 130, 134, 168
Kertzer, D., 154
Kirti Sri, King, 35, 41, 71–78, 112, 122–123, 125, 128, 162, 166, 170, 172, 174–175
Knox, R., 63, 67–68, 128
Kotte, kingdom of, 29, 31
Krautheimer, R., 154, 194
ksatriya, 32, 34, 122

Lacapra, D., 12, 16
lakes, 67, 76, 82–83, 97–107, 157
landscape
  Asokan, 6, 38, 57, 72, 78, 88, 155, 157, 162–163, 178–182
  kingly reading, 87–153, 156, 158–161
  nobles' readings, 88, 156, 161–171
  peasants' readings, 88, 156, 171–180
  reading, 4, 7, 13–15, 18, 59, 84, 87, 113, 154, 179
  rhetoric of, 17, 19–22, 106, 183
  Sakran, 6, 42–48, 55–58, 69, 78, 84, 88, 108, 155, 157, 159–60, 162–163, 170, 178–182
  and discourse, 5–7, 87, 156, 181, 183
  and political practice, 5–7, 11, 59, 72, 82, 87–88, 91–94, 106, 154, 156, 165, 171, 178–183
  and social process, 11, 13, 19, 184
  as a signifying system, 3–5, 11–24, 183–184
  as text, 4, 6, 17, 19, 22–23, 40, 49, 58–59, 84, 87, 106, 118, 154
Lawrie, A.C., 70, 76, 78, 123, 168
Lewis, J.P., 142, 144, 146–150
Ley, D., 7
liminality, 101, 113–114, 129, 146–147
literary theory, 13, 23, 154–155

Mahavamsa, 25, 27, 51, 164
Malalgoda, K., 72, 128
mandala, 93
media, 88–89
metonymy, 21, 57, 59, 89, 94, 101, 118, 147, 151
Mount Mandara, 46–48, 51, 98, 102, 108–110, 113, 130, 144, 147
Mount Meru, 21, 39–40, 43, 46–51, 55–56, 71, 84, 89, 98, 106–111, 113–117, 120, 124–125, 129–130, 132–133, 137, 146–148, 159
Mus, P., 50–51, 92, 154–155

narrative, 4, 6, 21, 23, 97, 181
  recurrent narrative structure, 22, 42, 59, 84, 88, 94–95, 106, 114, 120, 151–152, 181
  of the landscape of the gods, 42–48, 63, 88–89, 94–97, 101, 106–107, 114, 126–127, 134, 137–139, 148, 151–152
  of the landscape of the hero-kings, 48–53, 63, 88–89, 94–96, 107, 114, 126–127, 137–139, 151–152
Natha Devale, 59–60, 63, 70–73, 114, 122–123, 130, 134, 158, 168–170
Nayakkar dynasty, 32–33, 37, 40–41, 98, 105, 122, 204
  conflict with nobles, 37, 41, 158, 161–171
nobles, 32–37, 94, 146, 149, 151–152, 155, 158, 160–171, 177

Obeyesekere, G., 39, 41, 52, 55, 57, 67–68, 87, 97–99, 114, 116, 123, 137, 172–174, 176
Ocean of Milk, 21, 44–47, 51, 53–58, 67, 76, 84, 89, 97–108, 113, 125, 129–130, 133–134, 137, 159–160, 174
O'Flaherty, W., 102–105, 109, 111, 137, 179–180

palace, 49, 61–64, 71–81, 89, 108–111, 113, 145, 147, 157
Panawatta, S., 82
parallelism, 49, 54, 88–89, 92–94, 101, 107, 157, 159, 174–175
Paranavitana, S., 38, 52, 54–55, 114, 123

pataha ritual, 172–180
Pattini, 63, 72–73, 115, 130, 134, 158
perahara, 37, 63, 87, 128–139, 164
Pieris, P.E., 64, 99, 117, 134, 140, 142, 144–146, 148, 150, 170
Pieris, R., 34–36, 92, 99, 124, 163
Polonnaruva, 29–30, 51, 55–58, 98, 124, 126, 128, 157, 160, 171
ponds, 67
Portuguese, wars with, 31–32, 60–61, 64–68
Prematilleke, P.L., 70, 80, 82, 123, 147
Pybus, J., 144–145, 148

radala, 34
rajakariya, 35, 99, 155, 157, 162, 166–167, 170, 172, 176–177
Raja Sinha II, King, 66–69
religious festivals (*see also perahara*), 36–37
rhetoric, 4, 42
Richards, J.F., 119, 197
river, 76, 120, 122, 136, 144–145

Sakra, 20, 24–25, 38, 42–48, 98–99, 109–112, 122, 133–134, 136, 142, 144, 157, 171, 177
sangha, 23, 29, 35, 72, 88, 155, 160, 162, 164–165, 167
Sauer, C., 3–4, 13
semiotics, 4–5, 183
Seneviratne, H.L., 87, 92, 109, 116, 123–125, 129–130, 133–134, 136, 163
Shorto, H.L., 50, 92
simile, 21
Sitavaca, kingdom of, 31
Smith, B.L., 178
Sri Vikrama, King, 6, 24, 41, 78–84, 97, 100, 105, 125
  building program, 6–7, 78–84, 88, 93, 97–101, 108, 111, 132, 156–180
Stein, B., 128, 150
Stock, B., 16, 22–23, 155–156, 183
synecdoche, 20–21, 84, 88–89, 92, 94–97, 99, 102, 107–108, 112–115, 118, 120, 124, 126–127, 129, 136–137, 147, 149, 151–152, 181, 183, 185–193

Tambiah, S., 50, 93, 128, 154, 172, 199
Temple of the Tooth, 60, 62–63, 69–77, 87, 97, 99, 108–113, 130, 133–134, 157, 165, 168–169
text, 13–14, 16, 22–24, 28, 37–38, 172, 180
textual community, 23–24, 155–156, 172, 183
Tooth Relic of the Buddha, 36, 48, 60, 64, 92, 108, 111–113, 128–130, 132–134, 136, 164
tradition, 22, 24, 158, 165, 167, 169–170, 177, 180
trope, 4, 6, 19–22, 84, 89, 116, 181, 183
Turner, V., 4

viharagam, 35, 129
Visnu *devale*, 72–73, 114, 122, 130, 134, 157, 170
western rectangle, 92–94, 116–117, 125, 157
Wheatley, P., 48, 50–51, 92, 125, 128, 154–155
White, H., 4, 19–20
Williams, R., 4, 7, 15
world of the gods (*see* city of the gods)

Zimmer, H., 92, 136–137

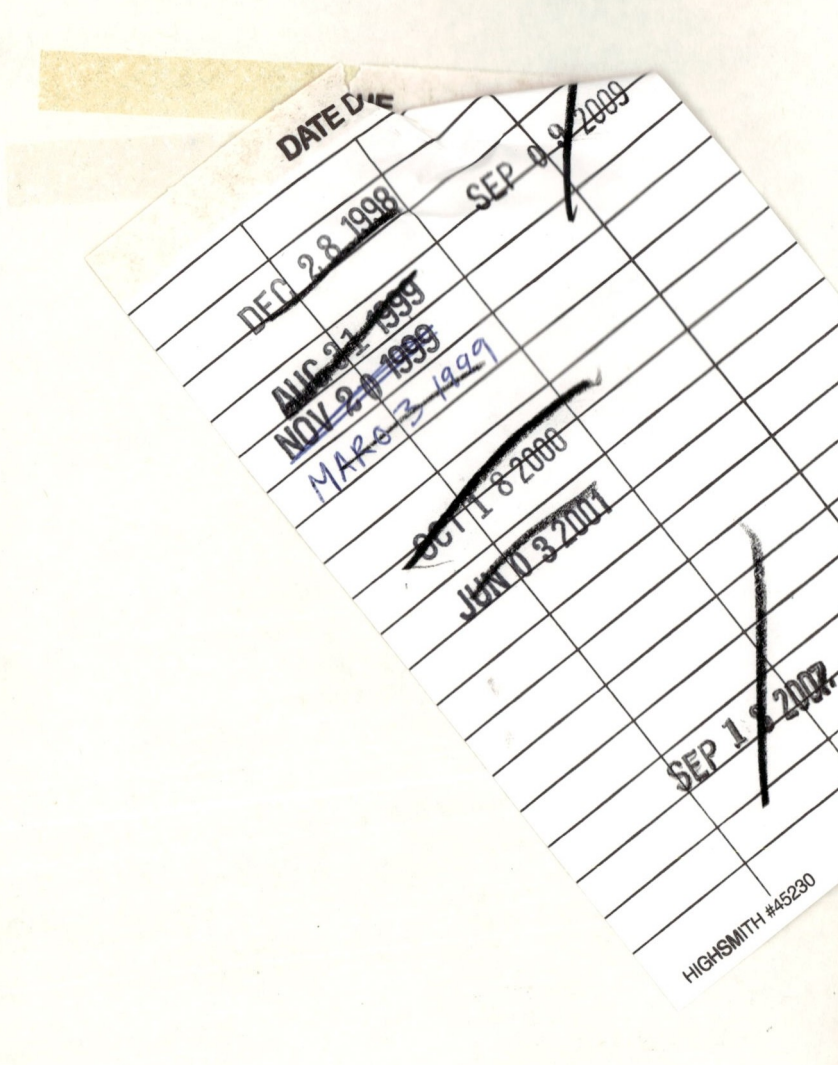